'This is a hugely interesting and provocative  graphical, historical and clinical sources to ma relationship between fascism and masculinity masculinity and on her knowledge of psychc Christina Wieland shows how the fascist stat _.__ a particular solution to the male struggle to avoid being ove᷒᷒᷒ᴄᴌᴍed by a phantastic maternal presence that threatens masculinity in times of personal and societal trauma. Hitler's personality and writings are used as examples of this state of mind in an attempt to understand why Hitler was the person in the right place at the right time, how he was just the sufficient mixture of charisma and craziness to overthrow common sense and tip a nation into societal and genocidal madness.' – **Bob Hinshelwood**, *Professor in the Centre for Psychoanalytic Studies, University of Essex*

'This is a valuable exploration of the madness at the heart of fascism. It employs psychoanalytic theory to generate new insights into the states of mind underlying totalitarian violence. It shows how a desperate pseudo-masculinity uses hatred and murder to stave off the collapse of selfhood, and adds to the foundations for a psychosocial understanding of contemporary extremisms.' – **Barry Richards**, *Professor of Public Communication, The Media School, Bournemouth University*

'Dr Wieland has proposed a wholly new understanding of the fascist mind, by posing the problem of what made a fascist group, with its combination of merging into nationalism, normally thought of as feminine, and heroic milita- rism, normally thought of as masculine. Together, they fed an illusion of rebirth through war as a rebirth of masculinity from a masculine womb. The psycho- analytic study of fascism, which goes back to the fascist period, enters a new stage with her book.' – **Karl Figlio**, *Professor in the Centre for Psychoanalytic Studies, University of Essex, and a Senior Member of the British Psychotherapy Foundation*

The Fascist State of Mind and the Manufacturing of Masculinity

The Fascist State of Mind and the Manufacturing of Masculinity: A psychoanalytic approach attempts to describe in psychoanalytic terms the psychological consequences of massive social trauma and national humiliation, and the regression that takes place within the individual under these circumstances. The book is not about understanding fascism as a historical, political or sociological phenomenon, but about understanding the special relationship between masculinity and fascism and *the state of mind* which both shaped, and was shaped by, the historical phenomenon of fascism.

Christina Wieland explores fascism as a product of certain forms of masculinity and focuses on the dynamics of masculinity as a mode of psychic functioning. She examines in detail masculine anxieties and defences and their interaction with the stresses of modernity and with the social and political unrest that followed the First World War.

The Fascist State of Mind and the Manufacturing of Masculinity is divided into four parts:

Part I – The meaning of fascism and the fascist state of mind – theories and definitions
Part II – Masculinity, its meaning and its vulnerability
Part III – Group and group theory, and the total environment
Part IV – Exploring the links between masculinity, groups and fascism

The Fascist State of Mind and the Manufacturing of Masculinity uses clinical material, literary texts, and extensive psychoanalytic interpretation of some passages from *Mein Kampf* to illustrate the interplay of the psychological processes with social and political events. This book will appeal to psychoanalysts and psychoanalytic psychotherapists, teachers and students of psychoanalysis and gender studies. It will also appeal to those interested in the application of psychoanalytic insights in the understanding of social and political phenomena.

Christina Wieland is a psychoanalytic psychotherapist in private practice, a training therapist, teacher and supervisor. She is a visiting Fellow and teaches at the Centre for Psychoanalytic Studies at the University of Essex.

The Fascist State of Mind and the Manufacturing of Masculinity

A psychoanalytic approach

Christina Wieland

Routledge
Taylor & Francis Group

LONDON AND NEW YORK

First published 2015
by Routledge
27 Church Road, Hove, East Sussex BN3 2FA

and by Routledge
711 Third Avenue, New York, NY 10017

Routledge is an imprint of the Taylor & Francis Group, an informa business

British Library Cataloguing in Publication Data
A catalogue record for this book is available from the British Library

Library of Congress Cataloging in Publication Data
Wieland, Christina.
The fascist state of mind and the manufacturing of masculinity: a
psychoanalytic approach / Christina Wieland.—First Edition.
pages cm
1. Masculinity. 2. Gender identity. I. Title.
BF175.5.M37W54 2014
155.3'32—dc23
2014009248

ISBN: 978-0-415-52645-6 (hbk)
ISBN: 978-0-415-52646-3 (pbk)
ISBN: 978-1-315-77434-3 (ebk)

Typeset in Times
by Book Now Ltd, London

To Volker and Stefan

Contents

Acknowledgements

In a study like this that has been developing over many years, many people, colleagues, students and others, have contributed with thoughts, comments, criticisms, and questions which helped to shape the book as it now stands. It would be impossible to trace every influence to its source so I thank collectively all those who took interest in this work and commented at different stages over the years. I would also like to express my deep gratitude to my patients who taught me a great deal about the workings of the human mind; and my own analyst who showed me the fascist state of mind in myself.

Specifically I would like to thank the following individuals for their generosity in finding time to read and comment on the book as it unfolded.

I want to express my deep gratitude to Bob Hinshelwood who supervised the original doctoral thesis which served as a basis from which the book developed, and who continued to take interest in the book as it unfolded. His insightful and encouraging comments kept me going despite the many crises of confidence I faced on the way.

I would also like to express my deep gratitude to Karl Figlio for finding the time in his very busy schedule to read and comment on the manuscript. His detailed, insightful and incisive comments, and often unsettling questions, helped me to refine and at times re-shape and re-think parts of the book.

Many thanks to Daniel Pick for reading one chapter of the book and for taking the time to discuss with me the central thesis of the book as well as many details.

Many thanks to Barry Richards who read and commented on an early version of the book and helped me re-shape and unify the book.

Last, but certainly not least, I want to thank my husband for being there and for being supportive and encouraging throughout the long gestation, discussing with me several aspects of the book, and putting up with me using every scrap of free time to this study. Not least his valuable contribution of IT knowledge, editorial and organizing skills in the final stages of the work have been invaluable.

Introduction

In Goethe's *Faust* the Devil appears for the first time as something ordinary and inconspicuous – a black dog, a poodle, circling around Faust and his assistant Wagner as they are taking a walk on Easter Sunday. He seems to be following them, circling closer and closer. No flames, no horns or bloodshot eyes, no infernal fires. Just a poodle. What more innocuous can this be?

Faust, however, is suspicious:

> FAUST: Look closer now, with care, and say what sort
> Of beast you think he is.
>
> WAGNER: Why, Sir, a hound
> Of poodle breed, who snuffs his way around
> To find a master.
>
> FAUST: Mark the spiral trail
> With which he comes from far, yet ever nigher
> Encircling us: unless my senses fail
> His track is traced with little tongues of fire.
>
> WAGNER: Some optical illusion, Sir, maybe:
> He's nothing but a poodle-dog to me. (pp. 68–9)

As they enter Faust's study the poodle follows in his uncanny ordinariness which, however, is soon transformed into an infernal monster:

> FAUST: The dog assumes a stature strange to see:
> Is it a phantom or reality?
> He rises up in might,
> No canine form has such a height. (p. 72)

As Faust recites a spell the monster changes into another ordinary creature – Mephistopheles now dressed as a travelling scholar appears.

> FAUST: So that is then the essence of the brute!
> A travelling scholar? Time to laugh yet! (p. 74)

A bit later Mephistopheles, the 'Lord of lies' and disguises appear as a noble squire:

MEPHISTOPHELES.
I come, your megrims to dispel,
In likeness of noble squire. (p. 82)

The Devil as a master of lies and illusions is part of all of us and is in this sense 'ordinary'. The Devil as an ordinary creature – a poodle, a travelling scholar or a noble squire – is maybe captured in Hannah Arendt's famous phrase 'the banality of evil' taken from her book Eichmann in Jerusalem. Many took offense at the time as Arendt was seen as condoning the Nazi crimes or Eichmann himself, or at least not condemning them enough. We all want to see evil or 'the Devil' surrounded by infernal fires. Yet Arendt was saying something more profound and more disturbing. She was saying, like Christopher Bollas later on, that we are all, or at least a sizeable number of us, capable of being seduced into participating in, or supporting, or turning a blind eye to terrible crimes. The history of the twentieth century is full of examples where ordinary citizens committed, participated in, supported, or turned a blind eye towards, criminal regimes and criminal acts while at the same time maintaining the love and care for their families and friends and the ordinary existence that these relations bestow on them. Millions of ordinary German citizens were able to ignore or simply 'not know' about the crimes perpetrated in their name. However, the seduction by the Devil in *Faust*, is not about ostensibly heinous acts but about power, lies and illusions.

So who is the Devil? The main characteristic of the Devil in *Faust* and in Christianity is that he is a seducer. He addresses himself to the wishes and desires of humans, mainly their wish to get rid of undesirable qualities or undesirable states of mind – weakness, ugliness, poverty, old age, loneliness and depression – and acquire instead beauty, power, love, sexual prowess. The price? Selling their souls to the Devil as Christianity would have it, or giving up their real self with all the unwanted qualities and take on the desired qualities in an act of delusion, as psychoanalysis would have it.

Melanie Klein described this process of getting rid of unwanted qualities of the self and putting them into other people in her concept of projective identification which she introduced in 1946 as the main defence of the paranoid-schizoid position (Klein 1946). Klein extended her concept of projective identification in 1955 to include a type of projective identification we can call 'total'. In this the subject does not just expel unwanted parts of himself but in a more aggressive and colonising way he puts himself in the place of the desired object which he takes over. The subject is now in the place of the object and has all its desired qualities. In the hybrid that is now created there is no subject and no object but a fraudulent entity.

Klein used Julian Green's novel *If I Were You* to explain this process (Klein 1955). In the novel a young man dissatisfied with himself, his insignificance and mediocrity, strikes a bargain with the Devil whereby he is given a formula that makes him capable of leaving his inadequate body and self and taking over other people's bodies in this way becoming whoever he wanted to be. This omnipotent transformation is one in which both the subject and the object cease to exist and the omnipotence of their fusion prevails. Members of some groups which I call 'homogeneous' undergo the same transformation as they give up their humdrum, despised or broken identity to embrace the leader's identity and participate in the group's omnipotence. I suggest that the fascist group functions in this way and that fascism was so successful because it offered people something impossible for which they yearned – the illusion of being reborn and re-shaped by being one with the Fuehrer or the Duce. Fascism's stress on rebirth and re-generation was not just a propaganda ruse. It was fundamental in its functioning as a religion to the masses that supported it. The phantasies surrounding this rebirth, especially the rebirth and regeneration of masculinity through violence and war, or even better the manufacturing of a new masculinity hard as steel, which would be clearly distinguished from a despised 'feminised' one, form part of the book's exploration of fascism.

Marinetti's Futurist Manifesto, a key proto-fascist text, puts it starkly:

> We want to glorify war – the only cure for the world – militarism, patriotism, the destructive gesture of the anarchists, the beautiful ideas which kill, and contempt for woman.
> We want to demolish the museums and libraries, fight morality, feminism and all opportunist and utilitarian cowardice.
>
> (Lyttelton 1973)

The fact that war 'belongs to man' as Mussolini declared, makes war not only the province of men but also and in a way unprecedented by older generations, *the making of a man*. In this sense not just man makes war but *war makes the man*. Militarism and violence become a way of being, or becoming, a man. As Adrian Lyttelton comments: 'Fascist ritual can be read at one level as a complex of virility symbols' (Lyttelton 1973: 28).

Anxieties about masculinity coupled with misogyny and anti-Semitism were rampant in Vienna (and in Europe in general) at the turn of the century and reflected the rise of feminism, the decline of paternal authority, and the loss of power and male authority for the ordinary man both within the family and within society. The new liberated, sexual woman in her guise as an insatiable 'femme fatale' was seen as dangerous and devouring. The male wish to be devoured, the male passive wish, has been hidden and forbidden only present as a projection onto the woman. In fact, as Freud discovered, this wish is the most repressed and the most forbidden wish in man (see Chapter 4). Freud saw the passive wish in men as part of the negative Oedipus complex, that is as a wish to be in the mother's place and be loved by father. My particular angle is to examine another part of this wish for passivity that exists *as a disavowal, or destruction* of the Oedipus complex and of all object relations. This is not dissimilar to the Lacanian view of the disavowal of the representation of the father in psychosis but my examination of it is within the Kleinian framework. The use of psychotic defences is, however, part of this analysis.

I shall examine this wish as part of the early relation to mother in its dual manifestation – firstly a totally passive wish to be absorbed into the mother's body – a wish that might be thought of as a manifestation of the silent Death Instinct, or the Nirvana principle, that Freud talked about; and secondly the more active and violent phantasy of the taking over of mother in an act of 'total' projective identification as Klein showed in her 1955 paper. In this transformation of the wish from passive to active, aggression is the main dynamic and the colonization and destruction of the object the main aim. However, the destruction of difference between subject and object is present in both. Klein described this wish in her concept of the 'femininity phase' (see Chapter 4).

This infantile wish is common to both boys and girls but it is only in boys that it is equated with castration and loss of masculinity. I suggest that with the decline of religion the representation of this passive wish as a wish for union with God also declined leaving the subject at the mercy of his primitive phantasies. This passive wish in men remained only as a prohibition and a projection.

This study follows this forbidden male wish, its perversion and its perverse fulfilment and simultaneous disavowal in fascism. The male container or male womb created by the fascist group, uses the cult of violence and militarism to prop the flagging masculinity of its members. In this sense the fascist group under an omnipotent Fuehrer *both fulfils and denies* the passive wish to be devoured, to lose one's self and one's identity within a bigger homogenised whole – in the unconscious the mother's body – while at the same time practices a monumental 'masculine protest'. In this sense fascism acts as both a religion and a perversion.

I argue that the phantasies of homogenisation within the fascist formation and the phantasies of being one with the Fuehrer or the Duce and participate in his glory are based on transformations of early phantasies to be one with an omnipotent version of the mother and partake of her power. In this sense the Fuehrer is not in the place of the father but more in the place of the early omnipotent mother taken over, robbed and appropriated by the son who is now truly omnipotent but, at the same time, in need of a ready-made masculinity manufactured in steel and violence.

So this book is not about the extreme violence and heinous crimes that fascism has unleashed on the twentieth century. All this has been documented countless of times before by historians and others. It is not an explanation or a description of fascism as a political system either. It is more about the insidious way in which we can slip from the ordinary to the grotesque, form civilization to barbarity both within the mind and within society following regressive wishes and their perversion. This includes the insidious way in which we can be seduced to becoming 'someone else', to be reborn, wiped clean and be re-invented following an ideology, a religion or a mere 'fashion'. As Christopher Bollas has observed the murderousness is already there in the way the self kills off its own contents (see Chapter 1).

I seemed to be saying two contradictory things here: (1) that we are all, men and women, susceptible to the seduction of fascism and (2) that fascism is a masculine phenomenon.

I think the contradiction is more apparent than real. The fascist promise of rebirth and regeneration and the totalitarian promise of a fusion of the individual with the whole appeal equally to the regressive wishes of both men and women. However, the central fascist doctrine of violence and militarism, of the survival of the fittest, of expansion and imperialism and of permanent revolution were essentially addressed to men. The rebirth and regeneration of the nation was essentially the rebirth and *regeneration of masculinity* – a masculinity that was seen as having been weakened and in a state of degeneracy by democracy, pacifism and the Jews. The Jews as emasculated and feminised men was a prominent theme of nineteenth- and early twentieth-century Europe (see Chapters 8 and 9). In this sense the theme of *contamination*, so prominent in fascism, applies equally to the Jews and to 'devouring' women.

However, the idea that fascism is a masculine phenomenon has been criticised by Lynne Segal (1990). Segal bases her critique on Claudia Koonz's detailed and well researched study of women in Nazi Germany (Koonz 1986). Koonz shows clearly and indisputably the enthusiastic participation of women in Nazi Germany and the efforts they made in ensuring the success of the regime. Koonz's book throws light to an area neglected by other historians and is extremely well researched. However, the fact that women collaborated enthusiastically with National Socialism and worked for its success does not make fascism less of a masculine phenomenon. It does, however, make it a less of a black and white phenomenon. Koonz seems to be describing two fascisms – one male, one female. And they are very different. Women's fascism, at least in Germany, was to embrace the National Socialism's dogma that women belong to the home and to their families and children. In this sense traditional ideas of gender, and virtual separation of sexes were welcomed by many women who seemed to have found them reassuring and protective of their domain. The adoration of the Fuehrer seemed to have been the common ground between men and women. As one leading Nazi woman put it: 'national Socialism is a male concern and we women will gladly retreat just as soon as our Fuehrer does not need us any longer' (Koonz: 54).

The separation of the sexes advocated by the fascists points to masculine fears of contamination and pollution, the same fears expressed in relation to the Jews. Men can be men only if they are separated from women and from the 'soft' feminine part of themselves. With the separation of sexes and the elevation of women, as mothers, onto a pedestal, idealised but kept at a safe distance, these fears were re-directed towards the Jews.

Historians have long debated the usefulness of the term 'fascism'. Many argue for the abolition of the term as it has been overused and abused. Others advocate a limited use of the term to describe at most Mussolini's Italy and the Nazi Germany. Yet others attempt to define a 'generic' fascism (Paxton) or a 'fascist style of rule' (De Grand).

Robert Paxton is one of the historians who argues for maintaining the term 'fascist' as a generic term that describes 'the most important twentieth century political innovation' and a post-democratic mass phenomenon characterised by certain 'mobilising passions' (Paxton 2004: 219). Paxton does not think that fascism is characterised by its ideology or certain immutable political arrangements but by the 'subterranean passions' that it ignites and represents. In this he seems to be close to what psychoanalysts call a 'fascist state of mind'.

As Paxton sees a set of 'mobilising passions' as the substratum of fascism a psychoanalytic understanding of these passions is a valid undertaking. I examine Paxton's 'mobilising passions' in Chapter 1. The special approach of this book, however, is to link these mobilising passions to masculine anxieties and defences.

It is important here to stress that it is masculine *anxieties and defences* I have in mind and not a 'masculinity' which is a biological, or even a social, *entity*. The stress on wishes, anxieties and defences is a stress on the psychoanalytic understanding of both masculinity and fascism. Following the fate of the 'passive wish' and its relationship to masculinity in fascism is the special approach of the book.

The relationship of masculinity to fascism, of masculinity to femininity, the relationship of man to the femininity in himself, and the male's relationship to the early maternal object are themes that are at the core of the book. The destruction of the object, and the destruction of difference and of masculinity, through total projective identification with the mother become central themes as fascism comes to acquire the meaning of a 'restoration' of masculinity.

I would like to stress here that this book is not conceived as an explanation of the historical phenomenon of fascism. It is conceived as an attempt to understand *the state of mind* that contributed to, and interacted with, the historical phenomena to create fascism.

A state of mind does not necessarily lead to social and political action. For this to happen many other conditions contribute which historians, social and political scientists examine and elaborate upon. Part of this study is to understand and attempt to define this state of mind. The other aim of the book is to examine the relation of this state of mind to masculine anxieties and defences.

So this book is about a psychoanalytic understanding of the fascist state of mind and its relation to masculinity, or more precisely to masculine anxieties and defences. I argue that this relation creates, or manufactures, a type of masculinity that we can call pseudo-masculinity. As there are two main concepts here – fascist state of mind and masculine state of mind – I shall examine each of these separately before I bring them together. As fascism is a group phenomenon and cannot be conceived without a particular kind of group in mind I shall also examine different types of group and different types of leadership always having in mind the inter-relationship between external and internal reality.

The seduction of internal tyranny (and by extension of external tyranny) is that it will free the individual from his own anxiety as the psychoanalyst Donald Meltzer has shown (Meltzer 1973, chapter 20). Anxieties about the dissolution of the self and the dissolution of society are core anxieties which come to the fore in times of crisis – personal or societal – when traumatic experiences predominate. That these anxieties are easily translated int
o castration anxiety, or loss of masculinity, was Freud's (and psychoanalysis') unique contribution to the understanding of masculinity. I argue that annihilation anxieties are translated into castration anxieties because the individual attempts to solve the problem of the dissolution of the self by retreating *in phantasy* into the protective container of mother's body or mind. Michael Roper's research on traumatised men during the First World War suggests something similar (Roper 2009).

I argue that the anxieties which brought about fascism were both universal anxieties about the dissolution of the self and of society, and specific masculine anxieties about the dissolution of masculinity. For, it is only masculinity (not femininity) which is threatened by the phantasy of retreating into mother's body.

However, internal fascism goes a step further than internal tyranny as described by Meltzer (1973) and promises not only freedom from anxiety but omnipotence – the rebirth of the individual and the manufacturing of a new masculinity, new 'men of steel' who defy vulnerability and femininity exactly because the new male body of militarism acts as a masculine womb. The Devil promises not just painlessness and power, but omnipotence – the rebirth of a new unspoilt and uncontaminated individual and a new pure society. And he can be very persuasive.

Part I

The fascist state of mind

Chapter 1

What is the fascist state of mind?

In his book *Benito Mussolini*, Anthony Cardoza wrote that Mussolini designed the movement to express and embody not a precise political project so much as a *state of mind*, a pervasive mood of post-war discontent and undirected revolt.

In attempting to define a 'fascist state of mind' the question begs itself whether it is legitimate to use a political term to describe a psychological state, and whether we can make the jump from the social and political levels to the level of the inner world (and vice versa) and have any confidence that we are talking about the same thing. This is indeed a serious problem which cannot be ignored, but I think that since human beings are social and political animals, and since fascist and totalitarian movements and regimes are human formations, we cannot ignore the question of what is in human beings that responds in such a way to the particular social, economic and political pressures of the twentieth century – and perhaps of modernity in general – to create systems that might be called fascist. However, caution is needed to distinguish these levels and not to confuse the one for the other.

I would like to stress right at the beginning that this book is not meant to be a psychoanalytic explanation of the historical phenomenon of fascism. It is conceived as an attempt to understand *the state of mind* that might describe the emotional forces that both emerged from, and interacted with, the historical phenomena to create what might be described as 'fascist regimes'. However, what is stressed throughout the book is that this state of mind is common to all human beings and can be mobilised when traumatic social and economic conditions predominate and threaten the individual and society with fragmentation.

It is not unusual in contemporary psychoanalysis to describe the self as comprised of different parts and different states of mind more or less integrated within the whole. However, a state of mind does not define the whole self. It only expresses a part of the self.

A theoretically healthy mind would be characterised by different parts of the self and different states of mind in communication with each other. However, splits within the mind exist in all of us and split off parts of the self, which are not in communication with other parts, can exert nevertheless strong influence on the whole personality – the way a terrorist underground organization can exert a great deal of influence on the rest of society in terms of how paranoid the society can be, what defences are mobilised to deal with this threat and so on. In terms of the individual he will be defined by the degree of integration or splitting that exists within the personality, by how autonomous the split off parts are, the relative strength of the split off parts in relation to the rest of the self, and by the defences that are mobilised to deal with these split off parts.

It is in this sense that I mean that a fascist state of mind is common to all human beings. However, this should not be considered that all human beings are dominated by a fascist state of mind, but rather that this state of mind (or at least the pre-requisites of this state of mind), co-exists with other states of mind and parts of the self. In this sense it is the balance within the mind that will determine whether this state of mind will take over the individual; and it is the balance within society, also between society and the individual, that will determine whether this state of mind will be externalised and will take over civil society.

I would like to add that the predominance of certain states of mind within the mind is not separate from society. It is a part of the big waves of emotions and passions that sweeps through societies and the institutions that are there to regulate human emotions and passions. Each era is characterised by a different and unique balance between human needs, emotions, passions, fears and anxieties on the one hand, and social institutions on the other. And each era has a different understanding of this balance. When the balance between individual and society breaks down, we can expect cataclysmic disturbances where regression to more regressive or 'debased' (Bion) states of mind takes place. We can say that this balance between social institutions and the needs of the individual broke down with the end of World War One and left individuals at the mercy of their uncontained human emotions. I suggest that fascism within the mind and within society is the alienated child of this broken marriage.

Views of historians and social scientists

Fascism is a term often used loosely in everyday speech to mean any extreme right wing party, government or individual and in this loose usage it can mean almost any authoritarian dictatorship. However, its more precise meaning developed in Italy in the 1920s when the Fascist Party was formed under Mussolini.[1] Most historians describe Hitler's National Socialist party and ideology as fascist (Kershaw 1993; Bracher 1973; Mommsen 2001; Gregor 2005; Paxton 2004; De Grand 1995). (From now on I shall use Fascist and Fascism when I speak about Italian Fascism and I shall use fascist and fascism when I speak of generic fascism and fascist states of mind.)

However, even in its academic usage the term proved to be quite 'elusive' and 'controversial' (O'Sullivan 1983). Summarising the different arguments and theories about the meaning of fascism Noel O' Sullivan concludes that the main characteristics of fascism are '… a condition of permanent revolution, a cult of despotic leadership draped out in democratic guise, and a highly theatrical form of state-worship that culminates in an ideal of self-sufficiency which makes a pro-gramme of conquest and expansion integral to the fascist philosophy' (ibid.: 5).

Other authors stressed also the idea of a national rebirth and the attempt to restore the nation to its past (mythical) greatness as central to fascist ideology in both Italy and Germany (Gregor 2005). The primacy of the group, community and race is also seen as a fundamental fascist characteristic (Paxton 2004). Also part of fascist ideology was a belief in a simplistic version of social Darwinism and the idea of the survival of the fittest which made war between nations part of natural selection. Thus, violence and war were idealised and democratic values denigrated as weak and ultimately harmful to the nation (Todd 2002: 7–12). The visceral hatred of democracy as weakening and 'softening' men is part of most definitions of fascism and of Mussolini's and Hitler's rhetoric.

Many historians gave up on the attempt to define a generic fascism and sug-gested that we should only call Fascist Mussolini's regime, or at most Mussolini's and Hitler's regimes. The historian Renzo De Felice (1977) concludes that no general definition of fascism could exist as every regime was unique.

Robert Paxton (2004), on the other hand, disagrees with this understanding of fascism, and in a recent book he sets out to define a generic fascism as a product of European democracies and of modernity in general. He argues for maintaining the term 'fascist' as a generic term that describes a twentieth-century political innova-tion and a post-democratic mass phenomenon characterised by certain 'mobilising passions'. In other words Paxton does not see fascism as described by either its ideology or certain immutable political arrangements. He sees fascism as defined by certain 'subterranean' or 'visceral feelings' which define fascism more accu-rately than the historical movement that they are enshrined in. Anthony Cardoza (2005: 38), writing about Italian Fascism, expresses a similar view namely that Mussolini designed Fascism, not to express a particular political ideology but a *state of mind* that characterised post-war Italy. Alexander De Grand (1995) on comparing Italian Fascism and German National Socialism talks about a 'fascist style of rule'. These authors seem to converge on the idea that it is not certain poli-cies or certain ideologies that constitute fascism but rather a *state of mind.*

Paxton (2004) looks at fascism not as a static entity but best described in action as it adapts itself to the conditions around it. He distinguishes five stages: The initial stage of creating a movement, followed by taking root, getting power, exercising power and the long term (radicalization or entropy). In this sense the historical movement defined as fascism may be changing its face, depending on the stage it is in, but the 'mobilising passions' remain the same. In other words the leopard may not change its spots, but in endlessly re-arranging them, looks like a different animal.

However, although fascism in these different stages may look like a different animal (for instance Hitler's party may have looked very different in 1936 from the one in 1925 or the one in 1942 or 1945), the underlying dynamics and the mobilising passions remained the same and led to a war of expansion and the poli-cies of the holocaust and finally to a war of self-destruction.

Paxton writes:

> Fascist regimes could not settle down into a comfortable enjoyment of power.
> The charismatic leader had made dramatic promises to unify, purify and ener-
> gise the community, to save it from the flabbiness of bourgeois materialism, the
> confusion and corruption of democratic politics, and the contamination of alien
> peoples and cultures; to head off the threatened revolution of property with a
> revolution of values; to rescue the community from decadence and decline. He
> had offered sweeping solutions to these menaces: violence against enemies,
> both inside and out; the individual's total immersion in the community; the
> purification of blood and culture; the galvanizing enterprise of rearmament and
> expansionist war. He had assured his people a 'privileged relation to history'.
>
> (Paxton 2004: 148)

Paxton's book seeks to define the essence of 'fascism' as a generic term, as
opposed to the essence of this or that fascist regime. He finally defines fascism
not by its policies, nor by its ideology or political arrangements but by a set of
'visceral feelings' and 'mobilising passions'.

To summarise Paxton's mobilising passions:

- a sense of overwhelming crisis beyond the reach of any traditional solution…
- the primacy of the group…
- the belief that one's group is a victim…
- dread of the group's decline…
- the need for a closer integration of a purer community…
- the need for authority by natural chiefs (always male)…
- the superiority of the leader's instincts over abstract and universal reason…
- the right of the chosen people to dominate others…

(Paxton 2004: 219–20)

Paxton's view that fascism as characterised by certain mobilising passions allows
a psychoanalytic understanding not only of the political phenomenon known as
'fascism' but also of the state of mind that can be called 'fascist' and which exists,
as most psychoanalysts would agree, *in all of us*. Attempting to describe this
underlying state of mind and how it might come to dominate both the mind and
society is the aim of this book.

Totalitarianism

"So we have established the first point in defining Fascism: its totalitarian nature"
(Giovanni Gentile 1934).

Part of the ideological underpinning of fascism, is its totalitarian ambition. The
term 'total' or 'totalitarian state' was adopted by Mussolini to describe the all
embracing type of the state he aspired to. His well-known motto 'all within the

state, nothing outside the state, nothing against the state' defines the totalitarian philosophy of Italian Fascism. However, it was Hitler, more than Mussolini, who attempted to develop the totalitarian side of fascism to chilling perfection.

Historians and political scientists differentiate between authoritarian dictatorships and totalitarianism and use these terms to describe qualitatively different regimes. Alan Todd, in his book *The European Dictatorships* (2002) summarises the views of one of the most eminent scholars on the subject K. D. Bracher:

> Authoritarian dictatorships . . . do not come to power as the result of a mass revolution, but come about as the result of an existing conservative regime imposing increasingly undemocratic measures intended to neutralise and immobilise mass political and industrial organisations. They can also arise following a military coup . . . (and they) are firmly committed to maintaining or restoring traditional structures or values. Totalitarian dictatorships, on the other hand, come to power as the result of a mass movement or revolution and are, at least in theory, committed to a radical ideology and programme of political, economic and social change.
>
> (Todd 2002: 12)

Adrian Lyttelton distinguishes totalitarian regimes as demanding 'not merely obedience but *active identification*' (1975: 35; italics mine).

He continues:

> it is probably true that the totalitarian ideal of unanimity can never be fully realized; the tension between obedience and fanatical enthusiasm, coercion and conviction, cannot be resolved except verbally, and the characteristic of any totalitarian regime is one of bad faith.
>
> (Ibid.: 36)

This contradiction of obedience or domination versus active identification of the individual with the regime makes totalitarianism difficult to define. This is perhaps the reason why some diametrically opposite definitions have been attempted.

Margaret Canovan maintains that 'there are almost as many senses on totalitarianism as there are writers on the subject' (Canovan 2000: 25). There is, however, the 'majority' view (Todd calls it the 'consensus' view) which defines totalitarianism as a coherent and cohesive system built on the image of an ideology with total control of all aspects of society by the state, using terror to prevent any change and any deviation from the ideology and working like clockwork according to a programme. It is a state frozen, unchanging and absolutely orderly (Canovan 2000: 25–6).

However, recent research casts doubts on this picture of the totalitarian regime as a frozen, stable regime where everything runs like clockwork and is co-ordinated from above. For instance, recent research on Nazi Germany reveals the chaotic nature of the regime spiralling out of control towards destruction (Mommsen 2001).

Ian Kershaw (1993) reviews the term and its uses and warns against the unthinking use of the concept sometimes as an ideological instrument and at other times as a conceptual tool. On the whole he finds only a limited use of the term useful. He concludes that what 'could be heuristically useful [is] ... the modest notion of the *'total claim'* of a regime on its subjects' (ibid.: 33).

The contradiction between the image of a regime totally controlled from above and frozen in time and the image of a regime out of control heading towards self-destruction can only be understood when we consider the underlying, unconscious structure of totalitarian and fascist regimes – their 'mobilising passions – and the difference between conscious aims and unconscious reality. The rest of this study is an attempt to throw some light on this underlying unconscious structure. In her own way Hannah Arendt comes very close to doing exactly this.

Hannah Arendt's theory of totalitarianism

Contrary to the 'consensus view', and preceding most of the writings on totalitarianism Hannah Arendt developed her own theory. In her classic book the *Origins of Totalitarianism*, published originally in England with the title *The Burden of Our Time* (1951), she puts forward a complete theory of totalitarianism. She sees totalitarianism as a radically new kind of regime and considered it a dangerous mistake to confuse it with other kind of tyrannies. She sees terror not as a means to an end, as in other dictatorships, but as the essence of totalitarianism, and sees its 'central institutions' being the concentration camps and the extermination camps' (Canovan 2000: 2). Not the enemies of the regime but whole populations of innocents were exterminated in both Stalinist Russia and Nazi Germany. This completely irrational element in totalitarianism is part of its nature and its reliance on the ideologies that are supposed to be based on Laws of Nature or of History. This view of irrationality and constant destructiveness as a part of the totalitarian regime is different from the consensus view. Canovan summarises the difference:

> Metaphorically, one might say that if the dominant picture suggests the rigidity, uniformity, transparency, and immobility of a frozen lake, Arendt's theory evokes a mountain torrent sweeping away everything in its path, or a hurricane levelling everything recognizably human. Instead of referring to a political system of a deliberately structured kind, 'totalitarianism' in Arendt's sense means a chaotic, non utilitarian, manically dynamic movement of destruction that assails all the features of human nature and the human world that make politics possible.
>
> (2000: 26)

For Arendt the totalitarian state is inherently unstable and relies on 'permanent revolution'. She writes: 'The point is that both Hitler and Stalin held out promises of stability in order to hide their intention of creating a state of permanent instability' (Arendt 1951: 377).

The total power of totalitarian regimes turns out to mean unparalleled destruction of plurality. But since plurality can only be destroyed by destroying humanity itself, the extermination of whole populations seems endless. Extermination continues and is part of the regime long after all the enemies of the regime have been eliminated. Enemies have to be invented and re-invented all the time. Reality itself becomes the enemy as 'the disregard for facts, the strict adherence to rules of a fictitious world, becomes more difficult to maintain' (ibid.: 378).

The real power in the totalitarian state lies with the secret police.

> Above the state and behind the facades of ostensible power, in a maze of multiplied offices, underlying all shifts of authority and in a chaos of inefficiency, lies the power nucleus of the country, the super-efficient and super-competent services of the secret police.
>
> (Ibid.: 378)

The expansion of the secret services takes place when the actual enemies of the regime have effectively been eliminated and no opponents to the regime are left. Now begins the systematic spying on 'potential enemies'. Arendt makes a distinction between a 'suspect' and a 'potential enemy' and argues that this differentiates the despotic from the totalitarian secret police since the latter is 'defined by the policy of the government and not by his own desire to overthrow it' (ibid.: 401).

Arendt continues:

> The category of potential enemies outlives the first ideologically determined foes of the movement; new potential enemies are discovered according to changing circumstances: the Nazis, foreseeing the completion of Jewish extermination, had already taken the necessary preliminary steps for the liquidation of the Polish people, while Hitler even planned the decimation of certain categories of Germans; while Bolsheviks, having started with descendants of the former ruling classes, directed their full terror against the kulaks (in the thirties), who in turn were followed by Russians of Polish origin (between 1936 and 1938), the Tartars and the Volga Germans during the war, former prisoners of war and units of occupational forces of the Red Army after the war, and Russian Jewry after the establishment of the Jewish State.
>
> (Ibid.: 402)

As the secret police carries the real power of the totalitarian state, every citizen becomes a suspect and every thought is suspect. 'Simply because of their capacity to think human beings are suspects by definition' (ibid.: 407) and mutual suspicion permeates the whole society.

Total domination is the aim of totalitarian regimes and as this is not possible as long as the individual has a sense of individuality and a sense of morality, the terror is directed towards the murder of the moral individual but also the individual who retains a loyalty in relationships outside the regime.[2]

Although criticised in the 1970s and 1980s Arendt's theory finds new support in contemporary scholarship (Villa 2000). Ian Kershaw writes in relation to her theory: '... her emphasis on the radicalizing, dynamic, and structure-destroying inbuilt characteristics of Nazism has been amply borne out by later research' (Kershaw quoted in Canovan 2000: 36). Hans Mommsen (2001: 37) also notes the 'cumulative radicalization and progressive self-destruction as structural determinants of the Nazi dictatorship'. He also observes that 'Nazi politics unleashed an unbridled political, economic and military dynamic with unprecedented destructive energy, while proving incapable of creating lasting political structures' (ibid.: 37). Michael Mann remarks that both the Nazi and the Stalinist regimes are examples of 'regimes of continuous revolution' and exhibit extreme use of terror and show 'persistent rejection of institutional compromise' (Canovan 2000: 37).

Hans Mommsen (2001: 11) exposed the last stages of the Nazi regime and the 'total claim' that it made on its citizens beginning with Goebbels famous speech in 1942 for a 'total war'.

What Mommsen is describing in the final months and weeks of the war is a totalitarian regime although he does not use the word. He uses, however, words and phrases identical to Hannah Arendt's description of totalitarianism such as 'the ruthless elimination of inimical elements', or 'virtual enemies of the regime', or 'the practice of annihilation of potential dissidents' (ibid.: 122), or '... the desire to eliminate all those who might be potential obstacles to the restoration of the National Socialist idea ... with the possible intention of liquidating them as potential traitors to the German people' (ibid.: 122–3).

Mommsen argues that the Nazi regime was on a course of self-destruction and that 'besides the military decay of the regime an accelerating process of internal dissolution accompanied its military setbacks and were without doubt related to them' (ibid.: 109).

Part of this process of internal dissolution was the utter 'atrophy of the political system which was completely paralyzed and unable to resist the suicidal course of the Nazi leadership' (ibid.: 123).

The preceding description by Mommsen of the last years of the Nazi regime has striking similarities with Hannah Arendt's description of totalitarianism and reminds us of the destructiveness of the quasi-religious fervour of utopianism embodied in totalitarianism and fascism alike (at least the Nazi type of fascism) and that the total domination that it aims for, is identical with total destruction.

If we take Paxton's view that fascism is best described by its 'mobilising passions' we can see that Hannah Arendt's description of totalitarianism comes very close to describing a regime dominated by a passion for total domination and annihilation of individuality and difference which amounts to total self-destruction. It is part of the thesis of this book that rational domination is not what fascism is about. Rational domination may be the dynamic of authoritarian regimes but not of totalitarian regimes. This book is an attempt to understand the unconscious dynamics of totalitarian/fascist regimes and their self-destructive passions.

The fascist state of mind: early psychoanalytic views

Attempts to apply psychoanalysis to understand the unconscious dynamics of fascism have been numerous and diverse. An early influential psychoanalytic analysis of fascism has been made by Wilhelm Reich in his book *The Mass Psychology of Fascism* (1933). For Reich, it was modern technological capitalist civilization which was to blame for the rise of fascism as it suppressed the biological and sexual needs of man. Reich argued that this technological capitalist culture developed within a patriarchal/authoritarian culture which created a personality that craved for authority. He stressed the mystical side of fascism which arose as a compensation for the suppression of man's sexual needs and the decline in personal relations. He states: '"Fascism" is the basic emotional attitude of the suppressed man of our authoritarian machine civilization and its mechanistic-mystical conception of life. It is the mechanistic-mystical character of modern man that produces fascist parties and not vice versa' (Reich 1946: 15).

Reich's approach is essentialist in that he assumes a human nature outside culture that is unchanging and suffering under the oppression of the authoritarian technological culture of the 1930s and 1940s (Parker 1997). His book suffers from a highly rhetorical oversimplification of the conditions that led to the European fascism since he does not tell us why some countries became fascist whilst others did not, although similar modern conditions of the suppression of biological needs existed in most European countries. However, his description of the mystical character of the Nazi ideology and its attempt to destroy human relations in the interest of a mass society is insightful and in my opinion accurate.

A more influential and less aphoristic approach to the problem of fascism and destructiveness concentrated on what came to be called the 'authoritarian character' (Horkheimer 1936) and the 'authoritarian personality' (Adorno *et al.* 1950). The thesis of the authoritarian character embodied in the authoritarian personality was further developed by the Frankfurt School who saw it as the answer to the question why the German people embraced fascism.

Fromm (1941) described the 'authoritarian character' along the lines of Freud's theory of sado-masochism that is he saw the psyche as being dominated by a cruel sadistic superego reigning over a weak and masochistic ego. Simultaneously the masochistic ego longing for submission gave itself to the power of the sadistic superego. He described in these terms not only the Nazi leaders but also the character structure of a great part of the German population. He sees such a personality as submitting masochistically to those above and dominating sadistically those below. Such a personality is also characterised by an admiration for the strong and hatred of weakness.

Fromm writes:

> The essence of the authoritarian character has been described as the simultaneous presence of sadistic and masochistic drives. Sadism was understood as aiming at unrestricted power over another person more or less mixed with destructiveness, masochism as aiming at dissolving oneself in an overwhelmingly strong power and participating in its strong glory.
>
> (Fromm 1941: 220)

In this work (Fromm 1941) Fromm saw Hitler and his close associates, but also the German people as being dominated by this internal structure. Fromm saw Hitler as being on the sadistic end of the structure dominating over masochistic crowds whose main desire was to submit to a strong leader. However, these followers are themselves sadistic in relation to powerless groups such as the Jews, the Gypsies and others. Fromm also describes the masochistic longing in Hitler himself – that is his wish to submit to a higher authority or power such as God, Fate, History or Nature.

The concept of the authoritarian personality was further developed by Adorno and his co-workers in their monumental empirical study carried out in the USA and attempting to demonstrate the relationship between 'the authoritarian personality' and racism and fascism (Adorno *et al.* 1950). They found that a correspondence existed between family relations and the way individuals responded in many different areas of life:

> ... a basically hierarchical, authoritarian, exploitive parent-child relationship is apt to carry over into a power-oriented, exploitively dependent attitude towards sex partner and one's God and may well culminate in a political philosophy and social outlook which has no room for anything but a desperate clinging to what appears to be strong and a disdainful rejection of whatever is delegated to the bottom.
>
> (Ibid.: 971)

Personality traits such as 'stereotypy, emotional coldness, identification with power, and general destructiveness' were found to be characteristics of the prejudiced personality (ibid.: 973). These characteristics gave the individuals readiness to break into violence. However, whether and under what conditions these individuals may erupt into actual violence was something that the authors were not prepared to speculate.

Whether there is a specific fascist personality has been also explored by the psychoanalysts Henry Dicks (1972) and Roger Money-Kyrle (1993). Their work was based on interviews with German civil servants and important functionaries in the Third Reich as well as interviews with SS[3] leaders.

Understanding the wider culture into which the Nazi ideology grew and took roots became an important issue for both these analysts. The German 'authoritarian personality' based on the submission to a harsh, murderous and omnipotent superego emerged as a basic national internal structure of that period. The family structure of the Wilhelmine period with its harsh father figure and a powerless, masochistic mother was examined. Dicks stressed the creation of a sado-masochistic relation between ego and superego and the idealization of a harsh, murderous superego that created a 'typical German male's oscillation between deferential conformity and harsh assertiveness' (1972: 35). He saw this as situated within the particular family structure of the Wilhelmine Germany.[4]

Both Dicks (1972) and Money-Kyrle (1978) distinguish between the general population, the civil servants, and the leadership and party fanatics. Their interviews with SS killers revealed the absolute fanatic worship of the leader and the ideology, and the lack of guilt with which they faced their participation in the extermination of human beings. This internal structure is more paranoid and goes beyond the sado-masochistic defences of the authoritarian personality and a submission to the superego. This is a more delusional and more paranoid state of mind which they distinguish from the majority of the followers of the regime who adhere more to an authoritarian personality structure.

Erich Fromm coming back to the theme of fascism in 1973, also came to the same conclusion that the paranoid state of mind that characterised Hitler and his SS killers went beyond the authoritarian personality. His search for a psychoanalytic understanding of fascism took him to examine psychic phenomena that are much more destructive than sado-masochism. In his book *The Anatomy of Human Destructiveness* he examined a character structure based on what he called 'necrophilia' or the love of death. Basing his theory on Freud's and Klein's concept of the death instinct he described necrophilia as 'the passion to destroy life and the attraction to all that is dead, decaying, and purely mechanical' (ibid.: 27). Fromm saw the fascist's fascination with violence, death and destructiveness as a part of the 'necrophilous character' but more than this he saw this potential in every human being under certain conditions. Like Reich he saw the modern social order with its worship of the machine and the mechanical as contributing to this character structure characterised by hatred of life itself.

The fascist state of mind: contemporary views

More recently psychoanalysts have talked about a 'fascist' (Bollas 1993; Lousada 2006) or a 'totalitarian' (Temple 2006) state of mind.

Bollas' seminal paper 'The fascist state of mind' (1993) re-opened the search for an understanding of the unconscious dynamics of fascism. I shall go into it in some detail as it bears similarities with, but also differences from, my own position.

Right at the beginning Bollas makes two important points: that the fascist state of mind is common to all of us; and that it is a state of mind that leads to genocide.

> As a psychoanalyst I turn my attention to that frame of mind which is the warrant for the extermination of human beings' he writes. 'I shall argue that there is a Fascist in each of us and that there is indeed a highly identifiable psychic profile for this personal state.
>
> (Bollas 1993: 196)

The fact that there is a fascist in all of us, that the fascist state of mind is an 'ordinary' state, makes us all susceptible, or at least many of us, under certain conditions, to either joining or condoning fascist regimes that sanction genocide. We have seen in recent times (post war times) how a regime like Poll Pot's, or to a lesser extent Milosevic's, can achieve this with the fanatical support of many ordinary citizens who become transformed under certain circumstances into mass murderers.

For Bollas the move is from a democratic, pluralist self or state of mind to a totalitarian one where the self is dominated by one idea, leader or ideology. Doubt or alternative views are banned from the mind and from the group. The elimination of all opposition and of all difference is at the heart of this state of mind. The search for a totally coherent ideology is at work.

Bollas continues: 'Thus something almost banal in its ordinariness – namely, our cohering of life into ideologies or theories – is the seed of the Fascist state of mind when such ideology must (for whatever reason) become total' (ibid.: 200).

The quest for *total* coherence and the elimination of difference and plurality lead eventually to the death of the symbolic but also to a moral void. The Nazi movement created a belief that everything was possible and nothing was forbidden, leading to an 'infinite moral space'.

Bollas refers to Janine Chasseguet-Smirgel's view that this infinite moral space is the 'pervert's accomplishment' eliminating all opposition, and having access to all objects. No (Oedipal) prohibition and no father is present in this state of mind where everything is permitted.

This 'moral void' simplifies violence. The empty subject must find a victim to contain the void 'and now a state of mind becomes an act of violence .... To accomplish this transfer, the Fascist mind transforms a human other into a disposable nonentity, a bizarre mirror transference of what has already occurred in the Fascist's self experience' (ibid.: 203).

Bollas talks about a change in the self towards simplification, cohesion and elimination of difference. The subject now exports his own sense of void – the empty self – onto the object who becomes empty, a nonentity, valueless. He sees grandiosity born out of the annihilation of the other. In this the very process of annihilation is idealised. The very process of annihilation brings with it emptiness and purity. What comes from outside contaminates and pollutes.

Such a state of mind extols the virtue of being pure, uncontaminated because nothing is taken into the self, the psyche living from its sense of antiseptic accomplishment by maintaining purity in its own right, achieved by the continuous evacuation of the noxious. We can find this phenomenon, however, in ordinary life, whether it be spoken by those who attempt to claim the position of pure Christianity, pure objectivity, pure science ...

(Ibid.: 204–5)

This continuum from the ordinary to the extreme and pathological is characterised by the increasing elimination of all opposition and the establishment of a delusionally narcissistic mind that is absolutely pure as it has eliminated all objects.

Bollas sees war as essential to the fascist state of mind – both externally and internally – war within the self and war against the self, the war to eliminate the contents of the self, ultimately the self itself, and replace it by a leader or an ideology. In this sense the elimination of the contents of the self is the most essential process in the fascist state of mind. Everything else follows from this.

> Thus the concentration camp, a metaphor of the psychic process of Fascism, is the place where, as the humane parts of the self are dehumanized and then exterminated, the death work is idealized in the death workers who cleanse the body politic.
>
> (Ibid.: 206)

In this sense Bollas sees *intellectual genocide*, the elimination of the contents of the self, as preceding genocide – the elimination of whole peoples. He identifies the difference between intellectual *committive genocide* and *ommittive genocide* and names several categories of committive genocide such as: *distortion* (the subject distorts the view of the opponent; *de-contextualisation* – points of view held by opponents are taken out of context; *denigration* – denigration of the opponent's view; *caricature* – a move from denigration to ridiculing; *character assassination* – discrediting the opponent's personal character; *change of name* – using derogatory names to refer to a group or people; *categorisation as aggregation* – the individual is lost and transferred to a mass.

Under omittive genocide Bollas lists: *Absence of reference* – an individual or group are removed from history books or from reference to them.

All the processes that he enumerates are a kind of simplification of the mind. So we come back to his concept of the simplification of the self by eliminating the contents of the self – a concept also central to Janine Chasseguet-Smirgel's theory of totalitarianism.

Janine Chasseguet-Smirgel's theory of utopia and totalitarianism

Chasseguet-Smirgel examined the utopian and destructive elements in totalitarianism as two sides of the same coin and linked them both to primitive wishes and anxieties described by Melanie Klein. In her book *Sexuality and Mind* she writes: 'The "totalitarian temptation" … cannot be understood, to my mind, by a simple reference to sado-masochism but by the seductive powers of fantasies linked to the archaic matrix of the Oedipus complex' (Chasseguet-Smirgel 1986: 102).

The 'archaic matrix of the Oedipus complex' is a term coined by Chasseguet-Smirgel to describe what she calls a 'primary wish to rediscover a universe without obstacles, a smooth maternal belly, stripped of its contents, to which free access is desired' (ibid.: 92).

She examines Melanie Klein's theory of the early Oedipus complex and Klein's descriptions of the sadistic attacks that the baby makes on the mother's body and its contents. For Klein, the mother's body represents the external world and reality, and as such it arouses both envy and sadistic impulses and the wish to appropriate all the riches of the mother's body – the babies, the father's penis and excrement. Thus in the description of the early Oedipus complex Klein describes the inevitable frustration and hatred that is aroused in the baby when he realises that the mother's body and its riches do not belong to him. The reality of separateness is now indisputable. With this goes a violent wish to appropriate, steal or violently scoop out, the contents of the mother's belly.

For Chasseguet-Smirgel there is a primary wish that goes with the attacks on mother's body and this is about getting rid of the contents of the mother's body (babies, milk, feces, father's penis) and getting access to the smooth belly of the mother, or in Lousada's words to become again 'the sole occupier' (Lousada 2006). In this sense the contents of the mother's body represent obstacles to the wish to go back to a place without pain and without frustration that is to a pre-natal existence. In her paper 'The archaic matrix of the Oedipus complex' she writes: 'It is a question of rediscovering, on the level of thought, a mental functioning without hindrances, with psychic energy flowing freely' (Chasseguet-Smirgel 1986: 77).

Chasseguet-Smirgel sees the destruction of the contents of the mother's belly not only as the destruction of obstacles but as the destruction of reality through the destruction of difference or differences. 'It is possible', she writes,

> to conceive of reality as being made up of differences. Rather than to speak of the difference between the sexes and the generations[5] as representing the only bedrock of reality, it would be more appropriate to think of reality as being entirely the result of differences.
>
> (Ibid.: 82)

This wish to rediscover a universe without obstacles is, of course, the pleasure principle. Citing compelling clinical material she describes the regression of thought that takes place under the sway of the pleasure principle. The phantasies are of a melting pot where obstacles are homogenised and rendered undifferentiated (ibid.: 84–5) like faeces or like ashes. The death instinct linked to the pleasure principle and the Nirvana principle, as Freud (1920) has shown, is evident here. The worlds of the father and of genitality are destroyed as they represent reality and differentiation. This finds expression in perversion which relies ultimately on an idealization of faeces. 'It is precisely this idealization', she writes, 'that permits the anal elements to pass through the barrier of repression' (ibid.: 89).

In her theory of utopia Chasseguet-Smirgel offered a description of totalitarianism. In this sense all utopias have an underlying threat of extreme violence: 'Everything that would prevent the establishment of utopian bliss must be annihilated' (ibid.: 105). The idea of a tabula rasa, of the destruction of the existing state of things, is often bypassed in the description of utopias. The violence of destroying 'the contents of the mother's belly' is not mentioned. The idealization of anality makes this omission possible and leads to the trap that is totalitarianism. 'The dream turns into a nightmare and the gentle maternal womb into a sadistic anus' (ibid.: 107).

To bring Bollas and Chasseguet-Smirgel together I wish to say that the simplification of the mind or of mental functioning is common to both of them but in different ways. In both of them the complexity of reality is avoided for a simplified version of the world and of others. In extreme cases, as in totalitarian functioning, both the subject and the object become homogenised and differences are not tolerated. Destructiveness prevails. Emptiness becomes idealised. Chasseguet-Smirgel stresses the utopian and perverse side of totalitarianism, whilst Bollas stresses the genocidal side. It should be obvious from the above that these are two sides of the same coin.

Fascism as a group phenomenon

It is in the nature of fascism that it is a group phenomenon and aspires to destroy any individual perspective that might exist apart from the group. Even when we are talking about the individual's internal world it is impossible to speak about a fascist state of mind without speaking about group psychology, mass psychology and group processes and dynamics as described by Freud (1921), Bion (1961), Rice (1965, 1969), Turquet (1967) and more recent authors like Otto Kernberg (2003a) and Hinshelwood (2006, 2007). In this sense a fascist state of mind will comprise an internal group that resembles a regressed group (see Chapters 6 and 7).

Rice's observations (1965, 1969) and Turquet's observation (1975) of large unstructured groups replicate Bion's description (1961) of narcissistic and paranoid reactions in small groups and the attack of the group on any individual who aspires to retain their autonomy and integrity (Kernberg 2003a: 686). What I want to stress here is the collapse of internal differentiation between the ego and the ego ideal and of the differentiation between the inner and outer world, or the individual and the group, in the members of such a group. When the group ideal takes the place of the ego ideal, any loyalty to internal objects is destroyed. In this way the collapse of differentiation within the self is mirrored within the group and vice versa. I shall examine the fascist state of mind as a group phenomenon in Chapters 6 and 7.

Conclusion

I have looked at two levels of description – one at the social/historical level and the other at the psychoanalytic/intra-psychic level. Pulling together the threads a convergence between the two levels emerges.

Firstly at both levels there is a differentiation made between authoritarian regimes and authoritarian states of mind on the one hand; and fascist or totalitarian regimes or states of mind on the other. Authoritarian regimes and authoritarian states of mind aim at stability. Their use of violence and domination has as its aim survival and the preservation not only of the regime but of the country or of the individual. The sado-masochistic structure of the authoritarian character creates, like other sado-masochistic structures, stability by limiting aggression to a strictly defined structure. Fascist regimes, on the other hand, embrace a 'state of permanent revolution' (O'Sullivan) and worship violence and instability whilst preaching stability.

Analyses at both levels describe the fascist regime – within the mind or within society – as fired by irrationality and self-destructive behaviour in its attempt to destroy plurality, individuality and difference and achieve a pure, homogeneous race and society or a pure homogeneous mind. The impossibility of this aim reveals a self-destructive frame of mind.

The impossible task of homogenising the world or the mind is driven by total irrationality, unreality and omnipotence. In psychoanalytic terms we can say that the fascist state of mind goes beyond the authoritarian personality and beyond sado-masochistic defences and embraces psychotic mechanisms and delusional states. However, the sado-masochistic character does not disappear but oscillates with the more delusional mode of functioning to create islands of stability and quasi-rationality within predominantly fascist regimes. The authoritarian sado-masochistic structure gives the fascist regimes whatever stability they may possess.

That human beings are capable, under certain circumstances, of acting in ways that are self-destructive, or perhaps more that this, *aiming* at self-destruction, defies common sense and the idea that human beings are rational creatures whose main aim is survival. Yet those characteristics of fascism, in its totalitarian ambition, that were revealed at the first and the last stages of the Nazi regime were exactly of this nature. A psychoanalytic understanding of this behaviour is, I believe, not only possible but mandatory.

However, my specific angle in examining the fascist state of mind is the part played by masculine anxieties and defences in the creation of fascism. It is part of my thesis that the ultimate destructiveness of the fascist state of mind can be traced not only to fears of annihilation but to the ultimate *wish for annihilation* (I believe that this is the same as what Freud called the death instinct). My own contribution in this book is to attempt to link the wish for annihilation or the wish for dissolution of the ego, to the masculine anxieties and defences that externalised themselves in fascism.

Passive wishes for ceasing to exist, for the dissolution of the ego, for being absorbed into a bigger entity, ultimately mother's body, are ordinary states of mind usually balanced by the will to live and to be an individual. Under traumatic circumstances these wishes may become dominant states of mind and in adult men difficult to be distinguished from losing one's masculinity inside mother. I suggest that the male passive wish for annihilation which is not to be distinguished from wishes and fears of being absorbed into, or devoured by, the mother is translated into the active wish for annihilating others and ultimately the self. Within a male fraternity and under a male leader the new masculinised mother, the fascist group, achieves both the dissolution of the ego and the manufacturing of a new hyper-masculinity born through a worship of purity, homogeneity, violence and war.

It is remarkable how few historians, social scientists or psychoanalysts have commented on the masculine character of fascist regimes as if dealing with the obvious is not their task. Certainly none of these historians, social scientists and psychoanalysts mentioned devote much space on the masculine character of the regime. Yet both Mussolini and Hitler boasted about the warlike masculinity that was at the heart of their regimes. Whether these theatrical hyper-masculine gestures were to be taken seriously the world was to find out at an immense cost to humanity.

I shall explore these themes in detail in the following chapters.

Notes

1 The Italian Fascist Party was formed in 1919 under Mussolini. The name Fascism is an amalgamation of two different sources: (1) *fascio* which is a group or a band of people. The term had been previously used by socialists and trade unionists; and (2) *fasces* which was a symbol of power and authority in ancient Rome. Originally the fasces was a bundle of sticks tied together to which an axe was later added to remind that justice included capital punishment. This was carried by the lictor (an official who controlled the debates in the Senate).

2 In relation to the destruction of relationships Arendt writes:

> In the Soviet Union a woman will sue for divorce immediately after her husband's arrest in order to save the lives of her children; if her husband chances to come back, she will indignantly turn him out of the house.
>
> (Arendt 1951: 423)

3 The intitials SS stand for Schutzstaffel which is translated as ProtectionSquadron, originally a nazi paramilitary formation which grew under Himmler's leadership to one of the most powerful and inhuman organizations of the Third Reich responsible for most of the crimes against humanity during the Second World War.

4 Ian Parker points out the contradictory accounts of the family during the nineteenth and early twentieth centuries that are given by different theoreticians. One account describes a very rigid family structure and a harsh and authoritarian father who shaped his son into obedience. A different account described the weakening of the family during the same period due to the absence of fathers away from home and the absence in the son of a strong identification with the father who then never freed himself from the illusion that a narcissistic fusion with the mother was possible (Parker 1997: 164–5).

5 Here Chasseguet-Smirgel refers to her previous view expressed in her book Creativity and Perversion (1985) where she defined perversion as the denial of the double difference between the sexes and between the generations.

Part II

Masculinity and its discontents

Chapter 2

Masculinity and violence

The next four chapters will be devoted to exploring masculinity, or more precisely, masculine anxieties and defences. It is a fundamental part of this study that anxieties about masculinity (what Freud saw as the castration complex) interacted with anxieties about the dissolution of the ego, and anxieties about the demise of a whole culture (from the end of the First World War onwards) and led to the creation of fascism as a particularly masculine ideology. In this sense an exploration into crucial points of masculine identity – wishes, anxieties and defences – is in my view essential for a psychoanalytic understanding of the fascist state of mind.

Of course it is possible to speak of fascism as if it were a gender neutral phenomenon which to some extent it is. The infantile wishes and anxieties that it expresses are gender neutral and this accounts for the appeal it has had for both men and women. The totalitarian/homogenizing element of fascism had universal appeal although this statement needs some qualification.

In Nazi Germany for instance men and women seemed to have been attracted to fascism for different reasons and at different times. Although some women marched together with SA[1] men in a military manner in the 1920s on the whole, women were not interested in the violent, military side of fascism. Paradoxically women embraced the side of fascism that advocated their disenfranchisement as well as the separation of the sexes and the return of woman to her traditional role as mother, wife and homemaker. The glorification of these qualities as womanly and the security and relative independence within these spheres that women were given had proved very attractive to them (Koonz 1987). In voting for Hitler and his party women, like most men, opted for security.

But we should not forget that women, at least in Germany, were attracted to fascism at a later time than men. The female vote lagged behind the male in the 1920s and it was not until 1932 that women's vote caught up with men's (Kershaw 1998: 409). Of course this was a time when Hitler was very careful to hide his military ambitions and his extermination policies from the wider public. In this sense we need to distinguish between the core fascism and the core Party in which the worship of violence, war, domination, military expansion and the internal policies of homogenisation and extermination are central; and 'sanitised' fascism presented to the voters in Germany after 1928.

Fascism as a mass phenomenon exemplified men's and women's hunger for authority, wish for security and wishes for merging with a bigger entity (Party, ideology, state, community). I shall examine this side of fascism, which constitutes its main attraction for the wider population, in Chapters 6 and 7 as part of my expolation of groups and group dynamics. However, for the core fascists violence, militarism and the will to dominate were the other side of the same coin to be hidden from the respectable, sanitised party that Hitler presented in the 1932 elections. And this core fascism never died as its dynamic of total domination, homogenisation and extermination led eventually to genocide and the collapse of the regime.

Nevertheless, the question remains whether the violent and militaristic side of fascism is a masculine phenomenon; and to what degree the mutual projections between men and women ensure that it remained a 'masculine' phenomenon.[2] In other words what I would like to examine here is the relation between masculinity and violence.

The masculine dilemma

I shall begin to explore the relationship between masculinity and violence by introducing a description of a young schizophrenic man presented by the psychoanalyst Herbert Rosenfeld in his paper on depression in a schizophrenic. 'He was preoccupied with being a woman' Rosenfeld writes,

> and he had a wish to be reborn a girl: '*Prince* Ann'. By analysing material … we began to realize that he attributed his dangerous, murderous feelings against his mother, and against women in general, to his male half and his penis. We also understood that his fantasies of being a woman were greatly reinforced by his desire to get rid of his aggression. When we began to understand this method of dealing with his aggression, his wish to be a woman lessened and he became less aggressive.
>
> (Herbert Rosenfeld 1965: 78)

The preceding passage is taken from the analysis of a schizophrenic young man with violent tendencies. The passage is not easy to understand in isolation but the main point that Rosenfeld makes here is his understanding that the patient's wishes to become a woman are a defence against his murderous 'masculine' self and his murderous impulses towards his mother.

However, we can equally say that his murderous masculine self was a defence against his wish (and the fears that go with it), to become a woman. In this second sense, not examined by Rosenfeld, violence acts as a defence against feminisation. The fear of feminisation can be linked with fears of being stuck with a mother without the presence, in reality or in the mind, of a father. (In fact the patient had a very domineering mother who treated him as her own possession.) The individual in this situation feels stuck in an endless vicious circle.

However, what is striking here is the association of masculinity and the penis with violence so that being a woman becomes a defence against violence (and vice versa).

I shall explore these themes in what follows.

One of the striking achievements of psychoanalysis in the domain of gender is to separate the biological sex from gender identity. Masculinity in women, as well as femininity in men, has been much explored by Freud, who developed Fliess's idea of bisexuality. Because of bisexuality anxieties and defences to do with contra-sexual identifications are always operative during development. For Freud optimal development has to do with firmly establishing the identification with the parent of the same sex and at the same time integrating contra-sexual identifications within the self. However, what Freud saw in the consulting room was the huge resistance that men exhibited in accepting their femininity. He attributed this to the castration complex, but in this he accepted that it was not only the fear of castration that precipitated the aversion to femininity, but more importantly the *wish* for castration, that is the wish to be feminine (Freud 1911, 1923b, 1924b).

Freud saw femininity in men as part of the Oedipus complex, that is as taking the place of the mother in order to be loved by the father. It was the love of the father therefore that determined men's feminine identification. This feminine identification which had the aim of being loved by the father, Freud saw as the negative Oedipus complex. Although Melanie Klein accepted the centrality of the Oedipus complex and in fact extended it to include the early Oedipus complex, she nevertheless examined a more basic and more archaic wish for femininity based on the early envy of the mother. The mother at this early phase (which Klein called the 'femininity phase' and which she situated long before the classical Oedipus complex) is seen as having everything – babies, milk and father's penis. So, at this stage, the father is only present as a penis inside mother which makes the mother truly omnipotent. The identification with mother at this stage is with an omnipotent mother and is based as much on feelings of deprivation as on feelings of envy. Although this first identification with mother is the same for both boy and girl, it nevertheless has different consequences for the two sexes. I shall examine Klein's theory of the early femininity phase in Chapter 4. Here I want to stress that the boy's identification with mother and his wish to be like her evokes eventually feelings of inferiority and reaction against the feminine role.

If the differentiation from mother has not been consolidated, the boy (and the girl) will be always in fear of being absorbed into the mother's body/mind. When these wishes and anxieties get projected outside persecution and violence are not far off. In this sense the boy's relation to father within the Oedipus complex, is, despite the conflicts between father and son, basically a protection from the fears of being absorbed into mother's body/mind. I shall examine these themes in what follows.

But first I shall examine the boy's position in a particular situation: the murder of the father and the retreat from, or the destruction of, the triangular situation of the Oedipus complex.

Oedipus and the Sphinx: masculinity and the retreat from the Oedipus complex

Consider Oedipus in front of the Sphinx. He has already killed his father at the crossroads and he is now in confrontation with the big primordial monster/ mother – the Sphinx. The Sphinx is a bloodthirsty monster that threatens Thebes by devouring all the young men who cannot answer her riddle. Since the death of Laius she has been dominating Thebes. Many classical scholars have argued of the redundancy or the irrelevance of the Sphinx in the Oedipus story. Some maintain that it is a relic of earlier cultures added onto the Oedipus story and that it does not serve any function in the story (Knox 1982). Yet from the psychoanalytic point of view the Sphinx is absolutely essential in this scenario of a murdered father and a son who is confused about his identity.

I suggest that the Sphinx represents the unavoidable reality of the boy who has murdered his father and finds himself confronted by the terror of being devoured by the mother. In this sense the encounter with the Sphinx represents the classic no-win situation. This no-win situation is the situation the son finds himself after he has murdered his father. It goes as follows: If Oedipus fails to answer the riddle correctly he will be devoured by the Sphinx. On the other hand if he does, which is actually the case, he will proceed to marry his mother and produce children with her. Either way catastrophe is at hand. In fact the catastrophe has begun with the murder of the father.

However, the situation is not how it appears either to Oedipus or to the people of Thebes. Oedipus is now the hero, the saviour of Thebes. He is now the most powerful and important individual in the land. The truth is deeply hidden – for the moment anyway.

But as we know the story does not end here. The murder of the father leads to unsolvable problems in the future – the plague that has spread years later and has reduced Thebes to a wasteland reminds us that guilt may go underground for a long time but, as long as there is sanity, it comes back to remind the individual of the terrible truth that a murder has taken place.

We can say that guilt keeps the object alive. Like a ghost that appears and re-appears until it is exorcised, so guilt will remind the perpetrator that a crime has been committed and that he is responsible. In this sense guilt establishes a link to reality and a link to the truth. It is in this way that guilt leads to reparation and eventually to symbolic thinking. For instance the murder of the primal father in Totem and Taboo results, through guilt, in the first law against murder and against incest – in other words it results in the beginning of civilization and of symbolic thinking. On the other hand, if omnipotent thinking prevails, no guilt and no mourning takes place. The dead father becomes a non-existent father and the mother/son merge takes a delusional quality.

This non-representation of the father in the mind is examined extensively by the Lacanian School of Psychoanalysis which sees psychosis as the 'disavowal' of the symbolic father, that is the inability of the individual to establish the symbolic father within the psyche. In a recent paper (2009) Rosine Perelberg examines clinically the problem of the elimination of the father from the mind. In this paper Perelberg differentiates between the 'dead symbolic father' and the 'murdered father' and links actual violence in a young man, Karl, with the phantasy that he was present at the time of his conception and that his father therefore did not exist as his progenitor.

Perelberg writes:

> Karl was thus expressing a belief that he was present at his own conception from which his (step)father was excluded. This left him experiencing himself as living in a world where only he and his mother existed from the beginning, a world in which he feels treated as an extension of her desires.
>
> (p. 726)

Perelberg's dichotomy of the 'murdered father' and the 'symbolic dead father' creates a division between concrete, psychotic thinking and symbolic thinking. The symbolic father is a product of facing the reality of one's murderous feelings that lead to guilt and reparation and to the symbolic world. On the other hand the murder of the father representation leads to a psychotic world where the very existence of the father as the other half in the process of conception is destroyed in the mind.

However, most patients we see in the consulting room are in-between these two positions or may oscillate between them. This intermediate place where a murder has and has not taken place is a position where guilt has not been accepted but has not completely been given up and reality has not completely been destroyed. The individual inhabits the position of the omnipotent father and guilt has gone underground but not destroyed. It is I suggest akin to Oedipal triumph where the son *usurps* the place of the father but has not murdered the *father representation*.

I shall carry the idea of the murder of the father a little further and introduce the idea of two types of parricide.

I suggest that there is a difference between murdering the father to take his place as the only owner of mother *within* the Oedipus complex; and murdering the father *in the mind* in the sense of eradicating the *representation* of the father and his function in conception (which is the case of Karl in Perelberg's example). I suggest that the first type of murder takes place within the Oedipus complex and leads to a relation to mother where father is around as a ghost threatening retribution. He is dead but not dead as his ghost and the guilt that it expresses is present. This type of guilt may or may not lead to reparation and to symbolic reality. It could remain present in the mind at an unconscious level as a force undermining the personality.

I call this a 'masculine murder' in the sense that the boy usurps the place of the murdered father in order to *have* the mother. In this sense he does not wipe the father out of the mind. He just takes his place. But neither is he able to face guilt and reality. The murdered father and guilt continue to exist in the unconscious and are revealed through the existence of various neurotic symptoms – impotence, undermining of possibilities of success, depression, perversion, obsessional symptoms. The type of aggression and violence that is triggered in this case is object related and is due to feelings such as love, hate, jealousy, rivalry, possessiveness, excessive competitiveness.

But much more destructive is the second type of murder – the murder that Perelberg is talking about which is a kind of erasing the father from the mind altogether. The omnipotence that results from this is not one of taking the place of the father, but one in which the father is eradicated from the mind. In this case the father does not exist and the boy can now be absorbed into the mother's mind/body. He can now be one with mother and truly omnipotent. This is not a wish to be in the father's place but rather a wish to be in the place of the mother, be one with her or be inside her – a wish that cannot be distinguished from 'being devoured'. This is not a masculine but a feminine identification. The omnipotence of being in the place of the mother is tantamount to the terror it leads to.

The anxieties here are psychotic. They are not guilt, punishment or retaliation but primitive terrors of annihilation which are the other side of omnipotence. As the father is wiped out of existence, the loss of masculinity follows. The son is absorbed into the mother's body. What was a wish becomes a terror. The persecution and the violence that result from this type of parricide are of a different kind to ordinary object-related violence. It is the type of annihilatory violence exhibited in fascist and totalitarian regimes at times when omnipotence and destruction reign supreme. In the consulting room we can see it only fleetingly in moments of momentary psychosis.

I shall now illustrate the above through a clinical example.

Clinical example

Paul a 21-year-old man has a history of drugs and violence. His father had left his mother when he was 2 and Paul never saw him again until he was an adult. Paul grew up with a mother who was over attached to him and quite abusive at the same time. His step father seemed a rather weak, passive man and he did not have much to do with him.

The sequence of sessions I wish to present took place some 2 years into the treatment which was a three times a week psychotherapy using, most of the time but not always, the couch.

On the Friday session Paul felt understood by me and expressed gratitude with tears in his eyes. This was a very unusual occasion as he mostly preferred to argue with me and avoid dependent feelings. In this occasion when the end of the session came he felt he was not ready to leave and expressed his reluctance to go. Eventually he left saying that I left him 'high and dry'.

The following Monday Paul came looking happy and rather manic. He opened the session by saying that he had repaired the 'hard drive' of his computer and was very pleased. He proceeded to tell me that he had spent the weekend with an old friend about whom he had talked previously and who had a shady history of drugs and violence. But now Paul was full of admiration for this man presenting him as brave, adventurous and independent. I thought that between the lines he meant 'masculine'. Paul related every detail of the weekend which included taking drugs and being 'high'. It also included taking photographs of tall buildings and 'skyscrapers'. Paul thought that he could make a career as an architect and build buildings as high as these, 'beautiful, tall, proud buildings'. He can then become famous and leave behind all this tedious existence.

He talked endlessly for 25 minutes. When I tried to say something in the minutely short break between his sentences he became frantic. 'Stop! Stop!', he cried. 'It's so important for me to say all these things, to make plans. You are destroying my plans.'

I managed to say that he felt invaded by me and my thoughts as if my thoughts would erase his.

He stopped and for a moment was silent. Then he remembered a dream he had on Friday evening after the session. In the dream he was in a house with a witch who was about to eat him. An old friend shouted at him to get the hell out of there. He woke up terrified. He associated the witch to Hansel and Gretel. I said that Hansel and Gretel were put out by their father and step mother to fend for themselves. That's how he felt when the session ended on Friday. He felt that I was throwing him out and abandoning him.

He did not answer but got up and paced up and down in the consulting room. Then he said that he felt trapped and claustrophobic with no way out.

I said that he felt trapped with me. If I understand him and he feels close to me, he feels the pain of separation at the end of the session and feels as if I had thrown him out to die. His wish to be one with me so that he will not lose me, feels like being swallowed up by me – the bad witch. He feels there is no way out of this dilemma.

Karl was silent for the rest of the session.

In the next session he came in an excited state and opened the session by saying that he spent the previous evening with a friend musician who plays 'that big instrument – you know the big one with strings'. I said that he might have felt at a disadvantage not playing such a big instrument. He said no, he felt that life was full of opportunities. He wanted to give up the boring college and his idiotic tutors and teachers and embark on a career in music. He could learn to play several instruments and sing – he knows he can. And who knows in the future he might even become a psychotherapist. He knows now what therapists do. The world is his oyster.

Then he talked about his flat mates who took all the space and he felt they were pushing him out. 'They are strangers really, not friends. They take all the space and push me out. I don't feel I have a home.'

THERAPIST: I think you experience me as somebody who takes all the space, who cuts across your thoughts and gets into your mind. I then become a stranger and you want to move out.

PATIENT (CALMER): I find it difficult here.

THERAPIST: I think that the last couple of sessions you've been very scared about any contact between us, about coming closer to me.

Paul calmed down and left calmer than he came.

However, the next sessions he became increasingly remote and inaccessible. He concentrated on events at college and how badly and unfairly he was treated by his tutors, teachers. He had been angry and the security men threatened to accompany him out of the building. They treated him like 'shit'.

He became angrier and angrier and seemed set on talking himself to a rage. He was treated like shit by a bunch of 'morons and 'retards', he shouted. When I said that he went back to an old way of relating that ignored all the work we did together and that he wanted me to believe that I have given him nothing, he went into a rage and became very angry and said that I did not understand what he suffered in the hands of these 'c...ts'.

He then stood up and walked into the middle of the room and began a verbal offensive against his teachers. He was going to set fire to their posh cars, to petrol bomb their houses, to push them down the stairwell, to smash their bones, beat their faces into a pulp. The more the images became gruesome the more vacant the expression in Paul's face became. It was as if he, as a person, was absent. This was a cold, detached hatred that sounded and looked psychopathic. At the same time there was a theatricality in it as if it was all staged for my sake, to scare me and tell me what a big boy he was, what he was capable of doing and how devoid of any 'soft' feelings he was.

I interrupted him saying that he was going into an unreal world where he did not have to take responsibility for what he said or did. He then turned on me with hatred. He said I was stupid and I did not understand how vicious the people at the college were and how much he suffered. He came very close to me and talked into my face. The rage in his eyes was immense. For a moment I thought he was going to hit me. Instead he turned around, picked up his bag and left banging the door behind him. I was reminded immediately of his wish a few sessions before 'to get the hell out of (t)here'.

Discussion

I shall now try to state my understanding of the preceding material.

As we have seen the next session after the patient felt helped by me and then felt abandoned at the end of the session, opened with the words 'I've fitted a new hard drive into the computer and I feel very good'. In my view the patient here lets me know that he is using phallic defences to counteract the 'softening' that took place in the previous session in feeling understood by me and the sense of abandonment at the end of the session. But I suggest that there is another softening that he created himself. I suggest that he felt unable to deal with the feelings of abandonment and attempted to get into me and become one with me. For the dream he had that night revealed the extreme anxiety or rather terror that he experienced in his attempt to deal with the sense of abandonment by getting inside me and becoming one with me which became the equivalent to being 'eaten up' by me, the witch. In his attempt to become one with me he felt terrified of being absorbed into me and, like Rosenfeld's patient, lose his masculinity. The hard drive, the tall, proud buildings, the big instrument are unmistakable symbols of phallic masculinity which he evokes to deal with the 'softening' that happened since the last session.

I understand the whole process as follows: The patient leaves the first session feeling vulnerable and experiencing abandonment and loss. To deal with these feelings, and with his greed to have more of me, he tries to become one with me and then feels in danger of being engulfed – 'eaten up' by a witch as the dream expressed. We can see the whole process as an expression of the 'core complex' as described by Mervyn Glasser (1985). But in this process of being engulfed not only his self but his masculinity is destroyed.

Glasser described the core complex as follows. There exists a wish in the infant for a state of complete satisfaction which is phantasised as a state of fusion with the mother. However, due to the projection of the baby's all consuming impulses, this fusion with the mother is felt as complete possession by the mother and as 'total annihilation' (for instance my patient's fear of being eaten by the witch). This fear drives the baby (and the adult) into flight, that is into a kind of narcissistic withdrawal from object relations (my patient's flight into phallic defences). This in turn triggers a state of utter isolation and abandonment that drives the baby back to mother and the wish to be one with her to avoid the fears of abandonment (my patient's fear of 'being eaten'). Glasser is describing the vicious circle that some patients can enter band which stifles any change.

But Glasser described another fundamental reaction to the threat of annihilation – aggression. When, due to the projective processes, the mother is seen as engulfing and annihilating, aggression becomes a rational response. But since the mother is also loved and needed this becomes an irreconcilable conflict. Glasser sees the development of perversion – basically sado-masochism – as a solution to the problem of containing aggression. In perversion the subject has an intense engagement with the object but not an intimate one. A safe emotional distance is kept to protect the subject from being absorbed into the object. We can see the perverse aspects springing up already in the first session presented here, but these perverse aspects have something of a mania in them. Paul's getting together with a man who had a history of violence and drugs and who suddenly appeared to him as an exciting person alerts us to the perverse processes that are developing to deal with fears of annihilation and the murderous impulses that they set into motion.

In this session we can see the manic and the perverse side of Paul as ways of dealing with both abandonment and fears of being devoured by me/mother, fears that lead to fears of loss of masculinity. In the next session he mobilised both sado-masochism and raw aggression to deal with these fears. But it is in the last session presented here that he went beyond sado-masochism and bordered on a psychotic micro-episode in a way that Kernberg describes in malignant narcissism (Kernberg 2003a).

If we look carefully at the sequence of sessions we can see that when I disturb his defensive resort to sado-masochism (his feeling that the teachers are looking down on him and think he is 'shit' for instance, or his description of the teachers as 'shit') he becomes quasi-psychotic, speaking and behaving as if he is not human, or has no human feelings at all, threatening his teachers and tutors with extermination in the most gruesome but impersonal way. We must not forget that Morgan and Ruszczynski (2007) saw sado-masochism as a way of controlling murderous aggression so it is not surprising that when I disturb his sado-masochistic engagement he becomes murderous. But the main thing here is the impersonal type of murderousness that he exhibited. What came to my mind was a robot kind of killer – a robocop – or a psychopath who has no human feelings of empathy. It was as if the rhetoric did not involve human beings at all.

When I interrupted this state he turned against me in a confrontation that was now about survival, but also it had the added advantage that it was now object related, that it was a kind of communication, asking me to experience, bear and subsequently interpret how unbearable he found me seen as separate from him and how absolutely terrified he was. The impersonal, cold violent state was substituted by a more object-related aggression that could be talked about in another session.

Masculinity and the fascist state of mind

The ranting and rhetoric of the last session and the way he delivered it reminded me of another ranting, one seen in the old newsreels of the 1930s – the rantings that nobody took seriously at the time – the rantings of Adolf Hitler. I didn't know what to do with this analogy at the time but it remained in my mind as an image that needed some decoding.

I now suggest that the impersonal type of violence that the patient engages in when he looks psychotic is the result of a destruction of object relations and of the Oedipus complex. It is equivalent to destroying the father representation in the mind that Perelberg talks about, which is equivalent to an attempt to destroy reality, or as Chasseguet-Smirgel put it – in an attempt to destroy differences. With this destruction of reality and difference, a loss of the symbolic meaning of words followed. Words became things and actions and human beings became words and cardboard figures.

A loss of humanity follows.

The destruction of symbolic thinking goes together with the 'destruction of the contents of the mind' which Bollas sees as part of the 'fascist state of mind'. As Bollas put it, 'the death of the symbolic is the first casualty' (see Chapter 1).

In this destruction of the father and of symbolic thinking there is a destruction of plurality. What is left is a self united with a mother – a state which cannot be differentiated from being 'eaten up'. My patient's own wish to be one with mother/therapist becomes eventually castrating and terrifying. To save his ego from being dissolved inside the mother's/witch's belly, he constructs first a phallic world of 'tall proud buildings' and 'big instruments' and then a sado-masochistic world where he has to fight to prove his dignity and masculinity. However, it is when I disturbed his sado-masochistic defences that he tipped into a semi-psychotic world where he was in the place of God (self united with an omnipotent mother) distributing cruel retributive justice on an unreal world.

I understand the violence recruited in the last few minutes of the session as an attempt to save the self and masculinity not only from humiliation and castration, but from annihilation. With the elimination of the father from the mind a loss of reality takes place temporarily. Instead a cardboard reality emerges where anything can take place. The violent vomiting of threats and gory images had a cardboard quality to it as if the people he threatened, or he himself, were not real human beings. For this very reason the dividing line between phantasy and reality became very fuzzy.

I suggest that it is this type of violence that permeates fascist and quasi-fascist organizations. However, to concentrate only on violence is to miss the attraction and seductiveness that these organizations exert on some males. It is to miss the allure of oneness, the seduction of merging – the appeal of a world without father, the world of homogeneity that these groups and organizations promote. It is this seductiveness that hides the extreme violence that permeates these organizations.

We can conceptualise this seductive appeal to homogeneity, whether in the individual or in the group, as a womb phantasy – as a kind of union with mother that has its prototype in intra-uterine life. Ferenczi argued that the wish to return to the womb is the most powerful wish of humankind (Ferenczi 1938). In my clinical example it begins with the terror that the witch/therapist will eat him up and ends with the threat to exterminate those who want to humiliate him that is castrate him. His own wish to be swallowed up and be part of mother/therapist is deeply hidden.

In everyday life the womb phantasy can be externalised in many objects and situations – drugs being the most obvious one. But I suggest that the homogenised group maybe its most prominent manifestation. The homogenised group has as its aim to erase any trait of difference between the members. To do this the differentiation between public and private, or life in the group and life outside the group has to be erased as well as the differentiation between members of the group. With this goes the elimination of the differentiation between different parts of the self so that ego, id and superego collapse into each other. A feeling akin to mania invades the group. The individual (and the group) is now his own ideal. All aggression is directed outside the group. I am describing here the prototype of a fascist organization whose basic aim is to erase difference. (I examine different types of groups in Chapters 6 and 7.)

Fascist organizations in their inception have been overwhelmingly male. They were, to start with, a kind of male violent fraternities, or gangs, which saw violence as both cleansing and masculine. We can see the ideology of fascism not in the years when fascist groups gained power (for Mussolini it was after 1922, for Hitler after 1933) but in their initial 'pure' revolutionary state where a state of unreality prevailed, where the socially and humanly unacceptable was openly declared as desirable in a flamboyant and provocative way. Hitler's war intentions as well as his genocidal intentions were unashamedly declared in *Mein Kampf* and presented as strengths. When in power, however, Hitler declared endlessly his peace intentions and fooled many foreign diplomats and heads of state as well as his own citizens (although he made endless preparations for war).

What I want to stress here is violence and war as part of a masculine denial of the wish to be one with mother and therefore feminine. The fascist group acts both as a *womb and as its denial* portrayed as a war machine – both as a big mother and as a huge machine for manufacturing new men – the 'men of steel'. It both affirms and denies the wish to be one with mother.

In this sense I suggest that the male fascist group based on an ideology of violence and homogeneity attempts to solve the insoluble problem of the wish to be one with mother *and* the wish to be masculine. The homogenised group has the advantage of being a concrete symbol (a 'symbolic equation') of the womb in which the members can immerse themselves and lose their individuality *but at the same time* retain their sense of being masculine, or perhaps more than that, enhance their masculinity. The merging of males together supplemented by symbols and paraphernalia of masculinity such as parades, oaths of allegiance, uniforms, weapons, salutes, create the manic phantasy of super-masculinity – a masculinity bigger than life and truly omnipotent. This manufacturing of masculinity is a real 'masquerade of masculinity' (to paraphrase Joan Riviere).[3]

I shall illustrate the preceding points by looking closely at some extracts from Hitler's book *Mein Kampf* which in my view encapsulates the fascist state of mind as a merge with mother and at the same time engaged in the manufacturing of masculinity. I shall treat the text in the same way I treated my patient's communications, trying to uncover its hidden meaning.

Mein Kampf begins in this way:

> Today it seems to me providential that Fate should have chosen Branau on the Inn as my birthplace. For this little town lies on the boundary between two German states which we of the younger generation at least have made it our life work to reunite by every means at our disposal.
>
> German–Austria must return to the great mother country and not because of any economic point of view; yes even if it were harmful, it must nevertheless take place. One Blood demands one Reich. Never will the German nation possess the moral right to engage in colonial politics until at last it embraces its own sons within a single state. Only when the Reich borders include the very last German but can no longer guarantee his daily bread, will the moral right to acquire foreign soil arise from the distress of our people. The sword will become our plough, and from the tears of war the daily bread of future generations will go. And so this little city on the border seems to me the symbol of a great mission.
>
> (p. 1)

I suggest that the opening statement of a book has the same unconscious significance as the first words a patient utters have for the session. In this sense we can say that the opening words of a book constitute a statement of the main unconscious theme of a book. In a way the rest of the book is an elaboration on this opening statement. I shall therefore look at Hitler's opening statement in some detail.

So let's look at the text more closely.

In the first paragraph Hitler speaks of his birthplace on the *boundary* between Austria and (mother) Germany and of his 'life work' to abolish this boundary. So right from the beginning we see the theme of the chosen son/hero, the theme of abolition of boundaries, that is of the father, and the deep wish for re-unification with mother Germany which turns into a threat: 'by every means at our disposal'. And, if is any doubt about what Germany means to him, he goes on to tell us at the beginning of the next paragraph: 'German Austria must return to the great German mother country' (We must not forget that Hitler was Austrian.).

In the original the word is 'Mutterlande' which literally means 'motherland'. As Germany is usually referred to as 'Fatherland' this change of words is striking. In my view it reveals the secret, unconscious and very powerful yearning for a union with mother that the abolition of boundaries makes possible. These deep yearnings are connected to a very powerful wish to destroy reality as the next half of the sentence shows. For the sentence continues: '… not because of any economic point of view; yes even if it were harmful, it must nevertheless take place. One Blood demands one Reich'.

Even if it is harmful, he tells us, this union must take place. Economic considerations and the reality they represent are not his concern (and this in the midst of a deep economic crisis in post-war Germany). Ideology and the powerful wishes it expresses and hides are the paramount guide and goal. The callousness and lack of humanity underneath the harangue is obvious. But, for my purpose, what is important here is that it reveals the irrationality of the wish – the fact that this wish does not belong to the realm of reality, that is the 'economic point of view' but follows its own irrational wishes – the laws of the unconscious. I suggest that the deep, regressive wish of uniting mother and sons and abolish the reality of boundaries, limitations and 'economic considerations' is here the main driving force.

After this he reveals a bit more: 'One blood demands one Reich. Never will the German nation possess the moral right to engage in colonial politics until, at least, it *embraces its own sons within a single state*' (italics mine).

From the point of view of this chapter this is a very revealing statement. Let's look at this very well-known phrase: 'One blood demands one Reich'. In my view Hitler reveals with this statement the redundancy of the father, or the destruction of difference that the father creates in the mind. The father who does not share the same blood with mother is firmly abolished from his world. The different blood of the father is eliminated. Difference is thus demolished both as a pre-condition for this world *and* as its aim. The omnipotence that this leads to is revealed by the next sentence. This union of mother and sons, he tells us, gives the 'moral right' to attack other countries which he calls 'to engage in colonial politics'. From now on everything is allowed and everything is possible as Hannah Arendt put it.

I suggest here that the Fuehrer as the father is not what lies behind Hitler's metaphors of the sons uniting with the mother. It is not an Oedipal wish he is expressing here. It is not a wish to be *in the place of the father* and have the mother. The abolition of boundaries and the 'one blood one Reich' principle points to a much more destructive process in which the very *reality of the father* is destroyed.

In my reading, the kind of 'union with mother' Hitler is talking about, spells the end of all libidinal positions and of all libido. It is truly synonymous with Ernest Jones' *aphanisis*[4] or with Klein's total projective identification as it is described in her paper 'On identification' (1955), and it is a manifestation of the death instinct. It is much more malignant and has much more to do with a destruction of difference in the mind and therefore the destruction of reality, the destruction of the existence of the father.

To return to the text, after he establishes the pleasure principle of unification with mother the text turns now to a distorted picture of both reality and morality that emerges as the only solution to the problems of the German people: 'Only when the Reich borders include the very last German, but can no longer guarantee his daily bread, will the moral right to acquire foreign soil arise from the distress of our own people.'

Here we see another dimension to this unification of the mother with the sons. The danger is that now the Reich can no longer guarantee 'the sons' their 'daily bread'. The fear of exhausting the mother's resources due to the sons' invading and inhabiting her body is very present in this passage. The threat of starvation is imminent. In this notion of the exhaustion of resources we have an inkling of the original phantasy of the baby as a parasite on his mother's body and the fear of exhausting her resources. Since there is no father to provide, or to put boundaries to greed and sole possession, the only solution seems to be appropriating other peoples' resources, or invading foreign lands. What is important to stress here is that the notion of the parasite, although not mentioned explicitly, is already present here and emanates from this union of the sons with the mother and the greedy and envious appropriating of her resources. The projection of the notion of the parasite onto the Jew, as in the endless passages in *Mein Kampf* and the Second Book[5], has its source in this union of mother and sons and the fear of starvation that emanates from the appropriation of the mother's body and contents.

In this sense the idealisation of war and the idealisation of the mother/son union go hand in hand and are linked through the notion of the exhaustion of resources and starvation.

The text continues with a militaristic mixed metaphor that borders on the poetic: 'Their sword will become our plough, and from the tears of war the daily bread of future generations will grow.' In this mixed metaphor I think that Hitler lets it be known that whatever the sentimentality of a return to mother might be, the real project is a war project and that the return to mother and war are closely interlinked. The 'beauty' and necessity of war, which is a fundamental fascist value, is revealed unintentionally here through the language.

And the second paragraph ends with: 'And so this little city on the border seems to me a symbol of a great mission.'

Conclusion

In this chapter I have distinguished two types of violence: one within the Oedipus complex and within object relations, and another the result of the destruction of the Oedipus complex in the mind. The first is ordinary human violence to do with strong feelings of love, hate, deprivation, exclusion and jealousy. This type of violence is not discussed in great detail here. I call it *ordinary* because it is object related and part of human society. The second type is the result of the destruction of the Oedipus complex and with it the destruction of the existence of the father within the mind and the destruction of separateness and of all libido and culminates in the destruction of civic society as we know it.

The second type of violence is linked to the destruction of difference in the mind and to the glorification of the immense violence which accompanies any attempt at homogenisation. It is synonymous with the destruction of the object as different and separate from the self.

The psychotic element of the elimination of the father representation from the mind smashes the very fabric of the ego as the seat of the reality principle. A cardboard world emerges which can be manipulated at will as omnipotent phantasy takes over.

My patient's pronouncement of annihilating his enemies and Hitler's pronouncements of taking over the world refer to this cardboard world where no empathy but also no reality need be considered. As the wish for total annihilation takes over, passive and active merge into one. That Hitler's Germany was able to use the reality principle to prepare for total annihilation was due to the co-existence of two different elements both in his personality and in the fascist state of mind – the sado-masochistic, authoritarian state of mind and the delusional state of mind. The authoritarian end of the regime – the bureaucratic certainty that the submission to father created – constituted what was stable in the Nazi regime. The rather stable, perverse sado-masochistic structure – the authoritarian structure – prepared and cultivated the soil for Hitler's total war without asking any questions or expressing any doubts. Within the authoritarian structure the father representation exists as the sadistic father who demands complete submission. The authoritarian structure made possible Hitler's omnipotent delusional structure to be ignored despite its very obvious presence.

The extreme violence of the tenet of 'One Blood One Reich' belongs to this delusional structure where anything is possible. It becomes only apparent when we consider that it relies on the elimination of both the father and difference. And although the elimination of either the father or difference is literally impossible, the pursuit of this goal can lead, and indeed has led, to unimaginable violence and to a state of mind that is difficult to distinguish from paranoid psychosis.

In Chapter 3, I shall examine in more detail the male wish to be inside mother in a concrete and unsymbolised way and the psychotic consequences of this wish.

Notes

1 The intitials SA stand for Sturm Abteilung translated as Assualt Division, otherwise known as Storm Troopers. The SA was a Nazi organization (founded in 1921) and in its early years was responsible for a great deal of street violence against Jews, communists, socialists, and trade unisionists. It eventually lost its power when Hilter used the SS to carry out a 'blood purge' executing its leaders in an operation known as 'the night of the long knives' (die Nacht der langen Messer).

2 The question of women's projection of their own aggression onto men is a very complex one and I do not intend to explore it here. To a certain extend I have explored it in my book *The Undead Mother* (2000/2002). Here suffice it to say that the psychological 'contract' between men and women about aggression seems to reassure the 'intactness' of masculinity and protect the male from fears of castration and humiliation – fears that have been aroused by the mother of his early childhood.

3 Joan Riviere's paper published in 1929 was called 'Womanliness as masquerade' (Riviere 1929).

4 Ernest Jones used the term *aphanisis* to denote the loss of all libido which constitutes the ultimate anxiety for both boy and girl. In this he disagrees with Freud that the boy's ultimate anxiety is castration anxiety. I suggest that the fear of the loss of all libido is synonymous to the fear of the loss of object relations and the destruction of the object. It is not a neurotic but a psychotic anxiety.

5 The *Second Book* is the title of Hitler's second book which he finished in 1928 but remained unpublished.

Chapter 3

Mad men and warriors

Femininity and paranoia in the male*

> It can hardly be doubted that the world of phantasy plays the same part in psychosis and that there too, it is the storehouse from which the materials or the pattern for building the new reality are derived. But whereas the new, imaginary external world of a psychosis attempts to put itself in the place of external reality, that of a neurosis, on the contrary, is apt, like the play of children, to attach itself to a piece of reality – a different piece from the one against which it has to defend itself – and to lend that piece a special importance and a secret meaning which we (not always quite appropriately) call a *symbolic* one. Thus we see that both neurosis and psychosis there comes into consideration the question not only of a *loss of reality* but also of a *substitute for reality*.
>
> (Freud 1924d: S.E. XIX, p. 187)

In this chapter I shall explore the violence and loss of reality that result from the destruction of the father representation, the primitive wishes to be inside mother, or to take her over and become her, and the terrors that this gives rise to, by examining Euripides' play *Bacchae* and Freud's case of Senatspraesident Schreber. I examine the way in which concrete phantasies of merging with mother or of taking her over destroy masculinity and lead to terror and paranoia.

Pentheus' deadly transgression

Arguably Euripides' most enigmatic play *Bacchae* is one of his two last plays performed posthumously in Athens in 405 BC (the other one being *Iphigenia at Aulis*). There exists an extensive literature about the play that centres around the decline of Athens, the disillusionment of its citizens and the dual nature of man – the rational and civilised side on the one hand, and the instinctual one on the other. I shall not attempt to cover this literature here but I shall concentrate instead on my own angle which has to do with masculinity.

The gender aspect of the play is prominent, but of course the play is, like any classical work, multi-dimensional and open to many interpretations. In fact it invites, through its enigmatic nature, multiple interpretations and multiple points of view. Having this in mind, I use Euripides' play of the tragic fate of Pentheus in his mother's hands to explore the thorny subject of male identity and the son's relation to mother, his unconscious wish to enter her domain and become indistinguishable from her, and the tragic consequences that follow when attempts are made to fulfil such an omnipotent wish. These tragic consequences include the fragmentation of both masculinity and the self.

The play begins with Dionysus, the god of wine, music and intoxication arriving at Thebes disguised as a priest, accompanied by a crowd of barbarian women followers who dance in a frenzy and praise Dionysus' glory. Dionysus is the son of Zeus and Semele. The legend goes that when Semele was pregnant she asked Zeus to show himself in his most powerful form. Unfortunately for her his most powerful form was Zeus the lightning carrier. Semele, struck by Zeus' lightning, died. Zeus, rescuing Dionysus from his mother's belly, implanted him in his thigh to continue his gestation time. In this way Dionysus was born out of Zeus' thigh and Zeus proclaimed him a god and invited him to reside in Olympus even though his mother was a mortal woman.

In Greek mythology Dionysus was at times represented as effeminate and yet at other times he stood for powerful animal masculinity. This ambiguity is also important in understanding the power of Dionysus to be outside civilization and reality, to challenge and denounce all civilised conventions, definitions and restrictions. In the introduction to their translation of the *Bacchae* Frederic Raphael and Kenneth McLeish write:

> Dionysus grew to be a god who could not be controlled. He took all limitations as an affront. He straddled the gulf between male and female, civilisation and barbarism, pleasure and pain. He neither respected 'normal' boundaries nor inspired routine pleasure.
>
> (Raphael and McLeish in Euripides 1998: XIV)

Dionysus is in fact the cousin of Pentheus, the ruler of Thebes, as his mother Semele is the sister of Pentheus' mother Agave. Semele was exiled from Thebes in shame when she got pregnant with Dionysus. Part of the reason why Dionysus is back to Thebes is to avenge his mother. He now wants to be recognised by Pentheus as a god and to establish his new religion.

Pentheus is young and immature, full of himself and his power. He is a rationalist, sealed in his small, rigidly defined world which excludes the terrain of ecstasy, mystery and intoxication – the terrain of Dionysus and the barbarian women. Pentheus' rationalism, however, amounts to tyranny as he excludes, and forcibly hunts down, any alien element and seeks to destroy it. He ignores Teirisias', and his grandfather's, exhortations to reconcile himself to this alien world of Dionysus and instead he sets out to destroy it. In the process he destroys himself.

As Pentheus is busy trying to destroy Dionysus, Dionysus' irresistible power drives the women of Thebes to Mount Kythairon and there, abandoning the controls of civilization, they dance themselves into a frenzy and create a world that is in harmony with nature and the beasts. The rumours speak of miraculous things taking place – they get water, milk and wine out of dry rock, but if they are attacked, or if their territory is invaded, they become fierce and can tear humans and animals with their bare hands. The herdsman who has just managed to escape their wrath talks to Pentheus about their power and exhorts him, just like Teirisias and Cadmus, to reconcile himself to Dionysus and accept him as a god.

> My lord, if you'd been there and seen such things
> The god you now abuse would see you on your knees.
>
> (Euripides 1998: 33)

But Pentheus is blind in his arrogance. He sees in Dionysus only a charlatan priest who is seducing the women of Thebes to abandon their ordinary lives and go and live outside the polis. He arrests and imprisons Dionysus, but Dionysus escapes from jail and causes an earthquake, a landslide and a fire that burns down Pentheus' palace. A half-crazed Pentheus emerges from the burnt-out palace. With his rationalist world in ruin and in a state of shock, he is now completely under the power of Dionysus and the regressive wishes he represents.

He has now only one desire – to join the women at Mount Kythairon. Dionysus helps him to dress like a woman and leads him to Mount Kythairon where the women's mysteries are performed. Pentheus' intention is to hide in the woods and spy on the women – to discover or uncover their mysteries.

We can see Dionysus as Pentheus' unconscious, stirring up all his wishes to be one with mother, everything he has repudiated in the way of becoming an adult male. The scene that follows reveals the tenuousness of Pentheus' adult masculinity:

DIONYSUS: Do you want to see them at it, in the hills?
PENTHEUS: See them? More than gold I'd give…
…
DIONYSUS: First my lord: a woman's dress.
PENTHEUS: A dress? I am to change my sex?
DIONYSUS: If you go as a man you are dead (ibid.: 38)

But further down the mood changes. The wish not just to penetrate the female domain but to be once again the baby in his mother's arms sets in. Dionysus exploits this very human wish in Pentheus:

DIONYSUS: You will be carried high
PENTHEUS: As I deserve
DIONYSUS: In mother's arms
PENTHEUS: She will cradle me
DIONYSUS: For all to see
PENTHEUS: She will spoil me
DIONYSUS: Spoiled you shall be (ibid.: 47)

As Pentheus reveals his secret wish to be cradled in his mother's arms, not as a man but as a baby, Dionysus alludes to his tragic death and dismemberment in his mother's hands. The juxtaposition of the two has indeed a tragic effect on the audience who know already Pentheus' fate.

It is obvious here that there is a twin desire in Pentheus when he yields to the seduction of Dionysus: First, to be his mother's baby, to be cradled in her arms; and second, to spy on her, to invade the forbidden place and uncover the female mysteries – to be one with the women. We can say that the forbidden place is mother's body – this place where all miracles take place, the mysterious place where we all come from. Thus to invade the forbidden place represents both an infantile wish to be in mother's arms and an aggressive wish to spy and invade. It is permeated by both yearning for mother's love; and envy of the mother and her riches. These two impulses get often confused not only in the boy but often in adult males as my patient described in Chapter 3 has shown me.

Pentheus arrives at the place of the female mysteries and lets Dionysus lift him to the top of a very tall tree (an allusion to a phallic delusion?) to be able to watch the women. This reification of the object in voyeurism and the superior position that the viewer has – high up at the top of a tree – hides the envy and the exclusion that the viewer experiences. The male, for ever excluded from the female scene, takes a superior voyeuristic position. The boy expelled from mother's miraculous domain without the promise of becoming a mother himself (unlike the girl) can take a 'high up' position as a compensation for this loss.

Pentheus does the one thing that males, who have not mourned this expulsion from paradise, often do – he watches, spies on the women from a place high up, a phallic place. He is apprehended and pulled down from the tree, and taken for a wild beast he is torn to pieces limb by limb by the women. His mother is the first to begin this orgy of murder and bestiality – signifying, I think, the projection of the wish for total dissolution and disintegration, for a return to an undifferentiated world.

One way of understanding the phantasy of Mount Kythairon and the miraculous women is to view it as a male phantasy of female omnipotence represented as a place where the women are – a place of plenty, a place of miracles from which men are excluded. In this sense the wish to enter the all female miraculous place, not as an adult man in sexual intercourse, but 'dressed as a woman', destroys masculinity and annihilates the individual.

Bacchae with its tragic dismemberment of Pentheus by his mother and the women points to something that is beyond dread. It points to a male wish, a male longing. Beware what you wish for, it might come true, goes the saying. Pentheus' seduction by Dionysus, like any seduction, trades on the illusion that infantile wishes can come true, that boundaries and differences created by civilization, as well as the laws of nature, can be overcome, ignored, demolished. The promise of omnipotence is the real seduction. The women on the hills are truly miraculous and Pentheus can join them. Pentheus can regress to the point where he does not have to decide whether he is a man or a woman. He can be both and can be truly omnipotent (exactly like Dionysus).

Pentheus' tragic death reminds us of the dangers and horrors surrounding an insecurely established male identity – the phallic grandiosity and its collapse into a parody of itself.

As Frederic Raphael and Kenneth McLeish writes:

> The horror in the play is so grotesque that it challenges the distinction between tragedy and comedy. The climax of the action is certainly terrible and – since the young king brings death on himself by his own vanity – it can almost pass for a proper instance of the hubris in the traditional 'flaw' of the Greek tragic hero. Yet Pentheus' fate lacks tragic dignity. Is it worthy of a hero to be caught spying on a bunch of women while dressed in drag? Is it a noble fate to die after running like a stag from a party of crazed huntresses?
>
> (Euripides 1998: XIX)

In this sense the play examines among other things the fragility of phallic masculinity and the comic undertones of pompous tyrants and their tragic/comic end.

In my reading, Euripides describes a world of dangerous women and masculine terrors – a world created by deep infantile longings and terrors. Dionysus is a very ambiguous figure in the play and in Greek culture as it transcends all boundaries and differentiations. Not born by a woman but from Zeus' thigh he seems to be both a man and a woman, both man and god, both Greek and barbarian and seems to excite these deep longings in humans. His seductive, effeminate appearance evokes all infantile wishes and masculine terrors about feminisation. But his mysteries, the cult of Dionysus, bind and contain the terror and turn the yearnings into religious knowledge and artistic creation (we must not forget that tragedy itself has its origins in the cult of Dionysus). The possibility of transforming primitive yearnings into religious knowledge and artistic creation is what Pentheus rejects when he rejects Dionysus. The possibility of transforming masculinity by integrating femininity within the masculine self is also what Dionysus is offering. Pentheus by rejecting Dionysus he rejects all possibilities of transformation. By rejecting his own primitive desires Pentheus ends up living them out and is destroyed by them.

We can read *Bacchae* as a failed attempt to create a container for these overwhelming human yearnings and primitive terrors. Dionysus himself, the god of ambiguity and transgression of boundaries, the god of instinctual life and of the Unconscious, offers nevertheless ways in which mortals can enjoy this madness, this transgression of boundaries, within a well-defined structure – a symbolic framework. The theatre, which has arisen out of the cult of Dionysus, is one of these symbolic structures as well as dance and music. The cult of Dionysus, the Dionysiac mysteries, where initiation took place, is another. Dionysus represents both instinct and its transformation into symbolic activity. He represents both mad yearnings and mad desires *and* their symbolic representation. When he is ignored or met with contempt his revenge is truly terrible – as we witness in *Bacchae*.

I think that with *Bacchae* we reach the deepest level of the unsymbolised wish to return to mother – a wish to be one with her, ultimately a return to the womb or its mental equivalent, an idyllic place of no conflict and no difference. Side by side with the wish there is an aggressive, invasive trend to appropriate what the child does not own – the mother's world and its riches. This idealised place – the womb or the place of the female utopia – is full of hatred towards the reality of difference and separation and the knowledge of what belongs to whom. The new reality is therefore delusional. In this new reality any difference, including sex difference, is viewed as hostile and will be hunted down.[1]

We can see Mount Kythairon and the women's domain as delusions in Pentheus' mind, a delusion that begins with the arrival of Dionysus, the alien in Pentheus' psyche. This alien unconscious world, his own unworked through infantile wishes, has burst its inadequate, pseudo-masculine, rationalist container and plunged him into a world of delusion – a female utopia from where he was excluded. His delusion of entering the female utopia, of being one with mother, spells his fragmentation symbolised by his violent dismemberment. In psychoanalytic language we can speak of a total projective identification with a delusional object that spells the dissolution of the ego (Rosenfeld 1971).

In this sense Pentheus' retreat from reality is not a regression to infantile longings. Rather, his infantile longings and his infantile envy, unworked through as they are, set in motion the creation of a delusional world. Instead of integrating these powerful longings within a symbolic framework that would lead to creative living, Pentheus, taken over by the god of transgression, sets out to make them reality in a concrete, psychotic way.

Femininity and paranoia in Senatspraesident Schreber

That psychosis in men is often accompanied by fears not only of disintegration but of feminisation and castration is nowhere shown more clearly than in the Schreber case, a case made famous by Freud's treatment of it. Freud never met Schreber but based his analysis on Schreber's account of his mental illness immortalised in *The Memoirs of my Nervous Illness*. This is an extraordinary book where Schreber describes in detail the bizarre experiences he went through during his illness and the bizarre 'solution' he invented for himself to recover from his illness. It is obvious that Freud considered the book a very important document in understanding the deepest layers of the mind.[2]

Daniel Paul Schreber was the son of the eminent physician and pedagogue Daniel Gottlieb Moritz Schreber whose reputation as a doctor in the late nineteenth-century Germany was immense. To this testify the many 'Schreber Associations' that were created in Germany to carry on Schreber's theories. The 'Schreber Gardens' (a type of allotments), so characteristic of German cities, sprang up all over Germany after his death to carry on his legacy and vision of healthy living. This famous and venerable father wrote more than 20 books on health, callisthenics, orthopaedics and child rearing which were bestsellers in Germany in the mid-nineteenth century, advocating healthy living as well as new bizarre and, by any standards, cruel and somewhat mad child-rearing practices. Schreber's (the son's) psychotic illness has been attributed by some to the way these practices were applied to him a baby and as a child (Niederland 1984; Schatzman 1973).

These bizarre practices included the use of contraptions so that the body of the child would be kept upright, others to hold the head upright and prevent the child's head from falling forward or sideways. Other contraptions would ensure healthy development of chin and teeth by holding the chin in a certain place and yet others would prevent the child from turning in bed and ensure that the child would remain supine. A version of this last device was shown in the German film *White Ribbon* to keep the child immobile in bed and prevent him from masturbating. The film itself can be understood as an attempt to explain the corruption and perversion of children's minds through cruelty and bizarre practices. This generation of children would later on follow, or vote for, Adolf Hitler.

Doctor Schreber (the father) recommended early intervention in the baby's life which included the recommendation of warm baths only until 6 months. After that, cool and cold baths were recommended. For adults the recommendation was for cold baths every day before they began work. In the Schreber family 'one strict rule was: one got up very early, did some gymnastics, bathed and swam before starting work. Occasionally in winter the ice had to be broken first' (Alfons Ritter quoted in Schatzman 1973: 36).

This intrusion into the child's body and mind was seen as absolutely necessary to 'break the child's will' and make him obedient to the father. In this lofty mission the mother was seen as dangerous and not to be entrusted with the well being of the child.

A great deal has been written about this father who saw impingement as a pedagogic tool. William Niederland (1984) was the first analyst to look into the father's bizarre practices and to explain the son's psychosis in terms of this grossly interfering and abusive father. We can assume that this is the father whose own paranoia about mothers and women would leave nothing to chance. According to Dr Schreber (the father) women, were not able to carry out the immense task of shaping and controlling the child's body and mind. Only the father could and should control absolutely everything in the child's life – from the child's position in bed or at the table, to his sexuality, thoughts, feelings and will. The subordination of the child's will to the father was his main objective. To achieve this, the mother had to be superseded after the first 6 months. Kafka's extraordinary depiction of this subordination to the father/ authority, or the superego, and the terror that accompanies this, remains a lasting testimony of a whole generation of German men.

Daniel Paul Schreber was born to this household the third of five children (his older brother committed suicide when he was 19. His three sisters, however, seemed to have led normal lives). He studied law and worked in various legal capacities before he was made administrative director of the District Court on Chemnitz. He had his first psychotic breakdown after his defeat in the Reichstag elections of 1884 where he stood as a liberal candidate. This was a minor episode from which he recovered after 6 months of hospitalization to continue an eminent career in the civil service. His second breakdown, the one which the *Memoirs* describe, occurred a few months after he was promoted to Senatspraesident – or presiding judge of the Supreme Court of Appeals in Leipzig. However, even before he resumed his position as Senatspraesident, during the period when the appointment was pending, he began to experience various symptoms of his body being innervated with divine nerves. Dreams that his old nervous illness had returned haunted him. But more significantly from this point of view was that

> one morning while still in bed (whether still half asleep or already awake I cannot remember), I had a feeling which thinking about it later on struck me as highly peculiar. It was the idea that it really must be rather pleasant to be a woman succumbing to intercourse.
>
> (Quoted in Freud 1911)

Freud writes:

> The idea of being transformed into a woman was the salient feature and the earliest germ of his delusional system. It also proved to be the one part of it that persisted after his cure, and the one part that was able to retain a presence in his behaviour in real life after he had recovered.
>
> (Ibid.: 21)

Freud follows this remark with a citation from the Memoirs:

> … I am sometimes to be found standing before a mirror or elsewhere, with the upper portion of my body bared, and wearing sundry feminine adornments, such as ribbons, false necklaces, and the like. This only occurs, I may add, when I am *by myself*, and never, at least so far as I am able to avoid it, in the presence of other people.
>
> (Ibid.: 21; italics in the original)

It is important to stress the point at which his first fears that his previous psychotic illness would return appeared. This was when he was about to be appointed to a prestigious authority position within the culture he lived. Eric Santner calls this failure to accept his position in the social order a 'failed investiture' (Santner 2004). In psychoanalytic terms we would say that he was unable to step into the place of the father, or unable to identify with his father (i.e. unable to resolve his Oedipus complex). We can see that as Schreber's inability to step into the place of the father took hold of him, his infantile wish to be, like Pentheus, *in the place of the mother*, was triggered. This shattering of his inner world points to murderous hate and fear, rather than love, for his father. In this case taking the place of the mother has the same meaning as in Rosenfeld's patient in the previous chapter – can be seen as an attempt to control murderous aggression. But this attempt to control aggression in a libidinal masochistic way (i.e. 'like a woman succumbing to intercourse') soon gave way to more psychotic paranoid functioning where paranoia became rampant and being a woman meant first and foremost being abused and his body discarded and being left to rot.

Freud does not deal with Schreber's hatred of his father but sees Schreber's wish to be a woman as a homosexual wish to be in the place of mother in order to be loved by father. In this sense Freud did not differentiate between the wish to identify with mother as a flight from murderous hatred towards his father, and a wish to identify with mother in order to be loved by the father. That the first wish is an anti-libidinal wish is borne out by the fact that it did not prevent Schreber's psychotic breakdown but rather set it into motion. The flight from his own aggression led to the projection of this aggression onto Dr Flechsig – 'Little Flechsig' the 'soul murderer' as he called him – and the shattering of his personality.[3]

I cannot go here into Schreber's hallucinations in great detail but suffice it to say that being transformed into a woman was central to his psychotic illness and it contained both megalomaniac and paranoid features, for it made him (in phantasy) on the one hand the victim of unimaginable tortures and degradations in the hands of his male doctor; and, on the other hand, the Redeemer of humankind.

William Niederland and Mortimer Schatzman explained Schreber's delusions as a re-enactment of his early treatment by his father. In this explanation the painful methods of body training and the psychological pressure used by the father are re-lived in the delusional horrors that Schreber describes. As the father was loved and also highly esteemed all the hatred and contempt was directed towards Schreber's physician, the dreaded Flechsig.

This interpretation does not contradict my understanding of Schreber's breakdown but rather complements it. As the father is extremely important for the boy (as well as the girl) in his struggle to separate from mother, a hated father will pose severe problems of separating and differentiating from mother. An ambivalent/hated father can only help the child to separate from mother if the hateful father is split off and projected outwards, and the loving father remains as a model of masculinity. An ambivalent father would demand a great degree of splitting and projection which could lead to the weakening and finally to the disintegration of the ego.

The phantasy of the 'redeemer' appeared during the last stage of his illness and transformed Schreber's paranoia into a delusional grandiose system whereby he was slowly transformed into a woman to serve the 'Order of Things' and to be impregnated by divine rays to produce the new race of human beings. In this sense the paranoia was transformed into megalomania and omnipotence. In this final solution to his problem of murderous hatred, the transformation is to the early omnipotent mother who, like Mary, can reproduce through divine rays. Parthenogenesis as part of omnipotent femininity solves the problem of the hatred against parental intercourse, the hatred against the father and the hatred against difference. In this way Schreber was to be the 'Redeemer' of humankind, the creator of new, better human beings. The 'Redeemer' is in this way a man who is transformed into a woman and impregnated by God's rays. It is perhaps Dionysus himself in his dual identity as man and woman.

We can see that the mythical content of Schreber's delusions is not dissimilar to the Pentheus/Dionysus' duality – a duality that includes the deepest male phantasies about woman's/mother's power. In this sense Schreber's delusions of becoming a woman and being the 'mother' of the new race of men is not unlike

Pentheus' secret wishes to join his mother and the women on Mount Kythairon and become part of a new omnipotent, miraculous race.

But Schreber's transformation of his illness into a new mythology has something of a search for a symbolic framework of a new religion, a new myth that can allow male deep wishes and phantasies to be explored, understood and transformed. It is, so to speak, the beginning of the 'new man'. Perhaps at the misogynist time that Schreber grew up the only way this new man could look at the sub-stratum of his identity, at his own primitive fears and deep wishes, was in this mad and delusional way. The alternative, Schreber seems to be saying to us, are paranoid fears of being attacked, sexually abused, humiliated and being left to rot. The images of immense cruelty, rotting and disintegration, described in the first part of the memoirs, are not so dissimilar to the images evoked by Hitler, some 20 years after the Memoirs were published, to describe the attacks the Jews, as parasites, made on the pure German body (see Chapter 9).

At the peak of his illness Schreber became convinced that the world was coming to an end, indeed that the world had already come to an end and he was the only human left alive. Freud talking about the 'end of the world' phantasy in paranoia links it to the detachment of libido from objects and the internal catastrophe that follows: 'The end of the world is the projection of this internal catastrophe; his subjective world has come to an end since his withdrawal of his love from it.'

Freud continues with a quote from *Faust* where the spirits accuse Faust of having destroyed 'the beautiful world' and with the omnipotence of a demi-god he builds it again. 'And the paranoic builds it again' Freud continues, 'not more splendid, it is true, but at least so that he can once more live in it!' (Freud 1911: 70–1).

In this sense Freud sees the second part of Schreber's illness as characterised by a construction which aimed at recovery. In fact it was during this phase of his illness, when he developed his ideas about himself as the 'Redeemer' of mankind that he began to recover and eventually secured his discharge from the mental Institution and eventually published his Memoirs.

The rebuilding of the world by the paranoiac is reminiscent of Hitler's omnipotent dream of destroying the world and building it anew according to his specifications (see Chapter 9). This view is in agreement with Eric Santner's argument that Schreber's madness was the alternative to fascism (Santner 2000). This might explain Schreber's insistence, contrary to his family's wishes, to publish his memoirs to which he attributed a great deal of importance.

Not only Euripides' fifth-century Greece, but nineteenth-century Europe, had difficulties in integrating the feminine identification within the masculine self. In Schreber's fears about his body being disposed and left to rot, we can read fears about the state of masculinity of his time, known to him most intimately through his father and the continuous fears and wishes of feminisation that this 'pure' masculinity evoked.

The type of masculinity that was promoted by Dr Schreber (the father) was based on the Enlightenment model of an independent, rational, self-sufficient individual. And this individual was, of course, male. The fact that in the process of creating this masculine individual a great deal of coercion, cruelty and demand for submission was used, experienced by the boy as feminisation, was part of the contradiction of the situation.

It is as if Schreber was saying, through his fears of being left to rot that there was something rotten in the state of this type of masculinity that was always and acutely in fear of feminisation. As if Schreber's breakdown had revealed to him the underside of the nineteenth-century masculinity. And as if he tried through his extraordinary Memoirs to say that only a man who was transformed into a woman (i.e. participating of both the masculine and the feminine) can transform humanity. This can be understood as a delusional idea of 'anything is possible' or, alternatively, as an attempt to integrate femininity within the masculine identity. Freud ends the Schreber case with an enigmatic sentence: 'it remains for the future to decide whether there is more delusion in my theory than I should like to admit, or whether there is more truth in Schreber's delusion than other people are yet prepared to believe' (p. 79).

What other people were 'not prepared as yet to believe' is, in my reading, Schreber's unconscious insight, that something was fundamentally wrong with the masculinity of his time. Having a father who used extraordinarily cruel practices to promote an independent masculine development may have helped him to understand at an unconscious level the paranoid base of masculinity as developed in the West since the Enlightenment. This paranoid base was the underside of the rational individual that the Enlightenment sought to bring about. This rational individual was, of course, male, and anything emotional, aesthetic or partaking of the physicality of life was deemed to be feminine. The mother–baby relationship steeped in physicality and emotionality was one of the victims of this state of affairs.

As we know Freud, being a man of his time, denied the importance of the mother–baby relationship in the development of masculinity. For instance when he speaks of the boy's 'pre-history' he talks about the boy's first identification with the pre-oedipal father (Freud 1931). I think that what Freud means here is that masculinity develops in identification with father. But in denying the importance of the boy's early relation to mother Freud excluded the substratum of masculinity from his theory of masculine development that is the phase before the identification with father takes place. In not daring to look into this domain Freud missed something important, something about the vulnerability of masculinity, something about the boy's first identification with mother, his envy of her and his wish to be like her. However, one could argue, as I do, that Freud's concept of the castration complex was an attempt to look into this substratum of masculinity. I shall look at Freud's theory of castration and femininity in the next chapter.

Notes

* Some parts of this chapter have appeared in my article 'Human longings and masculine terrors: masculinity and seperation from mother' (Wieland 2005).

1 Melanie Klein's 'femininity phase' (1928) describes the phantasy of the child invading the mother's body and her concept of projective identification describes his invasion of the object in more abstract terms. Janine Chasseguet-Smirgel's concept of the 'archaic matrix of the Oedipus complex' (1986) describes a similar phantasy but with the wish to eliminate the contents of mother's belly and gain access to the soft, empty belly.
2 In a very insightful book about Senatspraesident Daniel Paul Schreber's psychotic illness Eric Santner examines the connection between Schreber's paranoid psychosis, feminisation and the fin-de siècle fears of contamination and degeneration which became fertile ground for the fascist ideologies and Nazi ideologies (Santner 2004).
3 'Soul murderer' is how Schreber referred to Flechsig his physician.

Chapter 4

Masculinity in psychoanalysis.
I – Theoretical and clinical
considerations

In Chapters 2 and 3 I looked at the fears about the loss of masculinity that are the result of the destruction of the Oedipus complex and of symbolic thinking within the mind, and the violence and madness that this state evokes. Out of this exploration some basic questions have arisen about longings and anxieties in relation to the early 'omnipotent' mother as well as the solutions, ordinary and catastrophic that these anxieties could give rise to.

In Chapters 5 and 6 I shall examine the development of masculinity as described in psychoanalytic theory concentrating on these fundamental wishes, anxieties and defences.

Preliminary remarks

In this chapter I shall refer to masculinity, not masculinities (as it customary to talk about in non-psychoanalytic studies). In speaking about masculinity (singular) I do not mean to imply that there is an innate, pre-programmed entity. And I certainly do not want to deny the many variations that constitute personal and cultural solutions to the fundamental problem of gender. But I do argue that there is a fundamental problem we can legitimately call 'masculine' which is universal because it arises out of the human condition – out of the fact that both boys and girls are born by a woman and, the less universal fact that, on the whole, are looked after by a woman. What I call the problem of gender has to do with the vicissitudes of the early relation to mother – the phantasies surrounding her and the processes of projection, introjection, internalization, identification that are part of the relation to the primary maternal object. Separation and differentiation from the maternal object through the use of symbolic thinking constitutes the main dynamic of human development (Klein 1930). Failure of this process of symbolization plunges the individual into psychosis and the male into persecutory fears about masculinity. There is a particular masculine problem and a particular masculine set of phantasies that I explore in this chapter.

The solutions used in different cultures to solve this problem of a male child coming out of the a female body, and the phantasies that this gives rise to, vary according to what the masculine ideal in that particular culture is, what the cultural norms about the femininity within the masculine self are, and what type of defences are used against feminine identification.

Moreover, cultures vary as to whether they provide arrangements for male rites of passage, and whether there are arrangements that promote, or inhibit the integration of femininity within the self.

In previous studies I examined the solution that Western culture, beginning with the Greeks, has given to the problem of the male differentiating from mother and I named the masculine solution 'matricide' referring to Orestes' murder of his mother Clytemnestra and to the scotomization of the mother identification within the western masculine psyche (Wieland 1996, 2000).[1] Here I shall look at masculinity, concentrating on the formative moment of its development – the moment of the discovery by the boy of the sex difference between mother and himself, the envy and sense of deprivation that this gives rise to, and the defences that are formed to deny or attempt to overcome this early trauma.

Contrary to the traditional view that concentrates on descriptions of masculinity as dominance and independence, and as active and assertive, the psychoanalytic view of the last 40 years focuses on the vulnerability of masculinity (Alizade 2003; Breen 1993; Frosh 1997; Figlio 2000; Glasser 1985; Greenson 1968; Stoller 1975b). The vulnerability of masculinity, which is attributed to the first identification with mother and to an insufficient differentiation from her, is described by almost every contemporary psychoanalytic author who has written on the subject. Different authors have described this in different ways, using different concepts and different theories but the picture that emerges is one of instability in the constitution of masculinity which is always threatened by its demolition. In this sense the relation to father (pre-oedipal and oedipal, internal and external) is very important for the boy's identity. The importance of the Oedipus complex where the aggression towards father is worked through (or not), is therefore much more important for the boy than for the girl, as Freud (1931) has argued.

There exists an extensive literature on masculinity, femininity and 'the meaning of the phallus' based on Lacanian theory (Grosz 1990; Irigaray 1974, 1977; Kristeva 1986, 1989; Mitchell and Rose 1982). There also exists a vast non-psychoanalytic literature – R.W. Conell (1995, 2000), Victor J. Seidler (1993), Kaja Silverman (1992), John Stoltenberg (1999) and Judith Butler (1999) – to mention only a few. I shall not deal with this work, except occasionally to illustrate a specific point, not because I think it is not important, but because it lies outside the remit of my thesis which confines itself to a psychoanalytic framework. Non-psychoanalytic work on masculinity has helped us understand the political, sociological, historical and anthropological aspects of masculinity and has been used to promote social criticism as well as self-criticism and change in men. But on the whole these authors do not deal with the unconscious anxieties and defences that constitute the substratum of masculinity. This substratum is exactly the focus of this study. What I want to stress here is that this book is not about men but about *masculine anxieties and defences*. The difference is a fine one but, as I argue, it is a significant one that defines this work as psychoanalytic.

It was Freud who first remarked that he had the sense of 'preaching to the winds' when he suggested to male patients that a passive attitude is essential in many relationships in life (Freud 1937: 252). Part of this resistance is the cultural definition of masculinity as not passive, at least within western culture. In this sense a sociological analysis will also be helpful. But part of Freud's theory, is that passivity is not only feared. It is feared *because it is wished for* (Freud 1923b: 92). Freud's description of passivity is always within the Oedipus complex as he describes the boy's wish to take the place of the mother and be loved by father. I shall examine Freud's theory of masculinity through some of his case studies.

Freud and masculinity

> Masculinity has the appearance of being defined by something positive – that which the male has and the female lacks. However, emphasising this as Freud did and as Lacan appears to do, is a masculine strategy employed to deny the implications of the converse, that masculinity is defined negatively, as that which is not feminine.
>
> (Frosh 1994: 79)

Although Freud's theory has been called phallocentric and Freud has been accused of sexism by feminists and others, his theory is much more complex than this black and white view suggests. Central to Freud's theory of sexual development is the theory of the castration complex which he linked to his theory of the Oedipus complex. In fact it is the fear of castration that prompts the boy to put an end to the Oedipus complex (and it is the lack of this fear that makes the girl more likely not to resolve her Oedipus complex and stay attached to her father) (Freud 1924c, 1925, 1931, 1933). It is also the fear of castration that makes the little boy deny at first the biological facts and stick to the belief that his mother has a penis the way he does.

Part of the theory of castration is the assumption that Freud made, following Fliess, that human beings are bi-sexual, that is that masculine and feminine impulses are present to both men and women and that part of development is to repress the contra-sexual elements and accept one's biological destiny. In this sense the wish for femininity is there already in the male psyche from the beginning. That the wish for femininity is seen as castration says more about the cultural environment of Freud's world than of Freud himself. As we have already seen from Schreber his struggle to accept his feminine side could be done only through psychotic phantasies and delusions.

The theory of castration runs through Freud's work from the 'Three essays on Sexuality' (1905) to the 'Ego and the Id' (1923a) and to his papers on femininity (1925, 1931, 1932). He never abandoned it. The castration complex runs through all three approaches to defining masculinity – the anatomical (phallic), the object relations (by identification) and the activity/passivity pair of opposites: masculine as active, female as passive (intra-psychic).

The castration complex first arises as the boy sees the girl's genitals and assumes that the girl has been castrated. In that moment all the threats made by mother and father as a punishment for masturbation and all the fears around this seem suddenly real. The boy's fear of being castrated has its origins in this moment of recognition of the sexual difference. In this sense the anatomical difference lies at the bottom of castration anxiety and the boy's wish to preserve his penis.

However, side by side with it Freud introduced two other theories: (1) masculinity established through the working through of the Oedipus complex, and (2) the theory of masculinity as activity as opposed to femininity as passivity. These three theorizations of masculinity run through Freud's work but never quite being integrated into one theory of masculine development.

However the thorny problem of masculinity as difference from mother, the problem of the male being for ever exiled from the female body, so tragically depicted in Bacchae and in Schreber's struggle to accept his femininity, is only present by proxy in Freud, but the struggle with the femininity within the male is ubiquitous.

Castration anxiety: narcissistic wound or separation anxiety?

In 1905 Freud published three essays that were destined to become a landmark in the history of psychoanalysis (Freud 1905). The human body with its possibilities for pleasure and its centrality in the development of sexuality and of human imagination and fantasy became the focus of attention. The individual's relationship to a gendered body and mind and its development out of inchoate beginnings marked with deep wishes, anxieties and defences emerged as a problem for psychoanalysis. Far from being a straightforward correspondence between body and mind 'The Three essays' reveal the emergence of gender in the mind as a highly problematic process. Through this highly problematic process, masculinity emerges as an insecure state defined by castration anxiety.

Freud first looked at castration anxiety through the boy's unwillingness to accept sex difference: 'This conviction (that women have a penis) is energetically maintained by boys, is obstinately defended against contradictions which soon result from observation, and is only abandoned after severe internal struggle' (Freud 1905: 195).

The boy's denial of the biological facts, which has been confirmed by observational research (Roiphe and Galenson 1981), becomes important in perversion and fetishism (Freud 1924b, 1927). From the contemporary vantage point of Object Relations we can see this denial of reality on the part of the boy as a reluctance to accept difference and separation from mother. The gap that opens between himself and his mother is first revealed through sexual difference.

His attachment, fear of loss, and envy of the mother is proportionate to his inability to bear his separation anxiety. We know from Winnicott, Bowlby, Bion and others that a secure and good-enough mother–child relationship will equip the child with the necessary ego strength to face the reality of separateness and the loss of the primary object. Klein stressed the need to mourn the loss of the breast and the necessity to make reparation for the damage inflicted on the mother by the baby's phantasised and real attacks on her. For Klein the attempt to make reparation leads eventually to symbolic reality and to the ability to relate to an object which is separate from the self. However, all this research was not available to Freud. For Freud the anatomical difference, the fact that women do not have a penis, ushered in the fear of losing his own penis – either as a wish or as a punishment. At the end when the boy reluctantly accepts the reality of difference, his fear of losing his penis becomes part of his reality as a boy. With the advantage of Object Relations research we can say that the boy's castration anxiety is proportional to his not having accepted, not only the sex difference, but more importantly the loss of the early mother.

Although Freud talked about phallic superiority he knew exactly about the difficulty of being a boy and he encapsulated it in his theory of castration. To be a boy (at least within the western culture of the early twentieth century) was to be constantly threatened with castration – unmanning, emasculation, feminisation. Castration became central to his theory of masculinity, the Oedipus complex and emotional maturity.

Of course to be female is even worse – it is to be already castrated. But this shows already the wish of the boy to see everything in terms of his penis and to project his own fears about the precariousness of his masculinity onto the girl. I suggest that the castration complex is Freud's major contribution to the understanding of masculinity – its precariousness, its ambivalence about the feminine within the masculine psyche, and its ambivalence about mother/woman. In the castration complex Freud saw not only a dread but also a wish. The wish to be the same as mother. The wish to be part of her. The wish not to grow up and be 'one half of a person'. This wish led inevitably to the horror of the wish being granted – to the horror of castration. Freud looked at the wish for castration when he looked at the negative Oedipus complex in the 'Ego and the Id' (1923a) and in many other papers (1923b, 1924b, 1924c, 1927).

Freud saw castration anxiety as central to male psychology and sanity because it was about accepting reality – the reality of sexual difference and ultimately *difference* as a fundamental part of reality. Later on, Freud linked the castration complex to the Oedipus complex (1923a, 1924c) and to the distinction between the sexes (1925, 1931, 1933). He could now delineate a male Oedipus complex and a female one and they were distinguished by the different relation of the boy and the girl to the castration complex: the boy put an end to the Oedipus complex because of his fear of castration, whereas the girl entered the Oedipus complex because she was castrated (Freud 1923a, 1924c, 1925).

As Freud developed his theory of the Oedipus complex his language began to be more object related. Now he talked not only about erogenous zones and genitals, but also about the relation to mother and father. Eventually the castration complex was linked to love and hate for mother and father in the positive and negative Oedipus complex. Now the boy could take the place of the father after he eliminated him in phantasy and, therefore, would fear castration as a punishment; or take the place of the mother that is become feminine in phantasy and fear castration as a precondition (for being feminine). Either way, Freud says, castration is inextricably linked with the boy's Oedipus complex (Freud 1923a, 1924).

As Freud put it so eloquently:

> The Oedipus complex offered the child two possibilities of satisfaction, an active and a passive one. He could put himself in his father's place in a masculine fashion and have intercourse with his mother as his father did, in which case he would soon have felt the latter as a hindrance; or he might want to take the place of his mother and be loved by his father, in which case his mother would become superfluous ... His acceptance of the possibility of castration, his recognition that women were castrated, made an end of both possible ways of obtaining satisfaction from the Oedipus complex. For both of them entailed the loss of his penis – the masculine one as a resulting punishment and the feminine one as a precondition.
>
> (Freud 1924: 176)

The meaning of castration comes from the recognition that women do not possess a penis, so the mere recognition of sexual difference evokes the fear of castration. But, if instead of castration we read *feminisation*, we have the picture of the boy being in constant fear of losing his masculinity and be feminised either as a punishment, or as a wish, as the preceding citation shows. As Freud linked femininity, not only to a castrated state, but also to passivity he talked more and more about the male's (and female's) fear of passivity. In 'Analysis terminable and interminable' he declared with obvious resignation that:

> At no other point in one's analytic work does one suffer more from the oppressive feeling that one's repeated efforts have been in vain, and from a suspicion that one has been 'preaching to the winds', than when one is trying to persuade a woman to abandon her wish for a penis ... or when one is seeking to convince a man that a passive attitude to men does not always signify castration ...
>
> (Ibid.: 1937: 252)

What both sexes are afraid of is passivity, Freud is saying, and the penis is wanted as a signifier of activity and as a protection against passivity. In this sense both sexes are in a kind of flight from passivity and femininity and the formation of masculinity rests on this repudiation. Karen Horney described the fear of passivity and the flight from femininity in both men and women in her paper 'Flight from womanhood' (Horney 1971a).

But this is not as straight forward as it sounds. Passivity, which Freud equates with femininity, is not just feared and abhorred. In fact they are feared and abhorred because there exists a strong wish to be in that state. This is obvious from the preceding citation where Freud describes the wish to be in the place of the mother.

To be sure the equation of femininity with passivity[2] reads like a reversal of reality as it is the baby that is passive (or at least helpless) in the hands of the mother (not the mother). We can easily see projective identification operating here whereby as a concept in the mind masculinity (in both boys and girls) emerges out of splitting off the baby's passivity and helplessness and projecting them into the woman/mother. Masculinity is now endowed with power, activity and agency. Any wish to return to mother and be her little boy again, passive in her hands, is then met with intense anxiety and fear of feminsation that is castration.

Freud reserved the term castration for the fear of the loss of the penis and refused other suggestions. However, he uses castration and femininity, femininity and passivity, and femininity and male homosexuality as meaning basically the same thing (Freud 1909, 1918, 1923a, 1924, 1925, 1931). In a footnote to 'Little Hans' (Freud 1909) added in 1923 he speaks of the contributions of Lou Andrea Salome and Franz Alexander who linked the castration complex to the loss of the breast or the loss of the stool, in other words castration as a loss of the object as well as of something in the child's body. Freud insisted, however, that the term castration complex was to be retained 'for the excitations and consequences which are bound up with the loss of the *penis*' (Freud 1909: 8; italics in the original).

Narcissistic wholeness, narcissistic loss and separation anxiety

In my attempt to link the castration complex to the moment of separation and differentiation from mother, I would like to make clear two different relations to mother: the mother as an object in an object relation; and the mother as an extension of the baby's body and mind (a narcissistic object). To these two different mothers belong two different losses – an object loss and a narcissistic loss. The loss of the mother as an extension of the self or of the baby's body is a narcissistic loss. The narcissistic loss is the loss of the illusion that the baby has everything – penis, breast, milk, capacity to have children, in other words that he and mother are one omnipotent system. This is an omnipotent phantasy. It is a phantasy of perfection and wholeness. This stage of illusion has been movingly described by Winnicott (1945, 1956, 1960, 1962). For Klein the illusion is part of a projective identification with the ideal mother that exists as part of the splitting of both the ego and the object during the paranoid schizoid position (Klein 1946).

When this illusion is lost, usually with weaning or with the birth of another child or with the awareness of the father as a third person, or simply because it is no longer sustainable, the child transfers this phantasy onto the mother. It is the mother who has everything – milk, breasts, babies and penis. To be separated from this mother is to be left out in the cold – alone and without resources. Klein describes the phantasised attempts of the baby to get inside mother and scoop out all the riches and claim them for him/herself (Klein 1928). This act of projective identification confuses the boundaries between mother and baby and increases guilt and anxiety, but also the reality of difference that gives rise to envy. Accepting the reality of difference is not a simple task for the little boy.

The struggle to accept reality

The boy's struggle to accept his difference from mother is movingly portrayed in Freud's paper on 'Little Hans'. The full title of the paper, published in 1909, is 'Analysis of a phobia in a five-year-old boy' but is better know as 'Little Hans'. I shall not discuss the paper as a whole but will concentrate on Hans's struggle to accept his difference from mother – to accept that his mother does not have a penis and that he will not have children the way his mother does. The two seemed to be related and both denied the anatomical difference between Hans and mother.

Freud 'analysed' Little Hans through the notes Hans's father made of his son's everyday life. Prominent among the problems that Hans was facing was a phobia he developed to do with horses. The phobia had to do with the fear that a horse will bite him and became so acute that Hans refused to leave the house. The mere encounter with a horse made him panic. Freud interprets the phobia as a fear of the father although Hans had linked it to mother. The horse's 'big widdler' was linked to mother's 'big widdler' which Hans insisted that his mother had. However, if he were to accept the reality that his mother did not have a 'widdler' like his or like the horse's he would have to also accept that *he* will not be able to have children like mother.

Freud did not comment on the boy's loss of the mother when his little sister was born and his possible identification with her (mother) as a compensation for this loss. Neither did he comment on Hans's envy of her ability to have children. Instead he concentrated on the anatomical difference from the sister and on the penis as an external, visible organ.

We can deduce Hans's reasoning as follows: If the mother is not like Hans, then *he* will not be able to have children like mother. The narcissistic loss of not being able to have children is perhaps the biggest loss that comes with the boy's realization of the sexual difference. We can see that Hans hangs on to the idea that he will, one day, bear children although he knows that boys can't. He knows and does not know.

Freud described several aspects of Hans's wish – his wish to be in his mother's bed and have her all to himself (a baby's experience on the one hand, or an Oedipal wish on the other) and his wish to be like her and have babies just like her (which can be either narcissistic, or part of the negative Oedipus complex). Thus his wish to have a baby has three different and antithetical parts: to have a baby – as part of the positive Oedipus complex – that is as the wish to take his father's place and give his mother babies; as a wish to take his mother's place and be copulated by his father that is part of the negative Oedipus complex; and as a narcissistic phantasy to have a baby by having a 'lumpf' that is passing a stool.

Hans's struggle to retain the narcissistic state, which is a retreat from the Oedipus complex, is obvious in the case. In this narcissistic wish he eliminated his father and became like an omnipotent mother – having babies all by him/herself. At the end, however, the distinction between the two in the development of little Hans is quite clear and the giving up of his illusion that he could have babies himself led to his recovery. As the boy's father reports:

> Seeing Hans playing with his imaginary children again. 'Hullo', I said to him, 'are your children still alive? You know quite well a boy can't have any children'. Hans: 'I know. I was their Mummy before, *now I'm their Daddy*'.
>
> (Freud 1909: 96; italics in the original)

We can see the transition here from Hans's phantasy that he is, or can be, like mother to accepting the fact that he is like father. In the next few days Hans's phobia disappeared. Hans chooses the road to reality which includes the acceptance that one cannot have it all or be everything, that a boy cannot have children.

Although Freud speaks of the birth of his sister as the most important event in Hans's life he did not exactly relate it to Hans's phobia. He explains the horse as the father, although Hans had linked it to mother. Biting is, of course, an oral impulse and is related not only to aggression but also to eating and incorporation. It is maybe not too far-fetched to look at this as one of Hans's regressive wishes that is to be incorporated by his mother, like the baby in her belly, and never be separated from her. (This is reminiscent of my patient's dream in Chapter 2 and his fear of being eaten up.) Or as a punishment for such a wish to be incorporated? For such a wish would entail the loss of his masculinity that is the loss of his penis.

As we know, a symptom is over-determined and one explanation might not preclude the other. To be with mother, to be mother's baby, to be in mother's belly, to *be* mother and have babies himself might all be subsumed under the rubric of a *return to mother*. The last, to *be* mother, can exist within the Oedipus complex as a wish to be impregnated by father; or as an omnipotent, auto-erotic wish to have a baby the way the boy has a stool. This set of wishes can co-exist with another set of 'having mother' which exists within the positive Oedipus complex – that is displacing or eliminating father to take his place.

Although it is obvious that part of Hans's wish was to *be like* mother, Freud did not assume a feminine wish in him. He explains that the wish to have children and look after them was not a wish to be feminine:

> There is no necessity … to assume in Hans the presence of a feminine strain of desire for having children. It was with his mother that had had his most blissful experiences as a child, and he was now repeating them, and himself playing the active part, which was thus necessarily that of mother.
>
> (Freud 1909: 252)

The distinction seems unclear as if an identification with mother does not include a feminine wish. By 'feminine wish' Freud clearly means passivity so that being an *active* mother is not feminine. As Freud did not examine the boy's identification with the mother, or his early relation to her he could not examine the *narcissistic* wish to be feminine and to lose his masculinity, although he examined the object-related wish to be feminine within the Oedipus complex.

The Wolfman

The same reluctance to see the predominance of oral sadistic impulses as part of a relationship to mother is also present in another of Freud's cases 'From the history of infantile neurosis', better known as 'The Wolfman'. Freud's analysis of the young Russian aristocrat took place between 1910 and 1914 but Freud delayed publishing this paper until 1918 fearing that his young patient would be identified.

Unlike Little Hans whose observation of his childhood neurosis was made by the child's father at the time it was taking place, Freud had to reconstruct the Wolfman's childhood and the incidents that led to his infantile neurosis (an animal phobia, obsessional behaviour, loss of appetite, sado-masochistic practices). Central to the whole analysis was the dream with wolves from which the paper took its popular name. The patient had this dream when he was 4 years old. The patient's account of the dream is as follows:

> I dreamt that it was night and that I was in my bed. (My bed stood with its foot towards the window; in front of the window there was a row of old walnut trees. I know it was winter when I had the dream, and night time.) Suddenly the window opened of its own accord and I was terrified to see that some white wolves were sitting on the big walnut tree in front of the window. There were six or seven of them. The wolves were quite white, and looked more like foxes or sheep-dogs, for they had big tails like foxes and they had their ears pricked like dogs when they pay attention to something. In great terror, evidently of being eaten up by the wolves, I screamed and woke up.
>
> (Freud 1918: 29)

The patient himself associated the dream with a book of illustrated fairy tales and in particular Red Riding Hood. (The other fairy tale that has similar content is 'the wolf and the seven little goats'). In both stories there is a strong association between being eaten up and pregnancy and birth; as in both stories the wolf's belly is opened up and the grandmother (in Little Riding Hood) and the seven little goats (in Seven Little Goats) come out alive and well. Yet throughout the paper Freud insists that the wolves in the patient's dream represent the father. He writes: If in my patient's case the wolf was merely a first father-surrogate, the question arises whether the hidden content in the Red Riding Hood may not simply be infantile fear of the father (p. 32).

Freud continues to weave the themes of the fear of the father, of the boy witnessing the primal scene in his infancy, of castration with the repression of homosexual feelings towards the father, the rejection of passivity and femininity and the use of sado-masochism as an expression of the fear of castration. Mother plays no role whatsoever in all this although femininity as equivalent to both homosexuality and castration is referred to a great deal in the study. The fact that oral impulses and the fear (or the wish?) of being eaten up are themes that are connected with mother is not examined by Freud. However, towards the end of the treatment he refers to his patient's complaint that 'the world ... was hidden from him by a veil' (p. 99). Freud sees this as a 'wishful phantasy of flight from the world. It can be translated as follows: "Life makes me unhappy! I must get back into the womb!"', he writes (ibid.: 100).

Here at last appears the mother, or rather the womb, as a powerful presence and wish. The wish is a flight from life – a death wish disguised as life, or being in the womb. The wolf as a powerful androgynous mother corresponds to the patient's wish to be in his mother's belly and be one with her. To be unborn. The fear of the father may well be the cause of this flight from life, and flight from masculinity but that is not how Freud saw it. Freud explains the wish to be back in the womb as a homosexual wish, as a wish to be in the place of the mother and be copulated with by his father, to obtain sexual satisfaction by him and also bear him a child:

> The wish to be born of his father (as he had at first believed was the case), the wish to be sexually satisfied by him, the wish to present him with a child – *and all this at the price of his masculinity*, and expressed in a language of anal erotism – these wishes complete the circle of his fixation upon his father. In them homosexuality has found its furthest and most intimate expression.
>
> (Ibid.: 101; italics mine)

Although Freud touches on the theme – both wish and fear – of a retreat from masculinity, his explanation is in terms of the negative Oedipus complex and of the primal scene as well as of a transformation of homosexual feelings into symptoms and anxiety because of their forbidden nature. The retreat from any kind of sexuality into the womb which spells the negation of sexuality, ultimately the Nirvana principle, is very close to the death instinct and belonged to Freud's future discovery. At the time of the Wolfman's treatment (1910–1914), Eros was seen as the only force operating in human development.

There was, however, a phantasy of re-birth as well which Freud interprets as a wish to be in mother's genitals, or in other words to have intercourse with her. So Freud here describes the complete Oedipus complex – both positive and negative. What he ignores, however, is the fact that the patient saw his retreat into the womb as a kind of retreat from the world. Freud's libido theory could not explain such a retreat from life and the anti-libidinal elements in it. The anti-libidinal force that co-exists with Eros within the human psyche Freud eventually named the 'death instinct' (Freud 1920). Kleinian theorists explained this further in terms of narcissism and particularly 'destructive narcissism' (Rosenfeld 1971; Steiner 1993; Meltzer 1992).

This wish to retreat from the world into the womb could be seen, having in mind Freud's later developments of the death instinct and of the Oedipus complex, as an attempt to *destroy* the Oedipus complex and with it all relationships – a retreat into primary narcissism as Bela Grunberger sees it (Grunberger 1971, 1989) or a destruction of the father representation as Josine Perelberg saw it (see Chapter 1). It can be related not only to destructive narcissism but also to such concepts as Ernest Jones's 'aphanisis', Harry Guntrip's 'anti-libidinal ego', and Bion's 'ego-destructive superego'. Freud himself saw the death instinct encapsulated into the type of superego that was a 'pure culture of the death instinct' (Freud 1923a, 1930).

In the case of the Wolfman, we know that the patient thought he was special because he was born with a caul around his head and that this specialness created a kind of veil through which he saw the world. In this sense this specialness was bestowed on to him by his mother whose body he carried with him into the world. Freud does not comment or wonder about the child's wish to be one with mother not in a sexual way but in a way that negates sexuality and gender – in other words *as a flight from sexuality*. He comments instead on the patient's phantasy of re-birth which was achieved via an enema administered to him by a man, which he saw as sexual satisfaction by his father. However, in terms of separation from mother the man/father helping him to be re-born stresses the role of the father in helping the son to accept separation and difference from mother and therefore enter the turmoil of life and sexuality.

The Wolfman is an extremely rich and complex paper and it is impossible to do justice to its complexity in a few pages. From my point of view what Freud achieves here is to give us a lively picture of the polymorphous perverse sexuality of childhood, the defences that are erected against it and the instability of gender identity. What he also conveys is the difficulty that boys have in accepting their feminine impulses and their femininity. However, as the discussion of the primary pre-oedipal relation to mother is missing, Freud is obliged to see femininity always related to the Oedipus complex. In this way he identifies femininity with homosexuality and uses the two terms interchangeably. The little boy's wish to have a child is tantamount to his wish to be copulated with by his father and bear him a child. The more omnipotent wish to have a child in an act of parthenogenesis, as a complete system of himself merged with an omnipotent mother is a more primitive narcissistic wish that Freud does not comment about. (I shall examine later the malignant and perverted type of this childhood wish in examining the Nazi pre-occupation with re-birth, regeneration and creating a new world.)

In the same way Freud interprets cannibalism, the wish to devour and the fear of being devoured as a wish to be 'copulated with by the father' (p. 106). He relates this to anorexia which he sees as an aversion to sexuality. An aversion to sexuality is, however, also an aversion to life and an aversion to the reality of separateness, and separation. In this sense we can link together the Wolfman's wish to retreat inside mother, the destruction of object relations that follows it, and his anorexia.[3] The anti-libidinal force that governs all three phenomena is part of the wish to destroy reality and build it according to one's pleasure principle. In this we can discover a subtle link between primitive human longings and the wish to destroy the world and re-create it.

Freud continued to describe men's struggle with their feminine side and saw this as part of the wish to be in the place of the mother and be copulated with by the father that is the negative Oedipus complex. That's where he disagreed with Adler who saw in the 'masculine protest' only a wish for power. Femininity was loathed because it was seen as weakness and passivity, Adler was saying. For Freud this was to ignore the whole area not only of the Oedipus complex but also of the polymorphous perverse childhood sexuality, the negative Oedipus complex, as well as the whole area of perversions and of human sexuality. The attraction of femininity for the boy, the repression of feminine impulses as well as the inadequacy of repression in cases of masochism or other perversions was stressed by Freud throughout his writings. But nowhere did he stress the men's feminine wish to be in the place of the mother more than in the Schreber case where the wish became a delusion and eventually a cure for his paranoia (see Chapter 3).

Freud continued his exploration into the male wish for, and terror of, femininity in another paper 'A seventeenth century demonological neurosis' (Freud 1923b). Here Freud tells the story of a seventeenth-century painter Christoph Haizman who after his father's death and his ensuing depression he sealed a pact with the Devil for 9 years after which he was to belong completely to the Devil. Freud emphasises the fact that Haizman's depression began after his father's death and stressed his ambivalence towards him. Freud also emphasises the fact that what Haizman wanted from the Devil was not riches, fame or women but the wish to call himself his 'bounden son'. ('I, Christof Haizman, subscribe myself to this Lord as his bounden son till the ninth year' the contract said (ibid.: 81).)

The German word, 'leibeigener Sohn', has, however, a different connotation from the 'translation 'bounden son'. The German word includes the word 'Leib' which means body – his body belongs, like a slave or like a serf, to the Devil, he says. In fact the word means in German 'serf'. Freud does not comment on this but he writes that the Devil undertakes to replace the painter's lost father for 9 years. However, the thesis of the Devil as a father substitute, runs soon into trouble as Freud discusses one of the illustrations of the Devil that Haizman made – the second one in fact. The first one Freud explains portrayed the Devil as an honest citizen but in all the subsequent illustrations the Devil is portrayed 'naked and misshapen' and, surprisingly, has breasts. In the illustration reproduced by Freud in his paper Haizman portrays the Devil with two pairs of female breasts. The breasts are present in all the subsequent paintings of the Devil, Freud informs us. Freud finds this hard to explain as he has already seen the Devil as the father. But eventually he finds 'two explanations which compete with each other without being mutually exclusive' (ibid.: 90). He continues:

> A boy's feminine attitude to his father undergoes repression as soon as he understands that his rivalry with a woman for his father's love has a precondition the

loss of his own male genitals – in other words, castration. Repudiation of the feminine attitude is thus the result of a revolt against castration. It regularly finds its strongest expression in the converse phantasy of castrating the father, of turning *him* into a woman. Thus the Devil's breasts would correspond to a projection of the subject's own femininity on to the father-substitute.

(Ibid.: 90)

In the second explanation Freud sees the breasts as a displacement of the child's tender feelings towards his mother onto the father. This suggests, Freud tells us a previous strong attachment to the mother. Freud seems to be implying here a certain confusion between mother and father in the painter's psyche maybe born out of a wish not to give up his primary attachment to his mother or his wish to be part of her, or the wish not to have to decide whether one is a man or a woman – that is a wish to stay in a state of confusion which, like the Wolfman's veil, obscures reality. Freud, however, does not discuss all this. He discusses, however, the fact that there is 'a strong fixation to mother which, in its turn, is responsible for part of the child's hostility towards his father' (ibid.: 90–1).

Freud continues:

If our patient's repugnance to accepting castration made it impossible for him to appease his longing for his father, it is perfectly understandable that he should have turned for help and salvation to the image of the mother. This is why he declared that only the holy mother of God of Mariazell could release him from his pact with the Devil.

(Ibid.: 91)

However, Haizman is finally freed from his pact with the Devil by entering the Order of the Brothers Hospitallers – a male religious order. It is not difficult to see here that Haizman resolves his problem of deficient masculinity, due to his inability to identify with an ambivalent father, by seeking male identification of a brotherly nature. The religious brotherhood, a brotherhood that pays homage to some kind of femininity through the wearing of robes and through the practice of passivity and abstinence, may have been a solution for Haizman's confused mind. The impossibility of accepting the father – even the Devil is a woman – led him to problems not only of depression but to fears of annihilation. A group solution, a belonging to a male group which pays homage to being feminine in front of a male God may have been the 'order of things' that he craved. (As I will show later the fascist male group and the fascist solution is a different kind of fraternal group although the underlying masculine problems are similar.)

In discussing masochistic phantasies towards the end of the paper Freud refers to another male patient who suffered from obsessional neurosis and who revealed an unresolved conflict between a masculine and a feminine attitude – what Freud called 'fear of castration or desire for castration' (1923b: 92). Freud continues:

The patient had developed masochistic phantasies which were wholly derived from a wish to accept castration; and he had even gone beyond these phantasies to real satisfaction in perverse situations. The whole of his state rested – like Adler's theory itself – on the repression and denial of early infantile fixations of love.

(Ibid.: 92)

Freud concludes this section of the paper by referring to Schreber 'who found his way to recovery' by accepting his feminine role and giving up the struggle against castration. 'After that', Freud continues 'he became lucid and calm, was able to put through his own discharge from the asylum and led a normal life …' (ibid.: 92).

In 'The economic problem of masochism' (1924b) Freud makes it quite clear that what he is talking about is the male's *wish* to be in the place of the female:

If one has the opportunity of studying cases in which the masochistic phantasies have been especially richly elaborated, one quickly discovers that they place the subject in a characteristically female situation; they signify, that is, being castrated, or copulated with, or giving birth to a baby.

(Freud 1924b: 162)

However, masochistic phantasies do not only express the wish to be in the female role because of the love of father. They express the wish to inflict pain and cruelty which are projected onto the sadistic partner, real or imagined (Morgan and Ruszczynski 2007). In this sense masochism and wanting to be in the place of the woman is one way of restraining and containing violence as the Rosenfeld quote from p. 32 explains. We now enter another meaning of femininity, which Freud does not examine, which has to do not only with a wish to be in the place of the mother and be 'copulated with' by the father, but with a wish to avoid the violent feelings of the male towards both mother and father (towards mother for weaning him and frustrating him and for loving father more than him; towards father for taking mother away from him and threatening with castration).

Masochism remains within the realm of object relations and is an attempt to maintain relationships and protect both the self and the object. Freud, however, discusses another form of masochism – moral masochism.[4] In discussing moral masochism Freud re-opens the discussion about the severity of the superego and the need of the ego to submit to the superego. The need of the 'moral' masochist to be punished, that is to be beaten by the father is the same feminine wish of 'feminine masochism' except that in moral masochism the object-related wish is de-sexualised. What is now sexualised is morality. The individual shies away from a relation to objects and idealises morality or ideology. The violence that was projected onto the sadist in sado-masochism is now projected onto different ideas, ideologies cultures, groups. The violence of ideologies and the submission of the ego to them is born here.

Freud writes: 'Conscience and morality have arisen through the overcoming, the desexualization, of the Oedipus complex; but through moral masochism morality is sexualized once more' (Freud 1924b: 169).

With moral masochism Freud reached a state of mind that is destructive of relationships. The sexualization he refers to is not of another person but of the superego – of a superego that is a 'pure culture of the death instinct'. The superego is now in the place not only of the father/mother but in the place of the sexual object. Submission to this type of superego spells the destruction of a lively exchange between objects that constitutes life. It is synonymous with destructive narcissism as expounded by Rosenfeld (1964, 1971, 1987).

Beginning with the male's wish and fear of castration within the Oedipus complex Freud eventually reached more severely pathological and destructive states where love and sexuality were stripped of their base in object relations. In moral masochism, Freud discovered the reign of the anti-libidinal superego which played such an important role in the fascist movement.

We can see that in the concept of masochism, both libidinal and moral, Freud encapsulated a masculine pathology that is based on the wish to be feminine (see Kaja Silverman 1995, 2002 for a full discussion of moral masochism).

I argue that Freud's description of masochism is important not only in understanding the role of the feminine wish in male perversion but also in its role of male violence and violent ideology. De-sexualized sado-masochism, that is the submission of the ego to a cruel superego, has been seen by the Frankfurt School and by others (Adorno *et al.* 1950; Dicks 1972; Fromm 1936, 1941; Money Kyrle 1978) as the main dynamic that defines the 'authoritarian personality' and therefore the fascist psyche (see Chapter 1). In this sense we can understand, via Freud's understanding of masochism, the link between fears and wishes of feminisation, the authoritarian personality and the fascist psyche. Although my own position is that sado-masochism and the authoritarian personality cannot fully explain the fascist mind, I do think that it constitutes a big part of it (see Chapters 9 and 10).

Freud in his description of moral masochism and its relation to the death instinct gave us a whole way of looking at the relation between gender, sexuality and social violence. In moral masochism Freud separates the wish to be feminine from the love of the father and from any homosexual desire – or from any desire whatsoever. Eros is substituted by the death drive within a landscape empty of objects. We are already in the dark regions of submission to a deadly ideology which is the subject of Chapters 6–10.

Melanie Klein's theory of masculine development: the boy's early relation to mother

What remained unexplored in Freud was the child's early relation to mother which Melanie Klein made her main focus of research. With her theory of the early Oedipus complex and the introduction of a 'femininity phase' Klein altered

Freud's theory of gender development fundamentally and opened new horizons for the exploration of gender. I shall discuss here only the boy's development.

In her paper 'The early stages of the Oedipus conflict'(1928) Klein introduced the notion of an early Oedipus situation beginning around the end of the first year of life (Klein 1928). Furthermore, she describes the child's turning away from the breast as a result of the frustration caused by weaning, and turning his oral impulses to the penis and eventually to father. At the same time the child – boy or girl – *identifies with mother*. This is the beginning of what she called the 'femininity phase' in which both boys and girls identify with mother.[5]

The femininity phase is characterised by intense envy of the mother and by attacks on the inside of her body. It coincides, Klein tells us, with the ascent of the epistemophilic instinct and of sadism. The helplessness the child experiences after weaning is connected to the onset of the Oedipus situation and the primal scene which is a mystery to the child. The helplessness and grievance associated with not knowing gives rise to both the epistemophilic instinct and to sadism. Like in 'Little Hans' issues of separation, separateness, and the helplessness they give rise to, lead to a wish to invade mother's body and rob mother of all the riches.

The inside of the mother's body is now the object of both curiosity and a wish to appropriate its contents. Klein writes:

> So the epistemophilic instinct and the desire to take possession come quite early to be most intimately connected with one another and at the same time with the sense of guilt aroused by the incipient Oedipus conflict. This significant connection ushers in a phase of development in both sexes which is of vital importance, hitherto not sufficiently recognised. It consists of *a very early identification with mother*.
>
> (Klein 1928: 188; italics mine)

The femininity phase coincides with the anal phase so that faeces are equated with baby and the wish to rob mother from her babies also applies to faeces. The boy at this stage envies and wants to emulate mother's capacity to bear children. In relation to this Klein writes:

> As in the castration complex of the girls, so in the femininity complex of the male, there is at bottom the frustrated desire for a special organ. The tendencies to steal and destroy are concerned with the organs of conception, pregnancy and parturition, which the boy assumes to exist in mother, and further the vagina and the breasts, the fountain of milk, which are coveted as organs of receptivity and bounty from the time when the libidinal position is purely oral.
>
> (1928: 190)

The boy now fears retaliation by mother for the destruction of her body. He fears that his body will be mutilated and dismembered (one cannot help remembering Pentheus here! see Chapter 2). Fears of castration also arise. In the anal phase the mother who takes away the faeces signifies the castrating and dismembering mother.

The fear of the mother is combined with the fear of punishment by father whose penis the boy wants to steal from inside the mother where he assumes it is. These fears help create a powerful and vengeful superego which devours, dismembers and castrates.

The anxiety at this stage is very high and combines with fears of castration by both mother and father as well as humiliation and a sense of inferiority for not knowing and not possessing the mother's organs for the creation of children. The boy reacts now with a masculine defence – the over-estimation of his penis. 'His sense of being at a disadvantage' Klein writes, 'is then concealed and over-compensated by the superiority he deduces from his possession of a penis' (p. 191).

Klein calls these masculine defences 'excessive protestations of masculinity' (1928: 191). She goes on to describe the use that the boy makes of his aggression to compensate for the feminine role:

> A tendency in boys to express excessive aggression, which very frequently occurs, has its source in the femininity complex. It goes with an attitude of contempt and 'knowing better', and is highly asocial and sadistic; it is partly determined by an attempt to mask the anxiety and ignorance which lie behind it. In part it coincides with the boy's protest (originating in his fear of castration) against the feminine role, but it is rooted also in his dread of his mother, whom he intended to rob of the father's penis, her children and her female sexual organs.
>
> (Ibid.)

The anxieties of the femininity phase include not only an attack on mother and on the babies inside her and the fear of retaliation by her, but also an attack on father's penis which is seen to reside inside mother and fears of retaliation by him. These combined anxieties act as a force for separation from mother and help the child to turn towards the *external* father as an identificatory figure.

The struggle in the boy during the femininity phase is one between pre-genital and genital positions and culminates in what is known as the classical Oedipus complex between 3 and 5 years of age. The anxieties of the femininity phase drive the boy towards an *identification with father* but Klein does not consider this by itself an adequate base for a secure masculinity '... but this stimulus in itself does not provide a firm foundation for the genital position, since it *leads mainly to repression and over-compensation of the anal-sadistic instincts, and not to overcoming them*' (ibid. 192; italics mine).

Klein warns here against a pseudo-masculine solution where the identification with father covers up a split off early identification with mother full of violence, anxiety and guilt. I suggest that this pseudo-masculinity covering the split off feminine wishes is the substratum of what Freud explored in his work on the repressed femininity in men. Freud, of course did not put it in this way and insisted that the feminine position was always a homosexual one. Klein, although sees the femininity phase within an 'early Oedipus complex' this primitive Oedipus complex is characterised by the fact that father's penis is 'inside mother'. This is a mother who has everything including a penis. In this sense she distinguishes between a wish to be feminine based on the envy of the early omnipotent mother who has swallowed up father and his penis, from the wish to be feminine so that the boy will take the mother's place within the Oedipus complex. Although at this stage Klein had not yet formulated her concept of a primary envy, she seemed to be hinting at an early envy in describing the attacks of the baby on mother's body.

Klein's description of the early phantasies of the attacks on mother's body and the wish to get into mother's body and steal or take over the contents of her body form the basis of Klein's later concept of 'projective identification' which she defined as the prototype of an aggressive object relationship (1946). In this phantasy a part of the ego dislocates itself from the subject and lodges itself in the object thus claiming the object to itself. The taking over of the object in this way disturbs not only the perception of the object but also the ego which becomes impoverished and dislocated – that is it has its centre outside the self. The colonization of the object in this way leads to a weakening, not a strengthening, of the ego.

The consequences of this process for the development of masculinity are difficult to overestimate. If the taking over of the object is in the unconscious the mother, a male subject that uses excessive forms of projective identification will feel trapped inside mother's body/mind, feeling easily castrated/humiliated/ feminised. A cursory look at male borderline pathology with its overuse of projective identification tends to confirm this. This point, however, is left for later discussion.

To return to the working through of the femininity phase Klein insists that a defensive identification with father is not an adequate base for a secure masculinity. For this the pre-genital phase with all the anal-sadistic instincts as well, as the genital phase and the Oedipus complex, need to be worked through. As the boy's genital trends grow, his ability to make reparation to both mother and father increases and his internal objects become more benign. With this benign world a more secure sense of gender and self emerges (Klein 1932).

Klein sees a more symmetrical development between boy and girl. In both boy and girl the anxiety and guilt associated with the attacks on mother during the femininity phase is the primary cause of all anxiety and can lead to inhibitions in the development of symbol formation and in difficulties in work and in sexual life.

Klein's theory of masculine development seems to have been far ahead of her time and did not spark the kind of furore that Freud's theory of femininity did. Instead it was quietly forgotten and the gender-neutral theory of projective identification took its place. However, a few very influential papers on the femininity complex in men were published in the 1920s and 1930s.[6]

Notes

1 The murder of Clytemnestra by her son Orestes, his persecution and final exoneration is the main theme of Aeschylus' trilogy Oresteia. Orestes, ordered by Athena to avenge his father's murder by his wife Clytemnestra, carries out his mother's murder and is immediately persecuted by the bloodthirsty maternal goddesses of revenge, the furies. He

eventually takes refuge in Athens, in Athena's temple, and a trial takes place whereby he is finally exonerated. The reason given is that the murder of the father (by Clytemnestra) is bigger than the murder of the mother. The play is often interpreted as portraying the victory of the paternal principle and of patriarchy over the maternal principle and matriarchy.

2 Although the equation of femininity with passivity was maintained in most of Freud's papers, in his last paper on femininity (1933) he asserted that all libido was active and that a great deal of activity goes into the pursuit of passive strivings.

3 Karen Horney in her paper 'The dread of woman' (1932) describes the deadly wish to be absorbed into the mother's/woman's body and therefore the dread of woman who represents this danger.

4 I am indebted to Kaja Silverman (2002) for the discussion on moral masochism,

5 Klein's concept of the femininity phase was superseded by her concept of projective identification which came to dominate Kleinian theory since its formulation in 1946 and proved very valuable in understanding object relations between individuals and between parts of the self. However, something has been lost by doing away with the body, and the phantasies about the body, something very valuable for understanding the human beginnings in the body and through the body. Gender has been one of the casualties of this neglect of the body in contemporary Kleinian thought. I wonder whether the traumatic disagreements on female sexuality in the 1920s and 1930s, which have threatened to split the psychoanalytic movement, prompted psychoanalysts to stay clear of gender issues. It was not until the 1960s that psychoanalytic studies on gender resumed mainly in the USA.

6 Early psychoanalytic contributions to the femininity complex in men were made by Felix Boehm, Karen Horney and Ernest Jones.

In his paper 'The femininity complex in men' Felix Boehm (1930) gives striking clinical examples from the analyses of many men struggling with the feminine part of themselves. Boehm looks at his male patients' phantasies of being female and of wanting to be, like Schreber, in the female position during sexual intercourse: 'I would note here that many male patients can describe in phantasy how pleasant it would be to be a woman and have intercourse as a woman – this is even when feminine tendencies do not play any special part in their life' (p. 453).

Even more than Klein he stresses the boy's and man's envy of woman's ability to have children. He writes: 'Envy of the woman's capacity to bear children (which I will call for short "parturition envy") is a considerable incentive to the capacity for production in men' (p. 456).

Boehm concludes: 'All the phenomena which I have briefly described so far may be summed up in the term "the femininity complex in men"' (p. 457).

In a series of papers in the 1920s and 1930s Karen Horney also examined male envy of woman and her capacity to have children. In her paper 'The flight from womanhood' (1926) also examines men's envy of woman's capacity to have children:

> When one begins, as I did, to analyze men only after a fairly long experience of analyzing women, one receives a most surprising impression of the intensity of this envy of pregnancy, childbirth, and motherhood, as well as breasts and of the act of sucking.
> (Horney 1971: 60–1)

In a later paper entitled 'The dread of woman' (1932) Horney examines the male 'dread' of the vagina and Ferenczi's idea that sexual intercourse is phantasised as a return to the womb – ultimately the 'death instinct'. Longing and fear go together here in a scenario reminiscent of the *Bacchae*.

Chapter 5

Masculinity in psychoanalysis. II – Contemporary perspectives

A man's neurosis may be rooted in being unable to adapt to his femininity.

(J. Wisdom)

... in most cultures and most eras about which we have information men seem more concerned to preserve their masculinity against real or imaginary insult than women their femininity.

(Stoller 1975b: 149)

(The epigraph from Robert J. Stoller was originally published in *Perversion: The Erotic Form of Hatred* by Robert J. Stoller [published by Karnac Books in 1986], and is reprinted with kind permission of Karnac Books.)

The 'dis-identification' hypothesis

In what proved to be a very influential short article entitled 'Dis-identifying from mother: its special importance for the boy' Ralph Greenson (1968) examined the boy's first identification with mother and his envy of her. Greenson, whose work with transsexuals enabled him to describe the early envy of the mother and the crippling effect it had on male development, maintained that boys had to dis-identify from mother, who was the boy's first identification figure, and counter-identify with father in order to develop their masculinity. Greenson's thesis was supported and developed by Robert Stoller who worked with him in the studies on transsexuals (Stoller 1968, 1975b).

Part of the dis-identification thesis is that there exists a blissful symbiotic relationship between mother and child for which the child (and the adult) always yearns, and which he is unwilling to give up. In this process the father helps the boy to dis-identify from mother and to make a counter-identification with him. The father in this scenario is not the Freudian castrating father but contrary to this he is the good, helpful father supportive of the boy's masculinity.

In this paper Greenson looks at a disturbed little boy, Lance, who dressed and acted as a girl identifying with his doll 'Barbie'. He referred to Barbie always in relation to himself as 'we', never as 'she'.

Greenson writes:

> This lively, intelligent, well-oriented boy was highly disturbed in two major interrelated areas of development. In the first place, he had not made the step in the maturational process which enables one to distinguish loving someone from identifying with someone. As a consequence he was consumed by the wish to be a female.
>
> (in Breen 1993)

Lance dressed as a girl and acted as if he were a girl. This was not mere acting, Greenson maintains, but a wish and a conviction that had it not been treated would have resulted in the child being a 'full-fledged transsexual or transvestite' (p. 260).

Greenson continues by describing how he helped Lance to distinguish between love and identification, thus helping him to make an identification with him as a father. This, in turn, helped the boy to dis-identify from his mother and make a counter-identification with him as a father.

In working with Lance, Greenson refers to an episode where Lance was telling him how he dressed up Barbie as a princess and danced with her in the ballroom. Greenson praised the princess and told her that she was very beautiful. He writes:

> Lance finally said to me: 'Go ahead, you can be the princess.' I replied, 'I don't want to *be* the princess, I want to dance with her.' Lance was baffled. I repeated this several times until the boy permitted me to dance with the princess. He watched this baffled and upset. Finally he asked me if I dance with my wife, love my wife etc. I said 'yes, I do.' The boy left the session deep in thought.
>
> (p. 261)

Greenson reports that shortly after this episode Lance stopped referring to Barbie as 'I' or 'we' and began referring to her as 'she'. Greenson stresses the child's unwillingness to leave the 'security-giving closeness that identification with the mothering person affords' (p. 261) and move forward to 'the less accessible father' (p. 262). In this scenario the father has the task of helping the boy to move away from mother and dis-identify from her.

But the blissful symbiosis between mother and child that Greenson (following Margaret Mahler) describes has an underside – the boy's envy of the mother and his fear of getting stuck with her. Perhaps it is inevitable that a blissful symbiosis would create an intense envy of the mother (who has all the good things) and no internal conflict. We must not forget that the patients Greenson and Stoller based their thesis on were transsexual males wanting to become females. In this scenario the father is usually denigrated and is kept, or keeps himself, at a distance. This was also the pattern in the case of Lance.

Greenson's and Stoller's studies revealed a surprising trend. Contrary to what might be expected from the thesis of penis envy and the social place of women, and contrary to their expectations, they found that many more men wanted to become women than women wanted to become men. The ratio was between two-third and three-quarter of all transsexuals were men hoping to become women (Stoller 1968). Greenson concluded that both men and women are envious of each other but that the envy of the male for the female and for the mother was much stronger and much more strongly repressed or hidden under a façade of contempt for women in the normal male (Greenson 1968).

Once dis-identification from mother and counter-identification with father are established the male boy and adult man will defend his masculinity against any wishes for a symbiotic relation with mother or woman.[1] The danger is not only the loss of individuality, or ego loss, but also the loss of masculinity. Stoller coined the term 'symbiosis anxiety' for this type of anxiety: 'The ubiquitous fear that one's sense of maleness and masculinity are in danger and that one must build into character structure ever-vigilant defences against succumbing to the pull of merging with mother, I shall call symbiosis anxiety' (Stoller 1975b: 149).

Stoller's theory of perversion concentrates on the need of the boy to regulate the anxiety he feels about the intense feelings and desires that threaten his masculine identity. In this sense symbiotic anxiety is an anxiety about his ability to maintain ego boundaries and to safeguard his masculine identity when in close contact with a woman. What we might call perverse or deviant practices are used to maintain boundaries by rigidly regulating behaviour, and therefore anxiety, while at the same time satisfying forbidden wishes (Stoller 1968).

The dis-identification thesis was based on Margaret Mahler's hypothesis of a blissful symbiosis between mother and baby which the child was very unwilling to leave (Mahler 1975). The simplicity and clarity of the dis-identification thesis contributed to its immense influence in the USA. However, its very over-simplification of the process of gender development led inevitably to criticisms and to more sophisticated and accurate models of male development.

Jessica Benjamin (1990) writing also within the Margaret Mahler tradition describes the dyadic relation to father that facilitates the moving away from mother and paves the way into the Oedipus complex. This is 'the father-hero of the Rapprochement', the preoedipal father who represents the ego-ideal and makes the father a narcissistic object (Benjamin 1990). This pre-oedipal father facilitates the transition to the Oedipus complex.

The importance of a loving father facilitating separation from mother has been stressed by many other authors working within different psychoanalytic traditions (Abelin 1975; Campbell 1999; Davids 2002; Target and Fonagy 2002; Gaddini 1976; Greenspan 1982).

Critical review of the 'dis-identification' hypothesis

In a series of articles Michael Diamond (1998, 2001, 2004a, 2004b) has challenged the Greenson/Stoller hypothesis criticising its over-simplification. Diamond argues that the moving away from mother during the Rapprochement phase can be observed empirically but that this turning away is defensive and *transitional* and does not constitute a dis-identification. He contends that 'dis-identification' is a misnomer and it would be more correct to speak about 'denial' or 'disavowal' in this way pointing the defensive nature of this movement away from mother:

This *transitional* turning or stepping away from the mother helps the boy *differentiate and separate* from his primary, external object. However, this is not the same as *'dis-identifying' from his internal maternal object*. In fact, the early process of separation and the particular experience of loss actually facilitate the boy's internalization of key aspects of his relationship with his mother. The maternal identifications that do occur are founded upon neither symbiosis nor primary femininity. In contrast, these crucial and lasting early identifications evolve from the separation-individuation process.

(Diamond 2004a: 364; italics in the original)

Diamond here differentiates clearly between turning away from mother and dis-identifying. He argues that the very term dis-identification is based on a mis-understanding about the nature of identification and whether dis-identifying, as opposed to repressing or denying, is at all psychically possible. He points out that the very identification with mother is a way of separating from her. Diamond refers to Leowalds' dictum that objects which are relinquished as external are 'set up in the ego' (Leowald 1962). Freud was the first to point this out (Freud 1917, 1923a, 1924c). It is as if loss is not possible for human beings. What is lost externally is set up internally. A difficulty in separating from mother points to difficulties (possibly due to traumatic circumstances) in seeing her as separate.

This agrees with Klein's description of the first identification with mother as prompted by weaning and by dissatisfaction which trigger the perception of mother as separate. According to Klein this dissatisfaction leads to the move away from the breast and towards the penis (or the father) as an object and simultaneously the boy identifies with mother. (This is the same for the girl as well.) For Klein this is the first identification that the child makes. It is not a result of over indulgence but on the contrary it is a result of dissatisfaction and loss of the breast (Klein 1928) (see Chapter 4). However, what Diamond does not examine is the *nature* of the first concrete identifications as both Klein (1928) and Winnicott (1962, 1963) in very different ways pointed out. This is an identification with mother as an omnipotent system that is set up to counteract the child's helplessness.

As the first identifications are concrete and they confuse the boundaries between self and other they need to be eventually transformed if severe psychopathology is to be avoided (Klein 1928, 1946; Rosenfeld 1965, 1971; Segal 1955). This is the task of development for both boys and girls. The later, post-oedipal identifications, are symbolic and are based on the difference between self and object (Britton 1989; Segal 1955). However, identifications are always defensive and they occur as a result of failures of the primary objects (Kohut 1971) and not as a result of symbio-sis. In this sense the identification with mother is not a result of blissful symbiosis but a result of her perceived separateness.

In my opinion Diamond's criticism, that the dis-identification thesis is an over-simplification of the development of masculinity as it does not consider the long and complex development of gender identity and the various identifica-tions that constitute the self, is valid. As Diamond points out 'dis-identification' from mother is not possible. What is possible, however, as I see it, is the transformation of the original concrete identification with mother (and father) into a symbolic identification through the working through of the Oedipus complex and the depressive position.

Vulnerability of masculinity: attacks and defences

... in most cultures and most eras about which we have information men seem more concerned to preserve their masculinity against real or imaginary insult than women their femininity.

(Stoller 1975b: 149)

The insecurity and vulnerability of male identity has been stressed by many authors apart from Stoller (Alizade 2003; Chodorow 2003; Frosh 1994; Figlio 2000; Lax 2003 to mention only a few) and is usually seen as based on the male difficulty in integrating the femininity within the self. In this sense the feminine identification is experienced as a foreign object that seeks to undermine the stability of the masculine self.

A difficulty that is unique for the boy is that the first object, the mother, is also the Oedipal erotic object. The differentiation between the pre-oedipal and the oedipal mother is not always to be taken for granted and creates many obstacles in development. Ogden expresses this dilemma in the following way:

He (the boy) has known the pre-Oedipal mother as a primitive, omnipotent, partially differentiated object by whom he has been mesmerised and penetrated, whom he has ruthlessly used and omnipotently destroyed ad recreated (Winnicott 1954). She also has the glow of warmth and safety and makes him 'dissolve' in a way that is both blissful and terrifying at the same time, since this 'dissolution' causes him to begin to lose touch with his accruing knowledge of where he stops and where she begins.

(Ogden 1992: 148)

For Ogden it is the mother's identification with her own father, her own masculinity within herself, that will help the boy make a transition into the Oedipus complex and the Oedipal mother and father. This father within the mother (the mother's father) is an essential transitional object that helps the boy differentiate between the pre-oedipal and the oedipal mother. However, Ogden continues 'The male Oedipus complex is built upon a foundation that is vulnerable to erosion. For the little boy, the external object bears an uncanny resemblance to the pre-Oedipal internal object mother' (p. 167).

The pre-Oedipal relationship to mother, especially if the early father is either absent or hostile (not only in the external world but most importantly as an internal object), is seen by most contemporary authors as creating a particularly male problem that leads to a general vulnerability of masculine identity. The pre-Oedipal mother is not just frightening or alluring but is also poorly differentiated from the self. On the other hand the Oedipal mother creates a sense of smallness and inadequacy in the little boy compared with the potent Oedipal father with whom he compares himself.

Nancy Chodorow summarised the male problem in what she called the 'psychic fault-lines of masculinity':

> I have suggested that the psychic fault-lines of masculinity and male selfhood – the structure that is revealed when the crystal shatters – include two developmental and defensive fantasy components: 1. masculinity as not-female – the male self defensively separating from and warding off the female other- and 2. maleness as adult man rather than boy child, not humiliated, shamed, or defeated by another man.
>
> (Chodorow 2003: 103)

Chodorow went on to explore the idea that male violence including terrorism and mass murder are often a defence against being humiliated and (in unconscious phantasy) feminised or infantilised.

Recently a conference on Masculinity published in the *Journal of the American Psychoanalytic Association* stressed the fluidity of gender identity and the multiplicity of male identity, Nevertheless certain themes to do with the envy of the mother (Person 2006), bisexuality and the need for men to deal with their feminine half (Vogel 2006) and feelings of humiliation related to their feminine identification (Chodorow 2003) were prominent as masculine issues needing to be addressed.

More recently Karl Figlio (2010) refers to the male depressive anxiety about losing one's generativity. The fear of loss of the testes is a particularly masculine anxiety that has not been stressed by psychoanalysis which concentrated on the penis and on castration anxiety seen as the loss of the penis. Figlio argues that the anxiety about internal space and internal organs which cannot be checked to ensure their integrity is externalised onto the penis.[2] If so I wonder whether the anxiety relates to the bad mother inside who retaliates against the destruction of her internal organs by the child and the child's wish to steal and acquire these organs. I cannot help wondering whether this blind spot in psychoanalysis is another fear of femininity and the feminine within the male, in this case the bad mother within, and that it requires a great deal of maturity in the male child to allow for the experience of anxiety about his own internal organs.

I understand Figlio's contention about the absence of psychoanalytic studies on male internal space as part of a bigger problem of accepting the feminine identification within the male psyche. In this sense what is repressed by man, his internal space, is also repressed by psychoanalysis. However, one way of looking at Freud's stress on the penis and on castration is as an exploration of the defences against the *wish* for femininity and the fear of feminisation in men. His theory of castration came in fact very close to saying exactly this. In this sense his restricting the male castration fears to the loss of the penis only in itself expresses the very thing he is describing, that is fear of feminisation. If the male internal space has the meaning of femininity its repression, even by Freud himself, is maybe not so surprising.

In this sense I suggest that mature masculinity is based not only on the integration of femininity within the self but also on the integration of the male body image – the integration of external and internal male organs. To be able to do this the boy or man needs to clarify all the confusion that surrounds his own internal organs and mother's. Are the attacked internal organs his or mother's? And are the attacks from him or from mother?

In this sense the male has a similar task as the female – the task of working through the anxieties of the paranoid/schizoid position in which the internal mother is retaliating for the destruction of her own internal organs and babies. Establishing a secure good internal mother within the self will guarantee the internality for both boy and girl. The establishment of a good mother within the psyche is part of the working through of the depressive position and the Oedipus complex. Allowing the father to have his own internal objects, that is allowing the father to be the other half in the process of re-production, is allowing the parental couple to exist as independent of the child's omnipotence.

A contemporary Kleinian view of the integration of mother and father identifications in the working through Oedipus complex has been offered by Ronald Britton (1989).

Re-thinking the Oedipus complex

In re-thinking the Oedipus complex, Ronald Britton concentrates on the parents' relationship to each other as the crucial element the acknowledgment of which ushers the child into the 'oedipal situation'. This acknowledgment confronts the child with the reality that the mother does not belong to him and causes a profound sense of loss. A second reality that the child discovers is that the relationship between his parents is different to the one between the child and either parent. The difference is one of sexual maturity in the first case and the absence of it in the second. The discovery of these realities does not necessarily mean the acceptance of them. The struggle between maintaining the oedipal illusions and relinquishing them is recognisable as the classical Oedipus complex that Freud described. Britton describes the oscillation between the positive and the negative Oedipus complex as part of the working through of both the oedipal situation and the depressive position. As the good and bad parent change position in rapid oscillation, the split into part objects, ideal and persecutory, diminishes and more integrated objects emerge. The integration of good and bad objects into whole objects constitutes the working through of the depressive position as well as of the Oedipus complex.

Britton describes the outcome of the working through of the Oedipus complex in the acceptance of the parents' relation to each other as qualitatively different from the relation that each parent has with the child. This leads to the opening up of a new mental space which is a kind of 'limiting boundary of the internal world'.

This limiting boundary creates what he called a 'triangular space' (Britton 1989). Within this triangular space multiple positions and identifications are possible which include 'the possibility of being a participant in a relationship and being observed by a third person, as well as being an observer of a relationship between two people' (Britton 1989: 84). Being able to be outside and observe two people having a relationship is what Britton calls the 'third position' which involves also being able to observe one's self and inner world.

My reading of Britton is that the triangular space leads to the recognition and acceptance of a multiplicity of relationships that include both sameness and difference, both being inside and outside a relationship, both observing and being observed and culminates in a composite self in which different identifications are integrated including the identification with mother, that is it includes the integration of femininity within the male self. We can call this the *democratic self* which can recognise and accept plurality but is nevertheless rooted in its own identifications with its parental figures.

Discussion

However, this outcome, that is the creation of a triangular space, cannot be taken for granted. In fact, we can say that the human condition consists of different degrees to which defences against the perception and acceptance of the reality of difference, separation and exclusion are the common stuff of life. Different defences affect the personality differently. However, for the male child the denial of the reality of the parental couple, especially the denial of the meaning of the father as part of the parental couple, affects his gender identity in a way that the girl is not affected. A denial of the *reality* of the father constitutes an attack not only on reality but on himself as a male and may push the boy into the total projective identification with mother. It puts him in a position where he either has to *be* her, that is female, transsexual, transvestite or simply delusional, or to create an alternative parallel universe which can exist in an 'as if' way – a world of perversion and illusion.

Castration anxiety and the fear of being feminised are based as I have argued on the *wish* to be one with mother and avoid the unthinkable anxieties of helplessness and fragmentation that would emerge if separateness were to be acknowledged pre-maturely. The unthinkable state of being helpless (Freud 1926, Winnicott 1962) is defended against by an identification with mother. From now on the problem is not presented as helplessness but as omnipotence or as castration anxiety/feminisation.

A further step is now taken: to counteract the total projective identification with mother the boy resorts to projecting the omnipotence onto his own penis – an external organ the integrity of which he can constantly check. The over-estimation of the penis during the phallic phase is an infantile 'masculine' solution (whether it appears in boys or in girls) to the problem of identification with mother.

However, the problem of loss may find a more 'feminine' solution enacted either as a sado-masochistic ritual or in phantasies of being a woman, of having a vagina, and of craving the father's penis who will fill this huge gaping gap in the psyche. The attraction of being feminine might remain in the psyche, sometimes hidden, repressed or denied, but sometimes it creates a kind of a parallel world.

To illustrate this point I shall present two male patients who exhibited this parallel world.

Mr A. exemplified this parallel world by having a long standing loving sexual relationship with a woman and parallel to this having masochistic, one night (or more likely one hour) stands, with various men he picked up when cruising. These encounters were characterised by sado-masochistic rituals and the phantasies that accompanied his being anally penetrated were of being a woman and being humiliated. He really did experience his anus as a vagina wanting to be filled with the penis. He described his state of mind while he went cruising as if under the power of a hypnotic force. He also described the terrible emptiness he felt which took the form of physical sensations. The only thing that could fill this emptiness was the penis of another man in his identification with woman.

As he was a very respectable member of the community he put himself and his relationship under severe stress by exposing himself to the danger of being arrested as these rituals took place in public places. The danger was, however, part of the thrill. He described the world of cruising as something magical in his mind but at the same time he could see how sordid and absurd the rituals were. It never occurred to him to have an ordinary homosexual relationship neither did he want it. This kind of 'retreat' (Steiner 1993) expresses more the hatred than the longing of the father, although the longing was there and had to be punished through a painful humiliation of himself. The hatred, however, is more of the parental couple which is exposed as performing a sado-masochistic, absurd and meaningless ritual.

But the rituals had obviously another angle. Since they were performed with a man whom he desired they were to some extent the guarantee of his heterosexuality. They were the marginalised covert love and hate of the father in a relationship he never had with him. They could exist in the margins of his identity and guarantee his sanity and his ability to love with the rest of himself.

I don't know whether such a man could be classified as homosexual. He certainly craved for contact with a man. But more than this he craved to be a woman, and at the same time the only permanent and loving sexual relationship he ever had, and ever wanted, was with a woman.

As a child and adolescent he dressed regularly in his mother's clothes embarrassing his stiff upper lip father but at the same time longing for his attention. It was also advantageous being a girl as his sister was spared the belt – that is being punished by being flogged with father's belt. It is important to add here that many of his phantasies and practices had to do with his genitals being tied with a leather belt while he was beaten and penetrated.

As a child of two he was left with his aunt while his parents went on a 4-month cruise. After this he was left several times during his childhood for a few months and he recalls devising several sexual games with his male friends when he was a bit older, aged 4 or 5.

Far from an idyllic mother–son symbiosis envisioned by Greenson and Stoller this man's history shows neglect, cruelty and insensitivity by both parents. More than this, his early transvestism became transformed into what Freud has called 'feminine masochism' (Freud 1924b).

This combination of transvestism and masochism is also found in another transvestite patient with a history of neglect, cruelty and an absent father. I shall call him Mr B. In this second patient masochism became 'moral maso- chism' (Freud 1924b) and the relation to real men and women was minimised. He spent a great deal of energy castigating himself for not achieving a state of perfection where he would not have any negative thoughts towards any human being. His hatred for his mother was the source of a great deal of guilt and the attack on himself by his punishing, perfectionist superego drove him at times to a near psychotic state. In this sense his transvestism can be seen as an escape from guilt and from any feelings, loving or hateful towards any object, as well as from his 'ego-destructive superego' (Bion) through a near total identification with the mother. Like Rosenfeld's patient, being a woman was seen as the antidote of the 'ugly' male aggressive and murderous feelings towards the mother.

The hatred and punishment of both the self and the parental couple is obvi- ous in these patients. The attack on their masculinity is also obvious. But I think that the two men are very different in their acceptance of the parental couple. The first man operates in a world of feelings, suffering and the differ- entiation between men and women. He 'plays' at being a woman but in this he is able to *express* his love and hate for his parents and also have a space for a good relationship which he values enormously. The second patient, however, removes himself from any conflict and scotomises any feelings of love, hate or need when he dresses as a woman. He then exists within an idealised state, that is being a woman. This is a move from perversion to a delusory narcissistic state which annihilates any object relations, any needs and any aggression or envy. It is not surprising that at times he had several psychotic episodes and is constantly close to a new one.

It is inevitable that the two chapters on masculinity would be sketchy and selective in what is presented and discussed. I have aimed to show that below the fluidity and multiplicity of male identity lie a few conflictual themes that can be traced to the early relations to mother. I have particularly stressed the deep wish to be one with mother, or to take her over, which clashes not only with the development of the self but also with the development of masculinity. The importance of working through these early wishes and identifications is stressed throughout Chapters 4 and 5. The failure to do so leads to the creation of a persecutory object within the psyche that threatens the male subject with castration and feminisation and with the destruction of his own generativity. Or alternatively, it is projected out and those who carry the projections are perse- cuted and often threatened with extermination. These themes will be explored in the remaining chapters.

Notes

1 Janet Sayers in an experimental study of school boys and girls found that boys are more 'disconnected' than girls of the same age. She writes: 'Whether or not this is indeed necessary for their development, boys arrive at adolescence depicting themselves as disconnected from their mothers' (Sayers in Ussher 1997).
2 Disagreements with Freud as to the meaning of the phallic phase in both boys and girls arose from the British School of Psychoanalysis notably by Klein and Ernest Jones (see Jones 1932).

Part III

Groups, fascism and masculinity

Chapter 6

Groups and the internal world

Preliminary remarks

So far I have examined the problem of masculinity in terms of wishes, anxieties and defences and not in terms of masculinity as a social or psychological entity. I have explored the early relation to mother and the deep wishes and terrors associated with it, and I concluded that the vulnerability of masculinity can be traced in this early relationship with her. I linked these persecutory fears to the deep wishes for sameness and for merging with her – the deep longing for one-ness which is experienced as engulfment.

I hope to have shown that the deep longing for one-ness has two components: a passive and an active one. It is Klein's discovery of projective identification that helps us see more clearly the fight against separation and separateness. If the *passive* wish to merge with mother is a wish to be absorbed into her body, the concept of projective identification allows us to see the *active* side of this wish as part of an aggressive takeover of the object.

In this sense I interpret projective identification as the aggressive side of the silent longing for merging and for one-ness. Taking over mother's riches, or *becoming* mother, is an omnipotent phantasy that obliterates separateness. In ordinary circumstances it can be part of play and imagination and in this way the aggression can be worked through. But if this phantasy takes over the psyche in a concrete, delusional way, it can lead to psychosis or total destructiveness.

If aggression becomes too violent the individual may attempt to defend against it by retreating into a merging type of feminine identification in this way establishing a complete vicious circle. Trying to solve the problems of separation, loss or murderous aggression through phantasies of merging, or total projective identification, with mother, only compounds the problem of a persecutory feminine presence inside which demolishes masculinity.

In Chapters 6 and 7, I suggest that certain types of male groups constitute an attempt to solve this problem of male identity by performing a double role: the role of the early mother with whom the individual merges; and a fraternal masculine identity that creates an artificial mimetic masculinity – a 'masquerade' of masculinity. In this sense the male group as a 'male womb' both affirms and denies the original wish to merge with a bigger mother.

As the reader may remember 'the primacy of the group' is one of the 'mobilising passions' of fascism that Robert Paxton refers to. So my exploration into the relation between fascism and masculinity takes me to the exploration of groups.

In Chapters 6 and 7 I shall explore the function of groups in the external and the internal world and look particularly at the function that all-male groups have for the consolidation of masculinity.

Groups external and internal

We are born within a group and we acquire our identity within a group. Our original groups, the family, the community, the country we were born in become part of who we are. Our interaction with these groups forms our internal world and, if we are lucky, promotes a creative internal group, a collaborative internal world which can acknowledge both sameness and difference, both the individual and the community. Later on in life the groups we join are voluntary and they do not, on the whole, have the same pervasiveness into our internal world as our original group – our family.

The creation of groups as a way of co-operating in carrying out a certain task, or as a way of sharing meaning, knowledge, feelings and emotions is a basic human characteristic, part of being a social and political animal (Freud 1921; Bion 1961). Society, and civilization itself, would not be possible without this fundamental human trait. I suggest that Freud, by introducing the Oedipus complex, the internal family, introduced group psychology into the individual's internal world. Our internal group is therefore of the utter importance in who we are and how we relate.

The function of groups and social systems as containers of anxiety is less obvious, but equally central to the creation of groups (Jacques 1955; Menzies-Lyth 1992). Human beings, men and women, belong to many groups simultaneously during their lifetime and have several, usually overlapping, identities. The more democratic the institutions of a society are, the more groups the individual is bound to belong to and the more the diversity between them. Groups express both the sociality and the narcissistic element of individuals. In this sense the type of group an individual chooses to belong to can tell us a great deal about the individual.

Bion recognised the dual nature of humans when he wrote that:

> The human individual is a political animal and cannot find fulfillment outside the group and cannot satisfy any emotional drive without expression of its social component. His impulses, and I mean all impulses and not merely his sexual ones, are at the same time narcissistic.
>
> (Bion 1967: 118)

The psychoanalytic study of groups began with Freud's 'Totem and Taboo' (1913) and perhaps more importantly with 'Group Psychology and the Analysis of the Ego' (1921). In the latter study Freud attempted to explain psychoanalytically Le Bon's (1895) and Mc Dougall's (1920) insights into groups.

Freud explained the group processes – the relations between the members of the group and the relation between members and the leader in terms of the Oedipus complex. He looked at the libidinal and narcissistic ties that bound the members together and the libidinal and narcissistic ties that bound each member with the leader as each member projected his ego ideal onto the leader. He made a statement that opened new ways of seeing the inter-relatedness between the external and the internal worlds.

A group he said is a '... *number of individuals who have put one and the same object in the place of their ego ideal and have consequently identified themselves with one another in their ego*' (Freud 1921: 116; italics in the original).

In this sense he made identification a crucial mechanism in the creation and maintenance of groups. He saw identification as a relation between part of the self and an object. It is evident in the way he expressed this that the type of identification he meant is what Melanie Klein called later 'projective identification' (Klein 1946). The two-way identification he described – identification with the leader and identification with the members of the group – remains fundamental in understanding group dynamics.

Freud looked in some detail into two organized stable groups – the Church and the Army – and looked at both narcissistic and libidinal forces that formed the glue that held the group together.

Bion's theory of groups on the other hand was derived directly from his experience with therapeutic groups at the Tavistock Clinic in London. He confesses that he deliberately refrained from studying Freud's theory of groups, as he did not want his observations to be influenced by pre-conceptions about the nature of groups. In the Re-View part of his book *Experiences in Groups* (1961) he lays out his differences from Freud. These differences, he writes, are not disagreements but complementarities. Bion argues that Freud's explanation of the group as a family applies to more 'normal' groups (what Bion called 'work groups'). More pathological or regressed groups function along the lines of Klein's delineation of the paranoid-schizoid position.

In this way Bion differentiated between two types of group, or two states in which a group can exist – the *work group*, and the *basic assumption group*. The work group is task-oriented and follows a rational course to accomplish a particular task. There is co-operation between individuals who have differentiated roles and tasks.

The basic assumption group, on the other hand, is dominated by some kind of illusion that takes hold of the individuals and abolishes their differentiated function within the group. Basic assumption groups are irrational and function according to the psychotic mechanisms described by Melanie Klein. Projective identification, splitting, idealization and persecution, extreme dependence and messianic hopes play a big part in basic assumption groups, as persecutory anxieties oscillate with a fusion with an idealised object. Bion maintained that most work groups oscillate with basic assumption groups and in this sense a disturbance of the task of the work group occurs frequently. However, groups that persist over a long period of time have well-defined tasks and well-defined roles (Bion 1963).

The individual is born within a group – a family, a class, a country, an ethnic group. We can add to this religion and even such an obvious characteristic as gender. In the contemporary post-industrial, democratic society, however, the group one is born into, and the group one chooses to belong to, are not necessarily the same. Even gender is voluntary for some individuals. The type of group an individual chooses to join tells us a great deal about the individual's internal world – the degree of his narcissism, the degree of his omnipotence, the degree to which he is seeking security or fulfilment or development and so forth. One can say that the group an individual chooses to join corresponds to his internal group.

The internal group

I am here referring to the individual's internal world as an internal group. I suggested earlier that Freud by making the Oedipus complex the hub of his theory acknowledged the internal group as the fundamental structure of the psyche. What type of internal group a person adheres to, forms in a fundamental way his personality structure. This internal group may be a work group led by an ego-driven mentality of communication, collaboration able to tolerate anxiety and to work with conflicts; or it can be dominated by an idealised leader/idealised self or a tyrant; it can be organized like a mafia – an organised gang whose purpose is to use violence to retain the idealization of a perverse self based on deception and exploitation as Rosenfeld has shown (Rosenfeld 1971); or as in depression, it can be dominated by a cruel and idealised superego, an ego-destructive superego that oppresses every spontaneous and creative part of the self. Whether an individual is dominated by an internal work group or by a basic assumption group depends on whether the individual has worked through the emotional conflicts of early childhood and has achieved a capacity to tolerate anxiety and guilt. Ultimately it depends on the degree to which the individual has developed an internal space where symbolization and thinking can take place.

Ronald Britton described the way the individual comes to attain what he called a triangular space and a third position (Britton 1989; see Chapter 5).

Britton refers to the Oedipus complex in its totality: the relationship of the child to each parent as well as the relationship of the child to the parents as a unit – the parental couple. Britton looked at this third relationship within the Oedipus complex – the relationship of the child to both parents that is to the parental couple, which is different from the relationship that the child has to each parent separately. This 'missing link' – the relationship of the parents to each other – is perhaps the most difficult relationship within the Oedipus complex and requires an individual to accept his/her exclusion, smallness and redundancy. If love, hate, jealousy and wish for revenge make him feel important, the relationship to the parental couple makes him feel small, redundant.

However, something else is gained here as the closing of the triangle completes the feeling of belonging as part of a bigger whole that is called a family.

The family as a mini society with its own rules and its own guarantees of protection and caring is the first meaningful group for the individual. The acceptance by the individual of both his importance and unimportance within the family (the group, the society) is crucial in the development of a democratic group or internal world (I am talking here about a 'good enough' family and a 'good enough' society. Accepting one's role within a perverse or cruel family and a perverse society does not lead to growth but to a perverse or masochistic self.).

Britton's description of the three different relationships a child has with his parents opens a window through which we can see the creation of the democratic self. Through these different relationships different identifications emerge – a mother identification, a father identification and an identification with a parental couple. The difference in this last identification is striking. One can *possess* the mother, or one can *possess* the father. But one cannot possess the parental couple. This type of identification requires more than possession. It is, I suggest, a *symbolic* identification. Symbols proper arise here and they arise with this different type of identification which requires the giving up of omnipotence. This is in accordance with Segal's theory of symbols. A symbol proper, Segal says, partakes in a triangular relationship between the ego, the object and the symbol (Segal 1955). This is in contrast to what she called 'symbolic equation' where the symbol and object collapse into each other. In this case the symbol does not *represent* the object. The symbol *is* the object.

So with the working through of the Oedipus complex, and parallel with this the depressive position a leap in development occurs. Symbolisation proper arises and with this the ability to tolerate another point of view and another position both within the self and in the external world.

As we know not everybody achieves this space and this awareness. Accepting one's smallness, and the otherness of the other i.e. the relinquishing of narcissistic omnipotence, is not an easy task and is never completed even in the most optimal circumstances. The democratic self, like external democracy, requires constant vigilance against the basic assumption group – against temptations and illusions of omnipotence and idealisations, against the collapse into either chaos or tyranny.

The differentiated, composite nature of the democratic self (which I suggest corresponds to Bion's 'work group') is based on the influence that reality now has on the individual. This requires the differentiation between subject and object (obscured if projective identification is overactive); differentiation between different internal objects (again obscured if projective identification to an internal object is overactive); differentiation between the different agents of the self (ego, superego, ego ideal, id) and differentiation between external and internal reality (again obscured if projective identification is overactive). Herbert Rosenfeld and Wilfred Bion have shown the confusional states that result when projective identification is excessive both internally and externally (Rosenfeld 1965, 1971; Bion 1956, 1957, 1958).

Basic assumption groups are dominated either by murderous conflict or by panic, by submission to a leader, or by manic euphoria born out of messianic hopes and ideas. In all cases the group is dominated by one emotional idea. However, the emotions may change rapidly as the group oscillates between different basic assumptions. In any case the plurality of the group is lost and homogenisation sets in. Rational discussion, co-operation or rational conflict and the ability to work through it, is lost.

When internal murderous conflict (as in severe depression), or severe internal splitting (as in psychosis) threatens the individual with extinction or fragmentation, a homogenisation of the psyche may take place. This can happen temporarily under the influence of drugs, or hypnotic religious practices, or under the influence of manic states. In this state the individual attempts to empty themselves of all thoughts, all conflicts, all attachments and attain an internal cohesion to prevent the self from fragmenting. Other manoeuvres may involve obsessional practices, hysterical dissociation, perverse practices. Certain religious and political dogmas, with their simplicity and requirement for absolute adherence to them also simplify and homogenise the mind of the followers.

Isolated sociopathic and psychopathic practices can be thought about in this way.

The obsessive delusional ideas that lead to certain sociopathic crimes can be thought of as binding the self and prevent it from facing reality with all the fears of being invaded by foreign objects and being destroyed. For instance the Norwegian mass murderer Anders Behring Breivik, was dominated by an obsession of a pure, homogenised culture and was persecuted by a delusional idea that the contamination and destruction of western culture by foreigners was taking place. We can assume here the ruthless aim for a corresponding pure, homogenised internal world where uncomfortable conflicts and emotions disappear. In his trial, Breivik described a 'meditation technique' that he had developed to deaden his feelings of empathy and compassion and therefore the internal conflict that would arise. 'If you are going to be capable of executing such a bloody and horrendous operation you need to work on your mind, your psyche, for years', he told the court. 'We have seen from military traditions you cannot send an unprepared person into war' (Report by Helen Pidd in *The Guardian*, 21 April 2012). We can see that Breivik knew exactly how horrendous these cold blooded murders were yet he was capable of carrying them out as he had emptied his mind of everything except the will to carry out these crimes.

This emptying of the mind is characteristic of fanatics as well as mass murderers. It can be done in the service of an idea, an obsession, religion, war or crime, individually or in a group. We can assume from the violence and intensity of this 'technique' that the persecutory feelings inside were equally violent and intense. For what the preceding statement by Breivik gives away is the fear of guilt and the retreat from it. Guilt divides the psyche against itself and creates internal conflict. This internal conflict is a guarantor of the moral individual but only if it is part of a benign internal world where links with good objects are maintained and nurtured. A benign internal group – a good enough family – has to be sharply differentiated from the mafia gang type of internal group where guilt is abolished and idealisation of violence prevails. What the mafia promotes is a mono-culture – a world without conflict. Violence takes the place of internal conflict. If internal conflict has been wiped out, the individual has already committed internal violence – the wiping out of the contents of the self (as Bollas has shown; see Chapter 1).

The lack of an internal space: portrait of the Fuehrer as a young man

I shall examine this type of relating looking at the young Adolf Hitler.

Adolf Hitler as a young man seemed to be living already in an intense psychological mono-culture where internal objects had been wiped out. His adolescent years and early youth, have been documented by his friend August Kubizek in his book *The Young Hitler*. The book provides a valuable testimony of Adolf's teenage years and character traits which would become obvious later on. Although certain stories were obviously 'embellished' and the book needs to be read with caution, it is, however, unique in providing an insight into Hitler's teenage years by his only close friend (Kershaw 1998). The book provides a great deal of evidence about Hitler's already omnipotent personally. In this we can see a young man whose sense of reality was tenuous but very intense – a young man who could not bear a different opinion or a different approach. 'Adolf was exceedingly violent and highly-strung' writes Kubizek. 'Quite trivial things, such as a few thoughtless words, could produce in him outburst of temper which I thought were quite out of proportion to the significance of the matter …' (p. 100).

Kubizek and Hitler met at the opera in 1904 according to Kubizek's account. They were then 16 and 15 respectively. They were both opera lovers and at their first meeting they were rivals for the cheap, standing space in front of a pillar. Kubizek came from a background of artisans (his father was an upholsterer and he was training to become an upholsterer himself) and was obviously flattered by the friendship offered to him by the obviously more middle class Adolf. Their passionate love for music united them (Kubizek went on to become a musician).

Kubizek describes the teenage Hitler as 'far from sturdy, rather thin for his height and he was not at all strong. His health, in fact, was rather poor' (p. 15).

This skinny, spindly youth was, however, transformed when he began to talk or rather give a speech to his friend. Kubizek describes these speeches 'like a volcano erupting'. He had seen speeches like this only in the theatre, he says. 'But soon I realised that this was not acting, not exaggeration, this was really felt, and I saw that he was in dead earnest' (p. 11).

Kubizek attributes their friendship (possibly the only one Hitler ever had) to his own ability to listen:

> Soon I came to understand that our friendship endured largely for the reason that I was a patient listener. But I was not dissatisfied with this passive role, for it made me realise how much my friend needed me … Not what he said impressed

me first, but how he said it. This to me was something new, magnificent. I had never imagined that a man could produce such an effect with mere words. All he wanted from me, however, was one thing – agreement.

(pp. 10–11)

He also describes Hitler's utter possessiveness of him so that he had no time for other friends. However, this utter possessiveness was not based on love. To call this relationship homosexual is to miss the coldness of Hitler's utter will to dominate and to be mirrored. Love did not enter into it. This was an exclusive friendship that was based on one thing: Adolf finding a submissive listener who would replicate his thoughts and words. The homogenisation of speaker and listener is what Hitler sought in his early years, as much as later he sought it from the Party and the German people. His need for a submissive audience was absolute as his internal survival depended on this.

This wish for total control of his object is revealed in an episode which Kubizek relates regarding the funeral of his (Kubizek's) violin teacher where Hitler turned up although he did not know Kubizek's teacher. When Kubizek asked him why he came he answered 'I can't bear it that you should mix with other young people and talk to them' (p. 13). 'Sometimes I had the feeling' Kubizek writes a few pages later, 'that he was living my life as well as his' (p. 23).

This aim at total possession of his friend reveals a personality stuck at a stage of ownership of the object – the early femininity phase that Klein described in her paper 'The early stages of the Oedipus complex' (see Chapter 3). As we have seen (see Chapter 4), the invasion and takeover of the object that Klein described in this paper is what she would later subsume under the term 'projective identification'.

Young Hitler is also described by Kubizek as isolated and megalomaniac. The only person he really cared for was his mother but it was not clear whether he cared about his mother as a person he was attached to, or as a haven, i.e. as a refuge that gave his isolated life a purpose and a protection against an alien world. In this mother he seemed to have the admiring, mirroring object that erased all frustrating difference.

One thing is certain: after his mother's death he became more isolated, more megalomaniac and more distant from reality and its demands. We can speculate that his identification with his dead mother – not in a symbolic way but in a total projective identification – inflated his personality further and gave him a self-sufficiency that was devoid of any need for human warmth or relationship. Total projective identification with mother is only possible if the existence of father is extinguished from the psyche the way Rosine Perelberg has described (see Chapter 2).

In relation to his hatred of his father Kubizek writes:

There was no end to the things, even trivial ones, that could upset him. But he lost his temper most of all when it was suggested that he should become a Civil Servant. Whenever he heard the word 'Civil Servant', even without any connection with his own career, he fell into a rage. I discovered that these outbursts of fury were, in a certain sense, still quarrels with his long-dead father, whose greatest desire it had been to turn him into a Civil Servant. (We must not forget that Hitler's father was a civil servant himself.) So to speak a 'posthumous' defense.

It was an essential part of our friendship at the time that my opinion of Civil Servants should be as low as his.

(p. 13)

Hitler showed the same contempt and hatred towards his school and his teachers which he left at the age of 15. School was another subject Kubizek was not allowed to mention.

I would like to add here that the hatred of his father is in no way equivalent to 'erasing the father representation' at this mind from his mind. On the contrary it betrays a constant war with an *existing* object. I suggest that the final erasing of father representation from the mind took place years later as hatred towards existing authority and the external world took hold of him and the delusional wish to destroy this world and re-build it according to the homogenised self took over.

At this stage we can only admire the incisiveness of Kubizek's perception of his friend. Here, in Hitler's teenage years, we can see the beginnings of his rabid hatred and contempt for the established order (representing his father), his intolerance of difference (again representing father), and his wish to destroy both: the external father of the established order, and the internal father who was an exaggerated version of his real father, made perhaps more cruel and more corrupt through his own hatred of him.

Hitler's possessiveness and his wish to erase any difference between himself and his object go hand in hand with his hatred of his father and father's world represented by the external world and by plurality.

We can say that Hitler's internal group had collapsed into a narcissistic one-ness consisting of himself merged with the ideal object, his mother. As this merge is possible in the real external world only as total domination, he demanded absolute mirroring from his external object so that no separateness between himself and his object could be felt to exist. As long as such an external mirror existed – first as his mother then in the shape of Kubizek, the lodgers at the doss house in Vienna, the party members of the National Socialist party, or the German people – he could function and could retain his inner cohesiveness. The disintegration of his personality towards the end of the war could be explained by the disaffection of the German people and of the party members who began to disobey him, i.e. to differentiate themselves from him.

However, the rage with which he attacked anybody who disagreed with him, points to a tyrannical personality, or a mafia boss determined to violently eliminate anybody who disobeyed him. However, Kubizek's willing submission to him points also to the seduction involved in this mafia organization which poses as a savior.[1] Suffice it to say here that the transformation of the Oedipus complex, the internal family group, into a mafia gang points to the domination of the personality by a sado-masochistic and perverse type of relating to the object. Instead of love, hate and jealousy we have perversion, corruption and tyranny.

The rage that any disagreement triggered is the rage of discovering that reality was not what he defined it to be. In one word of disagreement the 'other' enters the scene, and with the entry of the 'other' omnipotence is shattered. Any frustration is a reminder of his smallness and helplessness. His legendary rage can be understood as a tyrannical response to the externality and 'otherness' of reality.

Hitler's omnipotent thinking and his utter disregard for reality are described by Kubizek with great thoughtfulness. For instance he describes Hitler's utter obsession with architectural designs which he carried out in his teens and through which he intended to re-build so many famous buildings in his home town of Linz. In fact the relevant chapter in Kubizek bears the title 'Adolf rebuilds Linz' (pp. 50–66): 'The first time I went to visit him at home', Kubizek writes,

> his room was littered with sketches, drawings, blue-prints. There was 'The New Theatre', there the Mountain Hotel on the Lichtenberg – it was like an architect's office. ... I was convinced that he must, long since, have acquired all the technical and specialised skill necessary for his work. I simply could not believe that it was possible to set down such difficult things on the spur of the moment, and that everything I saw was improvised.
>
> (p. 50)

Every public building in Linz was to be demolished and replaced by Adolf's new designs – the Town Hall, the old Castle, the Museum, the Cathedral, the railway station. But the boldest plan was the grandiose bridge over the Danube which was to span the river at a great height. He was obsessed with re-building Linz and by extension the world. But this obsession was not a mere youthful enthusiasm. He believed in it the way he believed that the sun will rise every morning.

'This was an unbridled will owing in sheer fantasy, but a well-disciplined, almost systematic process' Kubizek writes and admits that this 'Architecture set to Music' attracted him a great deal – the way it attracted the German people a few decades later, one is tempted to say.

Kubizek relates an episode when he gathered the courage to ask his friend the simple question of how he proposed to finance his projects (of re-building Linz). 'Oh to hell with money' replied Adolf. But it was obvious that the question had disturbed him. So he decided to buy a lottery ticket. Kubizek relates in detail the mixture of 'the most fantastic ideas with the coolest calculations' that characterised Hitler. He was already spending his winnings but at the same time he calculated the chances of winning and asked Kubizek to join him and pay fifty-fifty. He made sure that Kubizek's money came from his own earnings and were not given to him by his parents (one is tempted to ask where Hitler's money came from since he did not work, but this is not something Kubizek goes into).

When all conditions were fulfilled they went to the office of the State Lottery to buy the ticket. Hitler took a long time to choose the right one. 'But in the end he found his winner. "Here it is" he said, and put the ticket carefully away in the little, black notebook in which he wrote his poems' (p. 59).

Kubizek relates how happy they both were since the purchase of the ticket. They made serious and detailed plans what to do with the money. To spend it on one project would be foolish. It would be better to use the money to promote themselves into public life which will help to put into practice their plans. Hitler suggested buying a small flat where they could live in the meantime – nothing very luxurious. After careful considerations they chose a flat on the Second Floor of No. 2 Kirchengasse. Hitler did the drawings for all the furniture which was

> of most beautiful and superior quality … Even the decorations on the walls were designed by Adolf. I was only allowed to have a say about the curtains and draperies … Adolf's own faith had bewitched me into believing as he did. I, too, expected to move into 2, Kirchengasse very soon.
>
> (p. 60)

Kubizek relates what happened when the day came and the two friends did not win.

> Adolf came rushing wildly round to the workshop with the list of results. I have rarely heard him rage so madly as then. First he fumed over the State Lottery, this officially organised exploitation of human credulity, this open fraud at the expense of docile citizens. Then his fury turned against the State itself, this patchwork of ten or twelve or God knows how many nations, this monster built up by the Hapsburg marriages. Could one expect other than that two poor Devils should be cheated out of their last couple of crowns?
>
> (pp. 61–2)

One is reminded here of Hitler's similar rantings in *Mein Kampf* and in his public speeches. The similarity of vocabulary, the intense rage, the feeling of being defrauded and exploited by a monster Austrian state (which later became the Jewish/Marxist conspiracy) is striking. The rigidity of Hitler's internal structure, dominated by omnipotence and projective identification has also destroyed the passage of time and any kind of change that time can bring with it. The 15-year-old and the 30-, 40- and 50-year-old sound uncannily similar as his internal world was frozen and allowed no change or development.

Hitler's omnipotence and inability to accept anybody but his own thoughts points to an internal group where differentiation and plurality do not exist. This is a narcissistic world where the other becomes a mere echo/Echo.[2] Such an individual has destroyed an internal group that includes the father, the differentiated mother and siblings. What remains is a mother/son merge and a mirror/echo by the members of the group.

Adolf's disregard for reality is also very vividly described by Kubizek in his relation to his first love, a young woman called Stefanie. His infatuation with Stephanie lasted for a few years during which he exchanged no word with her, neither did he declare his love to her. During these years he made plans about their life together, designed the house where he was going to live with her and wrote poems to her. He was absolutely certain that Stephanie knew and shared his feelings and ideas for the future and that their love needed no words. When Kubizek asked him whether it was not a good idea to talk to her he answered 'what is in me, is in Stephanie' (p. 41).

At one point Kubizek learnt that Stephanie was fond of dancing and told Adolf to take dancing lessons. 'I shall never dance!' he screamed at Kubizek.

Adolf never talked to Stephanie for the 3 years that he was infatuated with her. He seemed to have some perception of the reality of his situation and of the strangeness of his position as a school dropout and having no profession and being in no training. In any case he rejected all suggestions by Kubizek to approach Stephanie. At one point he considered abducting her and at another he considered suicide, but in this fantasy she was, of course, to die with him. Kubizek concludes that:

> the young Hitler found the only correct attitude in his love for Stephanie: he possessed a being whom he loved, and at the same time, he did not possess her. He arranged his whole life as though he possessed this beloved creature entirely.
>
> (p. 49)

Hitler's later relation to women took the form of utter control. In the case of his first love, Stefanie, the control was achieved in his mind, by distancing himself from the real Stefanie and building a whole imaginary world in his mind. In the case of his future relations – for instance to his niece Geli, this absolute control coupled with terror drove her to suicide.[3] As for other women Eva Braun attempted suicide twice and Renee Muller an actress with whom he had a short liaison killed herself (Fromm 1974: 543–8).

Kubizek also describes Adolf's very close relation to his mother:

> I realised how much his nature resembled his mother's. Certainly this was partly due to the fact that he had spent the last four years of his life alone with her. But over and above that, there was *a peculiar spiritual harmony* between mother and son which I have never come across since. *All that separated them was pushed into the background.*
>
> (p. 85; italics mine)

We can only hypothesise that after his mother's death the omnipotence in Hitler's mind was accentuated. I suggest that as the caring for his real mother was gone, and as the loss of her was unbearable, the fusion with an archaic version of the mother took hold of him. Whatever vestiges of reality testing he possessed up to then he lost in this phantasised fusion. With no real mother to protect him he lost the last protective object in his mind as well. His years in Vienna were characterised by an inability to see the approaching disaster of ending up in a doss house, penniless and hungry.

The foregoing are not meant as an 'analysis' of Hitler but I present Hitler as an example of a personality where the internal group collapses into one-ness – either in a narcissistic echoing dialogue or, more destructively, as a mother/child omnipotent fusion – the taking over of the omnipotent object. In this way a homogenisation of the psyche takes place, similar to being within a homogenised group.

The group as the early mother

The group as an early all encompassing mother is described by Didier Anzieu in his concept of the 'group illusion' in which the members of the regressed group seek a fusion with the group/mother. The omnipotence thus created is due to the group illusion of being fused with the primary object. 'I use the term "group illusion"' Anzieu writes, 'to denote a group's search for a collective fusional state … The latent counterpart of this manifest content is incorporation of the breast as a good part-object partaking by all in the ideal of narcissistic omnipotence projected onto the mother/group' (Anzieu 2001: 57).

Anzieu refers to allegorical themes of an El Dorado or of a lost Paradise, or regaining a sacred place that are themes often expressed in groups and signify the hopes for complete fulfilment that the group will offer.

The myth of the El Dorado, of a place of Gold – a place of plenty – captured the imagination of the Europeans as Cortes returned from Mexico with unimaginable treasures. However, more importantly for my thesis, Anzieu refers to the myths of the Amazons that existed together with the myth of the El Dorado – the female warriors whose name was given to the river that flowed through South America. We cannot avoid the connection between the myth of the El Dorado and the Amazons and the wondrous women on Mount Kythairon in Bacchae. In this sense the El Dorado, the miraculous place, and mother's domain are inextricably linked.

Werner Bohleber (2003) in somewhat similar vein describes the regressed group's fantasy as one of a narcissistic fusion with the primary object, the mother. He relates the idea of purity, so prominent in fascist and fundamentalist groups, to the narcissistic fusion that allows no plurality. Such narcissistic union can only be achieved through the elimination of any sibling rivalry and any relation to father. 'Idealization and terror are closely related' he writes echoing Klein's description of the paranoid-schizoid position. Purity and idealization are also closely related. What pollutes is the other, the outsider. This other is often, in many religious groups, the feminine body. 'The feminine body', Bohleber continues, 'is charged with a particular strong power to pollute, seduce, and destroy. It also serves as a metaphor for the situation in society that sees itself as threatened by seductive, evil powers.' (Bohleber 2002: 122).

The projection of the femininity of the mother/son fusion outside feminises the 'other'. It is as if the omnipotence of the mother/son fusion is kept for the self, while the femininity involved in such a fusion, is projected outside. The demonization of the feminine, and the contempt for, and persecution of, the 'feminised' Jews are themes that took over the imagination of Europeans at the turn of the century. Misogyny and anit-Semitism went hand in hand. Otto Weiniger, the cult figure of the turn of the century, exemplifies this dual fear and hatred of women and Jews (Weiniger 1906). At the same time artists like Klimt and Oscar Kokoschka portrayed the fatal attraction to woman and the ecstasy related to the dissolution of the ego within a passionate sexual union. This passionate sexual union could be seen on the one hand as ecstasy and on the other as the devouring of man by a 'vampire woman' (see Karen Horney 'The dread of woman' 1971b).

The celebration of the dissolution of the ego either within sexual ecstasy or as a narcissistic fusion with the object seems to have been a desired state that expressed in secular terms a religious experience that had been made obsolete. The dissolution of the ego, within an all-male group, a fascist ideology and a fascist leader was a step beyond libidinal merge and fears of being devoured. It was the anti-libidinal wiping out of the differentiation between the various parts of the self and between the subject and object.

One also wonders whether the accusation by Christians that the Jews sacrificed babies and drank their blood wasn't also part of the paranoia about the woman vampire or the 'feminine' Jew. Is this a projection of the most feared, all-consuming early mother – the vision of the mother portrayed in Bacchae, the mother who dis-members her child? Bacchae stops short of cannibalism, but as Pentheus is taken for a stag, hunted down and dis-membered, the idea of cannibalism is already there.

Is it possible to see here the idea of the all-consuming mother/woman – the 'femme fatale', the woman vampire, of the early twentieth century portrayed in so many films and novels of the time – is it possible to see it as the projected form of the male child's wish to enter mother's body not in an erotic way but as a narcissistic wish to fuse with her – a wish that leads to his being 'devoured' by mother and being contaminated by her femininity? As we know from Freud the wish and the fear go hand in hand. And is all this unbearable conflict between wish and fear resolved by projecting the wish for femininity onto the Jews?

Groups and masculinity

I attempted to illustrate that Hitler's internal group seems to have revolved around one point – to force his object into becoming the same as himself. As merging is impossible in reality, the control of the object becomes increasingly important. His ambition to become a great artist or a great architect may have had the same aim – the forging of the object as a reflection of the self. In this sense the emptying of his mind and his megalomania go hand in hand as inner conflicts are avoided by the technique of taking over the object.

Hitler's megalomania distanced him from other people and from social norms and demands. He certainly did not belong to any group in his early life and his isolation and lack of a sense of reality led him eventually to homelessness. In the doss house in Vienna where he took refuge he discovered his ability to make inflammatory speeches and attract an audience. We can say that this group of social outcasts was Hitler's first group – one he identified with. We can speculate that his internal family group, by contrast, was fragmented and destroyed in his intense hatred of his father and in his pursuit of a grandiose and homogeneous self.

Maybe it is not surprising that the first organized group Hitler joined was the Army where his submission to a powerful structure and a (male) leader/commander gave him security and purpose. His submission to the authority of the army is in contrast to his rebellious rejection of school and Civil Service and begs the question as to what the army meant for him.

The army was, for Hitler, closely connected with the First World War which, as Ian Kershaw comments, was for Hitler 'godsend'. Hitler himself describes the years of the war as 'the greatest and most unforgettable time of my early existence' (quoted in Kershaw 1998: 87).

Kershaw comments on the fact that the army provided food, clothing and accommodation for Hitler, things he could not take for granted in his 'down and out' days in Vienna. In this sense he was once again a small baby in his mother's arms fed and secure without any worries or fears. This powerful mother/army had of course the great advantage of being masculinised and making a 'real man' out of the young vagrant artist lost in the Viennese Babel of multiple cultures and languages. By contrast to Viennese society, the German army was a homogeneous world with one language and one purpose: to be a man, to fight and win.

In *Mein Kampf* he refers to the outbreak of First World War in this words:

> I fell down on my knees and thanked Heaven from an overflowing heart for granting me the good fortune of being permitted to live at this time.
> A fight for freedom had begun, mightier than the Earth had ever been …
>
> (Ibid.: 148)

Men like Hitler – insecure about their identity and bitter with a society that rejected their omnipotence – were happy to submit to male authority and male rules and acquire a new identity. This male container has some of the features of the early mother – safety, omnipotence, and abdication of personal responsibility. 'For the first time in his life', Kershaw writes '– certainly the first time since the carefree childhood days as a mummy's boy in Upper Austria – Hitler felt truly at ease with himself in the war' (Kershaw 1999: 87). We can say that he exchanged 'the army' for the 'mummy'! In this sense the Army, and later on the Party, had all the hallmarks of a male container – or what I call a male womb. It was to be a masculinised mother.

In this sense the army, represented more than any other group, a safe male homogeneous group where masculinity was manufactured hard as Krupp steel:

> You are now the master race here. Nothing was yet built up through softness and weakness … That's why I expect, just as our Fuehrer Adolf Hitler expects from you, that you are disciplined, but stand together hard as Krupp steel …
>
> (Quoted in Kershaw 2000: 231)

In the next chapter I shall carry on with my exploration of the male homogenised group as a masculinised mother that provides a total environment as well as guarantees the survival of masculinity.

Notes

1 Herbert Rosenfeld's concept of a mafia organization (Rosenfeld 1971) represents a specific type of an internal group that he described in this paper characterised by 'pathological fusion' 'in which the psychic structure is dominated by a destructive part of the self (that) succeeds in imprisoning and overpowering the libidinal self, which is completely unable to oppose the destructive process'. (Rosenfeld in Spillius 1988a: 254).

2 Echo was the woman condemned by the Gods to repeat Narcissus' last words.

3 Geli killed herself with Hitler's gun in a hotel room in Munich while Hitler was away. There were rumours of violent mistreatment of her and speculation whether it was murder (by his henchmen) or a cry for help gone wrong but as Ian Kershaw writes 'the truth will never be known' (Kershaw 1998: 354).

Chapter 7

The homogenised group

Groups, masculinity
and the rise of fascism

The flaw in the pattern

In *Nineteen Eighty Four* George Orwell (1949) described the totalitarian state not only as a surveillance state, but as a state where the very free will of the individual had to be *freely* surrendered. It is not compliance that the totalitarian leader asks for. It is *homogenisation*. The aim is to change the individual's mind so that he becomes one with the leader.

> … why do you imagine we bring people to this place' O'Brien asks Winston when he stopped administering higher and higher degrees of electric shock. 'To make them confess', Winston answers. 'No, that's not the reason. Try again' O'Brien insists. 'To punish them' Winston tries again. 'No!' exclaimed O'Brien. His voice had changed extraordinarily, and his face had suddenly become both stern and animated. 'No! Not merely to extract your confession, not to punish you…. We are not interested in those stupid crimes that you have committed. The party is not interested in the overt act: the thought is all we care about. We do not merely destroy our enemies, we change them.'
>
> (Ibid.: 203)*

Further down O'Brien says:

> You are a flaw in the pattern, Winston. You are a stain that must be wiped out. Did I not tell you just now that we are different from the persecutors of the past? We are not content with negative obedience, not even with the most abject submission. When finally you surrender to us, it must be *of your own free will*. We do not destroy the heretic because he resists us: so long as he resists us we never destroy him. We convert him, we capture his inner mind, we reshape him.
>
> (Ibid.: 204–5)*

In intrapsychic terms we can see O'Brien, or any totalitarian leader, as the force in the mind that aims at homogenisation. The flaw in the pattern is the flaw of reality and the 'messiness' of life, the messiness of difference. I suggest that this force in the mind that fires homogeneous groups and homogeneous minds is what Freud meant by the Nirvana principle which he connected to the death instinct. To suggest that this exists only in fascist groups is to use projection and projective identification to get rid of the knowledge of this deep wish in all of us. Fascism has been so successful because it corresponded to this deep wish in human beings. I suggest that ultimately it is a death wish which explains the utter destructiveness of fascist and totalitarian regimes.

In contrast to this, Freud's portrayal of the primary group in 'Totem and taboo' is of a different kind. In Freud's description it is the wish for life and love that ultimately wins the day. For Freud in describing the male primal horde, focused not only on hate and wish for revenge, but also on guilt and love for the father that led the sons not only towards murder but also towards reparation and the creation of civilised life, that is the restoration of the father *at a symbolic level*. In this sense Freud described the 'longing for the father'. We can say that Euripides, in describing the phantasy of the female primal horde, described the 'longing for the mother', but an omnipotent, idealised, undifferentiated mother that encompasses everything.

Freud is describing the dynamics of the Oedipus complex and the feelings of longing, hate and deprivation that accompany it. In this he describes the steps towards accepting reality through guilt, mourning and symbolization.

I suggest that Euripides describes a much more deluded state of mind where longing for the early omnipotent mother becomes concretised and leads to an attempt to destroy reality and difference. I talked about this as a *destruction* of the Oedipus complex and of all differentiation. The destruction of symbolic thinking is both its pre-condition and its consequence.

The all-female primal group in Pentheus' mind seems to be beyond love, hate or human attachment. The mother does not recognise her son. Pentheus is not recognised as human – he is hunted down being taken for a stag. All human relations external to the group are eliminated. Together with this, difference is eliminated. Differences are dangerous to the group as they undermine the group's unity and self-idealization and have to be destroyed. The de-humaniza-tion of the other is tragically portrayed in *Bacchae*. The manic group could be said to be the prototype of the homogeneous regressed group where difference is not recognised. Pentheus is only a 'flaw in the pattern, a stain that must be wiped out'.

Homogeneous groups

I suggest that homogeneous male groups do not resurrect the father at a symbolic level. The leader is not the differentiated father of the post-Oedipal world. The leader is a father who can hardly be differentiated from the deluded creation of the miraculous mother in Bacchae – except for his masculine masquerade. The male leader of a homogeneous male group goes on protesting his masculinity in undoing real or imagined humiliations and affronts to his masculinity and to his group's masculinity. The destruction of differentiation and the destruction of the reality of plurality leads the group to a paranoid world and to destructiveness and violence *as an ideal*.

R.D. Hinshelwood (2007) differentiates between constructive and destructive groups. He describes constructive groups as the ones where the ego-ideal co-exists with the group ideal and in this way the internal object relations to parental and other figures remain intact. The separation between the ego and the ego ideal is also maintained. On the other hand he describes destructive groups as those where the ego ideal is substituted by the group ideal.

In the latter case,

> a new situation arises in which a group ideal can substitute for the ego-ideal. Something from outside substitutes for my ego-ideal; and this is where Freud's analogy with the hypnotist comes in. Like the hypnotist who takes over the agency of the hypnotised subject so a group by pressing the group-ideal on the individual member also takes away the individual's agency by this kind of substitution …. These group pressures induce an identity (or equation) between the ego-ideal and the group ideal which obliterates the distinction between them, and in the same process a similar identity occurs between the ego and its ego ideal or rather, it is now between the ego and the group ideal. As an end-result the group members decline into a homogeneous group state.
>
> (Hinshelwood 2007: 8–9)

To paraphrase Mussolini: everything within the group, nothing against the group, nothing outside the group.[1]

In another paper Hinshelwood discussing Freud's paper (1921) writes:

> Every one in the group accepts the same ideal. It appears to be independent of the past history of any individual. Indeed the members tend towards an anonymity, a homogeneity…. The important thing about the group-ideal is that it is common to all group members. Although this tends to homogenise the members, there is at the same time, a compensation. In such a group, the individual *becomes* his ideal. No longer aspiring to it, he is encouraged by all the others in the belief that he now *is* his ideal, as painted by the group. This compensation is the triumph of a satisfied narcissism, the excitement of the self-directed libido, and a perfect self-love. This triumphal state can be very appealing, even addictive.
>
> (Hinshelwood 2006: 89)

Otto Kernberg (2003) argues that regressed groups exhibit the same defensive operations as exhibited in severe personality disorders. Psychoanalytic understanding of groups has supported this view (Bion 1961; Rice 1965, 1969; Turquet 1975; Anzieu 2001).

Kernberg (2003a) distinguishes a narcissistic and a paranoid reaction to intense anxiety in regressed groups. He examines the emotional reactions in large unstructured groups where individuals are deprived of individualised relationships and the reassurance of mutual control. In this case primitive defences become operative such as projective identification, omnipotent control or denial of aggression and passivity to prevent the spread of panic. Kernberg describes two ways in which such a group can relieve its panicky state: one corresponds to the narcissistic and one to a paranoid organization.

The narcissistic group will select a narcissistic leader who enjoys being the centre of attention and who will reassure the group who now passively adheres to the leader in exchange for being taken care of and kept safe. Aggression and envy are denied and prevented from emerging through passivity and the cultivation of the image of a 'benign' leader.

In the case of a paranoid group the group selects a paranoid personality who prepares the group for a fight against its enemies. All aggression is projected outside the group and intra-group aggression is transformed into loyalty to the group and the leader. Mutual identification between the members occurs – which brings us back to Freud's original formulation in 'Group psychology'. However, Kernberg points out that Freud did not stress the aggression in such a group but only the libidinal ties between the members of the group.

But Kernberg talks about a third, much more destructive possibility – that of a condenzation of paranoid and narcissistic elements which he saw in the syndrome of *malignant narcissism*. He sees this as a frequent combination in totalitarian leadership. 'The leader characterized by malignant narcissism' he writes,

> experiences and expresses an inordinate grandiosity, needs to be loved, admired, feared and submitted to at the same time, cannot accept submission from others except when it is accompanied by intense idealizing loyalty and abandonment of all independent judgment, and experiences any manifestation contrary to his wishes as a sadistic, willful, grave attack against himself.
>
> (Ibid.: 693)

The concept of malignant narcissism coincides much more with my own understanding of the fascist leader and his group. The group of such a leader is not just submissive. The 'intense idealising loyalty' and the love and admiration that Kernberg talks about change the group in moments of elation. At this moment the submissive group ceases to exist. Instead the group partakes of the omnipotence of the leader and the followers are elevated to the level of his glorious existence. The extreme violence of the paranoid leader and the paranoid group become part of the elation. As in *Bacchae* violence becomes elating and triumphant. 'Violence is beautiful' the Italian fascists declared and Walter Benjamin saw war as 'the ultimate fascist aesthetic experience' (Benjamin quoted in Paxton 2004: 17).

As I have argued this regression to narcissistic feelings of elation and expansion in an identification with a bigger than life entity is a regression to a phantasy of a union with mother – the archaic, omnipotent mother who contains father in herself. At the same time the paranoia of being robbed of one's masculinity leads to the paranoia that characterises this phantasy. I have argued that Schreber's paranoia is a prime example of this phantasy.

The perfection of a mother/baby fusion is the prototype of narcissistic omnipotence and refers to a phantasy of a prenatal perfection, of a place of expansion (Grunberger 1971; Ferenczi 1924).[2]

At the same time the taking over of the mother and her contents, what Klein described as total projective identification, is an act full of greed, envy and grievance for what the subject is deprived of. Elation and grievance maybe the two sides of a coin but completely unacceptable in its duality to the idealised image of the group. Instead one side of this duality is projected outside: to the outsider, the Jew or the Gypsy who wants to usurp the body of mother and strip it of all its goodness. The body images that run through Hitler's *Mein Kampf*, the images of pollution, contamination and invasion by foreign bodies, are a sign of the psychic level at which the debate is carried out and of the primitive terrors that it describes.

In relation to the foregoing I suggest that the homogeneous male group is necessarily and by definition a paranoid group. As the spectre of femininity arises out of its central phantasy of one-ness with mother, the homogeneous male group is both elated and omnipotent on the one hand, and paranoid on the other. Castration, annihilation and humiliation threaten to reverse the tide of omnipotence.

Total projective identification

To some extent all groups function on the principle of sameness. There is something that binds the members together, something they experience as sameness – a goal or an ideal symbolised by the leader or the ideology. As Freud put it they share the same ego ideal. So to some extent identification with the group ideal and the leader is present in most groups which we would not describe as destructive. The question is the type of identification we are talking about, as well as how much it has erased or co-exists with other identifications and internal object relations.

Freud saw introjection as the main mechanism in identification. In this way we can talk about introjective identification whose function is mainly libidinal. The introjection of a loving object would lead to the creation of a benign internal world for instance. However, in Group Psychology he came very close to formulating Klein's concept of projective identification as he saw the members of the group putting their own ego ideal into the leader and identifying with him. This is a description that Klein would have recognised as her own description of what she called 'projective identification'.

In this sense projective identification is the mechanism in which groups function and we can say that the more regressed a group is the stronger and more pervasive the projective mechanisms will be.

Klein saw different types of projective identification often working together: the evacuation of an unwanted part of the self and the insertion of this part into the object; the taking over of the object and robbing it of its desired qualities which one claims for oneself; the intrusion of the self into the object and the taking over of this object in its totality.

I use the term 'total' projective identification for this taking over of the object in its totality. The prototype of this is offered by Melanie Klein in her paper 'On identification' (1955). I shall remind the reader here of Klein's paper already discussed in the Introduction.

In this paper Klein uses Julian Green's novel *If I Were You* (1950) to illustrate the mechanism of projective identification. I call the type of projective identification she uses in this paper 'total' as it includes the wholesale takeover of the object by the self (and of course the self by the object) and leads eventually to the death, or the near death, of the self.

Interestingly, at the beginning of the paper Klein refers to Freud's 'Group psychology and the analysis of the ego' and Freud's understanding of the type of identification that takes place in groups. It is as if she were implying that groups are the place where this type of 'total' identification takes place for people who in their ordinary life are not psychotic. This is in accordance with Bion's findings on groups.

Green's novel describes a young man Fabian who was unhappy with himself, with how he looked, his lack of success with women, his poverty, his inferior position. Fabian is full of grievance towards his parents who did not give him better opportunities in life and condemned him to an inferior existence.

'The essence of the story' Klein writes, 'is the magic power to change himself into other people which is conferred on Fabian by a pact with the Devil, who seduces him with false promises of happiness into accepting this sinister gift' (p. 146).

In this pact with the Devil Fabian is given a secret formula through which he can turn himself into whatever person he wished. His first choice is his employer Monsieur Poujars who the author, seeing him through Fabian's eyes, describes in these words: 'Ah! the sun. It often seemed to him that Monsieur Pujars kept it hidden in his pocket' (Klein 1955: 146). I think that a better description of the glorified image of a leader of a basic assumption group is difficult to find!

However, after Fabian becomes Monsieur Pujars new discontents arise and various transformations follow as each new identity, stolen from its rightful owner, has its own problems and takes him further away from his phantasy of finding a self without conflicts. With each transformation he is led further away from his original self and makes him feel trapped into somebody else's personality and body. Eventually he manages, with his last breath to recite the formula and return to Fabian's body which is lying unconscious looked after by his mother. The return of Fabian to his original body/self and the search for love for, and by, his mother lead to some kind of redemption.

'The intense affection which he experiences towards her (his mother) extends suddenly to the rest of humanity', Klein writes, 'and he feels overflowing with unaccountable happiness. His mother suggests that he should pray, but he can only recall the words "Our Father". Then he is again overcome by this mysterious happiness, and dies' (ibid.: 151).

The return of Fabian to his mother signals the restoration of the object and the restoration of links (in Bion's sense; Bion 1959, 1962) which were broken by the excessive use of projective identification. It signals the restoration of love and gratitude for his objects.[3]

A more ordinary loss of one's humdrum (and often despised) identity/self can take place within a same minded manic group which transforms ordinary people into heroic figures. This can be a temporary affair such as attending a political meeting, a religious meeting, a rock concert or even a football match. The participant of such a group merges with others and with the leader/performer and feels elated, bigger than himself. It can be a respite from the everyday struggle to cope with life's difficulties as an individual, or as Winnicott put it, a respite from 'the continuous struggle to differentiate between what is subjective and what is objective' (Winnicott 1971). However, when the group takes over all the functions of the ego something very disturbing and much more permanent takes place – the creation of a pathological organization. To paraphrase Freud – where a functioning self was, a pathological organization will be. Before I go on to describe the characteristic of pathological organizations, however, I would like to delineate the relationship between helplessness, the absence of a containing object, and a pathological organization.

Helplessness and dependence

What follows contains some repetition of earlier themes so I ask the reader for some tolerance. The reason for this detour into theory here is to probe further into the relationship between trauma, helplessness, identification with mother, and homogenised groups. As the creation of fascism followed the trauma of World War One, and the helplessness that millions of people experienced during and after the war, an exploration into the ways humans deal with helplessness is important. What follows is a psychoanalytic understanding of human development. Those who are familiar with psychoanalytic theory may want to skip this section.

Dependence on an object, usually the mother, is the original state of a relationship to an 'other', the relationship of a newborn to the mother, as the newborn infant depends completely on the care of others for his survival. Freud called the experience of the newborn baby *Hilflosigkeit* (helplessness) and we can say that ultimately all our defences are defences against this original state of helplessness. Needless to say some defences are more successful than others. Bion saw any change from one state of mind to another as accompanied by an experience of catastrophe (1977) which we can equate to an experience of helplessness. In this sense, all states of mind are containers for primitive anxieties, ultimately helplessness.

What we call trauma is an experience that exceeds the ability of the ego to defend against helplessness (Freud 1926). A traumatic experience crashes the container of normal, or not so normal, defences and plunges us into the original state of helplessness. More primitive defences are then called upon to deal with this extreme situation. This is usually referred to as regression to a more primitive state of mind or to a more primitive defensive system.

In an optimal environment the baby's experience of helplessness is contained by the 'good enough mother' who, with her care and understanding, shields the baby from the experience of helplessness that brings about annihilation anxiety. Winnicott sees the good enough mother adapting to the baby's need so completely that the baby experiences the mother as an extension of himself and the experience of helplessness is averted (Winnicott 1956, 1962, 1963). This is Winnicott's theory of holding and primary omnipotence. (We can use different models here – we can refer to Bion's mother who takes in the baby's primitive terrors and through her alpha function digests them so that the baby can accept his own feelings and integrate them in this way creating his own alpha function. Or we can talk about the introjection of the good object as a defense against primitive terrors described by Klein.) Whatever model we choose, the significance of the dependence on an object (usually the mother) as a defense against helplessness, or fears of annihilation, however, is central.

In this way we can see the development of the self itself as a defense against primitive anxieties. As we have seen the development of the self depends on the relation to the object/mother. So the development of the self proceeds through the child's dependence on his/her significant others and includes the relationships to objects. The type of relationship to the object defines the self itself. Klein's paranoid/schizoid position is already a defensive organization that attributes these original terrors to the bad mother/breast whereas the good mother who deals with the baby's needs becomes idealised. This first structuralization of the self through splitting has as its aim the protection of the good object and therefore the protection of both the self and the object – ultimately a protection against helplessness.

If the loss of the object threatens to plunge the individual back to the experience of helplessness, dealing with the reality of loss and separation is crucial. How the individual deals with it becomes a crucial aspect of the development of the self.

Here I would like to stress the original aspect of identification as a defense against loss (and we can add against dependence and against envy). Klein used it in this way when she outlined the child's first identification as an identification with mother (for both boys and girls). What she called the 'femininity phase' followed the loss of the breast. It is in this sense that Klein talked about the first identification for both boys and girls as the identification with mother (1928).

Klein's portrayal of the femininity phase describes primitive terrors and primitive impulses – aggression, appropriation, violence, invasiveness.

As the child struggles to come to terms with the loss of the breast and the realization of separateness, the spectrum of helplessness and fears of annihilation loom high. The appropriation of mother with all the aggression involved makes him feel strong and powerful but with the first mishap he comes crying and sobbing to mother.

Winnicott (1971) argues that only if the mother survives the child's aggression, can the child work through this aggression. For Klein the working through of aggression takes place through the displacement of aggression onto other objects, and onto the father, thus leading to symbol formation (Klein 1930) and to the Oedipus complex (1928).

In an optimal environment omnipotence and dependence balance each other. These impulses, anxieties and defences will be worked through mainly with the turning towards the father as a new object within a triangular relationship. This is now identifiable as the classical Oedipus complex. It is the triangulation that is established in the internal world that leads to Britton's 'triangular space' and to the symbolic function in the individual. Identifications at this stage are symbolic and multiple.

By contrast, the identification with mother during the femininity phase is not a symbolic one. It is a concrete taking over of the mother's body and is a defense against helplessness as the loss of the breast threatens the individual with the fragmentation of the self. This first identification with mother is of a concrete and delusory kind and based not only on fear of loss but also on envy: the wish to have mother's ability to create babies is at the centre of it. We have seen Little Hans' struggle to accept the reality, and the narcissistic wound that goes with it, that boys do not have babies. In contrast to this lively little boy we can hypothesise that Hitler and the Nazis never quite accepted this reality. The statement 'Hitler is Germany', so much used for propaganda purposes, equals the statement 'the child is the mother' – a delusional state of mind of early infancy.

I have looked at two antithetical ways in which helplessness can be contained. The one is through dependence on a loving and trustworthy object that leads to development. Development proceeds through the loss of the primary object, mourning for the object and re-finding the object at a higher i.e. symbolic level. Bion expressed this as the 'absent' object leading to 'thought' and to the capacity for thinking. So the first way leads through dependence on an object, to the loss of the primary object, to mourning and to the creation of symbolic thinking. Symbolic thinking changes the relation to the object from one of total possession (or total loss) to one of a *relationship* where the integrity of both subject and object is maintained.

In the second way the loss of the object is followed by a total identification with it in an attempt to escape the experience of helplessness. Mourning, and the sense of reality it creates, is not possible here. Loss is negated. I *am* the object is a statement of denial of loss but also a statement of grandiosity and narcissistic completeness. It is seductive as much as it is destructive.

Complete adherence to such a belief would lead to psychosis. However, often a sado-masochistic structure develops to forbid a regression to this primitive identification with mother which would be psychotic. Within the sado-masochistic structure the sadistic superego makes its appearance as a protector against the terror of helplessness on the one hand or of being absorbed into the mother's body/mind on the other. It appears as the authoritarian father who forbids the child the return to mother – not only the mother as a love object, but maybe more importantly, the mother as an object for primitive concrete identifications. This authoritarian father, whose own femininity phase has not been adequately worked through, will promote a masculinity that is only a 'repudiation of femininity'. This is a primitive kind of masculinity always on the defensive against threats of humiliation and castration. However, the authoritarian father does not resolve the illusion of a fusion with mother. On the contrary, the illusion is preserved but a sado-masochistic system is installed within the psyche which prevents the dissolution of the self.

As the authoritarian structure is not a real resolution of the wish to merge with mother the individual might, in times of crisis and collective trauma, revert to a more omnipotent type of being. This oscillation between an omnipotent state of mind (what I call 'total' projective identification with the object), and a sado-masochistic state of mind characterises, in my view, the fascist state of mind. It can exist in women as well as in men but it is the male individual who assumes the role of the 'saviour' – either as a Fuehrer, a Party member or a follower in identification with the Fuehrer. The sado-masochistic structure makes it easier for the rest of the population – men and women – to submit to the higher authority and every now and then be submerged into the ecstasy of belonging to an omnipotent system.

It is a central part of this study that if this concrete identification with mother is not worked through the boy will look, very much like Fabian, to colonise other men and take over (in phantasy) their identity. This is what takes place very often within a male group. In this sense this new identity is a group identity.

As I have argued, a total identification with the primary object, the mother, poses problems for masculinity. Identifying with mother at such a total level spells the death of masculinity. This is the problem that Schreber could not resolve as a man. He chose the way to peace and security by rejecting his masculinity in one part of himself. He seemed to have achieved a 'benign' split between his mad self, in which this total identification with mother existed, and his sane self who argued with judges, wrote letters and formulated elaborate arguments and finally achieved his discharge from the mental institution and the publication of his *Memoirs*. His solution was bizarre but peaceful and contained within the self. His solution to accept his femininity as part of himself was in itself an elaborate choice.

The fascist solution is of a different kind. The fascist does not make such a choice. In fact he does not make any choice whatsoever except the choice of omnipotence. In other words he chooses to retain the omnipotent phantasy of total identification with mother *and* at the same time retain his masculinity all this at an omnipotent level. But true to the level of his functioning, his masculinity is also of a total type. It is a kind of masquerade of masculinity that results from the repudiation of femininity. It consists of men banding together and merging into one, creating a huge male body that safeguards their weak and threatened ego and masculine identity. This bigger than life masculinity manifests itself in group rituals, uniforms, salutes, weapons, parades and so forth. In this type of masculinity violence is central and violence and war are idealised as cleansing – cleansing the morass of femininity and weakness.

Pathological organisations

When an individual is caught into the net of a basic assumption or a homogeneous group (internal or external) and becomes a permanent member of such a group something more lasting takes place in his personality and his object relations. Projective identification with idealised objects becomes a permanent feature and defences designed to protect him/her from reality are consolidated. His distance from his real self/body/identity increases. He is now, so to speak, somebody else. This 'born again' quality is characteristic of total projective identification. The fact that this identity is forged by stealth, stolen, or conquered makes his owner ruthless in his dealings with other human beings. If the self is manufactured everything else can also be manufactured, disposed of, bulldosed over and re-built as if nothing is real. If the self is not real, nothing that surrounds it is. Ruthlessness, intrigues, lies, corruption, cruelty are all used with utter indifference. The 'pack of cards' world of the Queen in *Alice in Wonderland* becomes the new reality in its nightmarish quality. 'Off with their heads' becomes not just a matter of power but also of total indifference as to the fate of human beings who are hardly real. This situation can be maintained by ordinary people through splitting and denial so that ordinary life can go on in one part of themselves and heinous crimes can be committed in another.

Hannah Arendt describing Eichmann's trial in Jerusalem in 1960 described him as an average, ordinary man. One of the psychiatrists who examined him

> found that his whole psychological outlook, his attitude toward his wife and children, mother and father, brothers, sisters and friends was 'not only normal but most desirable' – and finally the minister who had paid regular visits to him in prison after the Supreme Court had finished hearing his appeal reassured everybody by declaring that Eichmann to be 'a man with very positive ideas'.
>
> (Arendt 1977: 26)

This 'positive man' had arranged the transport of millions of Jews to the extermination camps and did this with utter efficiency and without any sign of guilt or remorse. Arendt reports:

> ... as for his conscience, he remembered perfectly well that he would have had a bad conscience only if he had not done what he had been ordered to do – to ship millions of men, women, and children to their death with great zeal and the most meticulous care.
>
> (Ibid.: 23)

Eichmann was obviously two people here. For he would not have done to his wife and children what he had done to millions of people with such indifference and lack of guilt, as if these people were not real but images projected on a screen. In one part of himself Eichmann identified with the Fuehrer and the people who had 'ordered' him to do what he did. In this sense both identification and submission to authority prevented guilt from emerging as the responsibility was shifted endlessly onto the 'superiors'. His feelings of love and caring for other human beings was erased from this part of himself.

This split in the ego points towards the formation of what in psychoanalysis today is known as a 'pathological organization'.

Pathological organizations act as split off parts of the self organized around narcissistic defences. John Steiner, who coined the term, saw them as 'psychic retreats' or resting places that avoid conflict, pain and guilt (Steiner 1993). Such organizations exist on the border between the paranoid-schizoid and the depressive positions and in equilibrium to them hence their durability and resistance to change as they avoid both the guilt of the depressive position and the chaos and instability of the paranoid-schizoid position (Steiner 1987). It is implied in this formulation that, if they exist apart from the paranoid-schizoid and depressive positions, the relation of the individual to real objects is obliterated. A fictitious reality emerges which is basically narcissistic and can be organized around obsessional, manic, perverse or even psychotic lines. What they all have in common is the avoidance of the reality of terror, conflict, pain, guilt, separation and loss. The distance from real objects makes the world of Eichmann chillingly possible. My patient in Chapter 2 entered temporarily this place when he talked in a detached and cold way about exterminating his teachers in many gruesome ways.

Herbert Rosenfeld stressed another aspect of pathological organizations as he described projective identification as their central defense. He stressed their function 'as a defense against any recognition of separateness between the self and objects. Awareness of separateness immediately leads to feelings of dependence on an object and therefore to inevitable frustrations' (Rosenfeld 1971 in Spillius 1988a: 246). Rosenfeld continues:

> The destructive narcissism of these patients appears highly organized, as if one were dealing with a powerful gang dominated by a leader, who controls all members of the gang .... The main aim seems to be to prevent the weakening of the organisation and to control the members of the gang so that they will not desert the destructive organization ...
>
> (Ibid.: 249)

It is interesting that the image Rosenfeld chooses to use here is an all-male criminal group – a gang or a mafia – whose main function is to fight against dependency and any kind of weakness. (Rosenfeld did not of course mention that it is an all-male group but the metaphor of the 'mafia' is just that). In itself it is a prototype of pseudo-masculinity. Within such an organization dependency and 'softness' are greatly feared and despised. Fears of feminisation reign high.

Rosenfeld also adds: 'This narcissistic organization is in my experience not directed against guilt and anxiety, but seems to have *the purpose of maintaining the idealization of the self* ' (p. 249; italics mine).

The maintenance of the organization is the maintenance of the lie at the heart of such organizations. Bion said that the truth does not need to be defended but the lie does. The lie has to do with the identity of its members – the fact that they are 'somebody else'. The lie has to do with heir fraudulent masculinity. The idealization of violence as power and as the making of a man is common to violent gangs and to fascist ideology alike. The internal gang or mafia might work silently and surreptitiously as Rosenfeld saw it in the consulting room, side by side with a more caring self; or it may be externalised into actual organized violence or socially sanctioned violence.

I suggest that the fact that Rosenfeld portrayed the pathological organization as a male gang is not a matter of chance. For both men and women violence (especially organized violence) is seen as masculine and belonging to men. Rosenfeld's schizophrenic patient in Chapter 2 shows this very succinctly. The patient is afraid that he is turning into a woman (maybe afraid that he *wants* to turn into a woman) to avoid his murderous feelings towards his mother. Rosenfeld implies in this quote that many disturbances of gender identity in men are due to the fear of their murderous feelings, also implying that violence is identified in the mind (and in society) with masculinity.[4]

The powerful organization described by Rosenfeld idealises itself and its destructiveness and at the same time moves away from human relationships into some kind of internal *fusion*. In other words it is different from the primal horde that was motivated by hate for the father and discovered, by killing him, its love for him and more importantly *guilt* for his murder. Rosenfeld's pathological organization exists as a defense against guilt. To achieve this it ensures the destruction of love and the dependent feelings it engenders. It moves away from external or internal object relationships of love and hate and becomes self-sufficient in its narcissistic perfection. Reality and meaning are what the organization (or the Party) says it is.

We are now far away from ordinary human relationships of love, hate, jealousy, guilt and reparation. Ordinary human emotions that are part of ordinary human relationships are annihilated. After all, what changes Winston for ever in *Nineteen Eighty Four* is not torture or persuasion, but his own renunciation of human relationships, of human love for another. The homogeneous group, like O'Brien's state of mind, has sacrificed human relationships to the one-ness of the group: Nothing outside the group. Nothing against the group. The aim is for the individual to be completely merged with the group and its ideology.

Hitler as an individual came very close to this ideal. When he was asked whether he would get married it is said to have answered 'I am already married – to Germany'. Rudolf Hess in addressing Hitler went a step further and declared 'Hitler is Germany'. (Hess addressing the crowds in Leni Riefenstahl's film *Triumph of the Will*.)

We can hypothesise that devoid of, or perhaps unable to form, any intimate relationships, Hitler merged with his own megalomania, and in this he became a convincing specimen of a leader who has no self apart from the Party and the Reich. As long as the Party existed he could have a self. The disintegration of his personality towards the end of the war points to his inability to survive without a powerful Party or a powerful army. Humiliation really meant for Hitler annihilation.

Maybe Hitler's internal group is an example of Rosenfeld's internal mafia, in as far as the idealization of the violent (masculine) self and of the mafia organization keeps the terror of being absorbed into the mother and being dismembered (castrated or annihilated) at bay. When the primary object is seen as devouring, and when the father is exterminated from the mind, the survival of the self is threatened (as in *Bacchae*). In this case the pathological organization acts as a retreat for the threatened self. The Oedipus complex with its relationships of love and hate is transformed into a mafia gang where relationships are cardboard-like and unreal.

When this happens the main dynamic is the preservation of the idealization of the organization and I would add: the idealization of an over-masculinised self. Criminality becomes idealised and war becomes cleansing. The world as we know it is now upside down. Mother's coveted warm body becomes a claustrum (Meltzer 1973).

The world of perversion and the strive for homogeneity

We usually call this reversal of values 'perversion'. As described by psychoanalysis perversion has two main elements: (1) the denial, or disavowal, of reality; and (2) the idealization of faeces. In fact both elements point to the same thing seen from different angles. Both have to do with the denial of dependence on a live object, the denial of loss, the denial of the other as other, the denial of difference, the idealization of the self and its products, the destruction of intimate object relations – finally the ruthless use of the object/other to preserve the sanity of the self.

Narcissistic object relations take the place of relations with real objects (i.e. with objects that are not controlled by the ego.)

In his understanding of the use of the fetish Freud (1927) explained it as the woman's missing penis – meaning I think that the wish is for a narcissistic world where everything is the same, a world where no difference exists. The boy builds the world and his objects in his own image. This world – a world where women have a penis – is a world where the vagina does not exist and therefore returning to mother's 'smooth belly' – the mad dangerous wish – is impossible. Freud did not follow this line of inquiry but instead insisted that in childhood the vagina is unknown and that the boy insists that women have a penis as a defense against castration anxiety. The argument goes that when the boy discovers that women do not have a penis he comes to see women as castrated and fears that the same thing may happen to him, that is it leads to the boy's castration anxiety. If the boy's castration anxiety is not worked through he may demand the penis in the woman in the shape of a fetish.

It was left to Melanie Klein (1932), Ernest Jones (1932) and Karen Horney (1971) to point to the defensive nature of the 'unknown' vagina and that an unknown vagina was only a *denial of the knowledge of the vagina*. But, whichever way we choose to see it, perversion includes a denial or 'disavowal' of the reality of difference.

Janine Chasseguet-Smirgel originally saw the denial of difference in perversion as having two axes – the denial of the difference between the sexes and the difference between the generations (Chasseguet-Smirgel 1985). Later on Chasseguet-Smirgel (1986) defined reality as made out of differences and the attempt to deny or destroy these differences she saw as part of an attempt to deny reality. This becomes equivalent to homogenising the world, that is to reducing everything to faeces. A better description of the death instinct is difficult to find. Chasseguet-Smirgel saw this homogenisation of the self as a necessary ingredient of totalitarianism (Chasseguet-Smirgel 1986). Faeces is the main object here. Idealising faeces is an idealization of death.

Within object relations perversion is seen as aiming at the control of the object with the intention of guaranteeing the survival of the object. Morgan and Ruszczynski (2007), following Mervyn Glasser, describe perversion as a way of maintaining some relation to the object/other but without any intimacy involved. Control through sado-masochistic practices or processes becomes the only way of relating. In this way the self retains some kind of sanity but under the strict control of the perverse part.

We are here reminded once again of the total control that young Hitler exercised on his own thought processes and on his friend Kubizek (see Chapter 6) – a preamble of what he attempted to do with a whole nation some 20 years later.

What is obvious from the foregoing is the reversal of reality. The world is now upside down. What was good and wholesome (valuing one's good objects and valuing one's fellow beings whoever they are, valuing one's thought processes and different parts of the self) is now declared bad, or 'a stain in the pattern' as O'Brien declares it. A Newspeak has to be invented. Fellow citizens who do not belong to the 'group' or the 'racial state' have to be exterminated as 'vermin', 'parasites', 'bacillus' who will contaminate the purity of the race (as Hitler called the Jews); or as 'enemies of the people' as Stalin and Pol Pot declared anybody whose thinking or status was seen to be at odds with the Party line.

This new, homogenised organization idealises violence and control. But in fascism, as opposed to gang culture, the ecstasy is retained – a quasi-religious ecstasy in unity and omnipotence (at least in the first stages of the fascist state). The illusion of taking over the magic place in an act of total projective identification turns the individual into anything they want to be. The magic tricks of a conjurer or a hypnotist, Mephistopheles' transformations, take over as the self disappears. One can now become anybody and anything one wants.

Albert Speer (1970) describes how Hitler could adjust his behaviour and his speeches according to the audience he was addressing. He describes the first time he heard Hitler speak. He was addressing the students of Berlin University at the Institute of Technology. Speer remembers his initial surprise at Hitler's appearance:

... his appearance surprised me. On posters and in caricatures I had seen him in military tunic, with shoulder straps, swastika armband, and hair flapping over his forehead. But here he was wearing a well-fitted blue suit and looking markedly respectable. Everything about him bore out the note of reasonable modesty. Later, I learned that he had a great gift for adjusting – consciously or intuitively – to his surroundings ... Then, in a low voice, hesitantly and somewhat shyly, he began a kind of historical lecture rather than a speech.... It seemed to me that he were candidly presenting his anxieties about the future. His irony was softened by a somewhat self-conscious humor... Hitler's initial shyness soon disappeared; at times now his pitch rose. He spoke urgently and with hypnotic persuasiveness. The mood cast was much deeper than the speech itself, most of which I did not remember for long. Moreover I was carried away on the wave of enthusiasm which, one could almost feel physically, bore the speaker along from sentence to sentence. It swept away any scepticism, any reservations. Opponents were given no chance to speak. This furthered the illusion, at least momentarily, of unanimity. Finally Hitler no longer seemed to be speaking to convince: rather he seemed to feel that he was expressing what the audience, by now transformed into a single mass, expected of him.

(Speer 1970: 45–6)

In choosing to join the NSDAP Party (the National Socialist Party) Speer says:

I was not choosing the NSDAP, but becoming a follower of Hitler, whose magnetic force had reached out to me the first time I saw him and had not thereafter released me .... I knew nothing about his program. He had taken hold of me before I grasped what was happening.

(Ibid.: 48)

Hitler's 'magnetic force' was his ability to become the depository of the primitive longings of the audience. He was the alchemist who transformed faeces into gold. It was as if he was leading the miraculous group on Mount Kythairon. He could achieve miracles and the crowd entered together with him in this manic dreamland. Fuehrer and followers were swept by one tidal wave of the idealization of feces. By a sleight of hand the mafia became a Dionysiac group heralding salvation.

Patient A in Chapter 4 speaks of the same magic he experienced when he entered the sado-masochistic world where he was humiliated and penetrated experiencing himself as a woman with a vagina. The bizarre magic of mount Kythairon was a living reality for him. However, I would like to differentiate the 'play quality' of my patient's perversion from the malignant perversion of fascism where violence, domination and rebirth ceased to be a matter of 'play' and took the place of reality. This malignant perversion was mixed with the psychotic processes of rebirth and paranoia and with the amplification of the group attempted to transform the delusion into reality.

This confusion between illusion and reality goes beyond ordinary perversion and points to psychotic mechanisms. Idealization and paranoia, amplified by the homogenised group, and declared as scientific reality became part of the twin policies of promoting the pure, German race and implementing the extermination of the Jews.

Perversion here is not in the service of life as the examples of sexual perversion that Freud and others gave. Perversion here is in the service of death and destruction. In line with Kernberg's terminology of a *malignant narcissism* I call this kind of perversion *malignant perversion*. This type of perversion is encountered whenever the primacy of the group and the group's illusions takes over and destroys all human relations. The destruction of human sociality is presented as a virtue and as strength.

The reversal of values, the world upside down, that constitutes perversion is exemplified by Himmler's chilling address to the S.S. regarding the extermination of Jews:

> Most of you know what it is means when a hundred corpses are lying side by side, or five hundred or one thousand. To have stuck it out, and at the same time – apart from exceptions caused by human weakness – to *have remained decent fellows*, that is what has made us hard. This is a page of glory in our history …
>
> (Quoted in Bullock 1963: 698; italics mine)

This type of reversal of values is one way of divesting the members of the group of their own set of values and their own internal group.

Robert Lifton (1999) describes the violent mental conditioning that members of the Japanese Aum sect and the Japanese United Red Army undergo to divest them from any trace of individuality or separate identity. Absolute control of all communication is exercised and violence is used and justified as a process of purification promoting an absolute separation of what is good or bad, pure or impure. *The very perception of reality becomes the property of the group* (quoted in Bohleber 2003: 128)

A description of an Islamic Jihad camp by a survivor goes even further and talks about the sacrifice of one of its own people as a formative experience for the rest of the group. One of the trainees is chosen to commit jihad in front of the group. The group witnessing their fellow trainee being blown up in pieces experience their own death and the terror binds them even more to the leader and to the cause (Bohleber 2003). Again here annihilation of the self, the unthinkable terror, is averted by the binding of the individual to the group.

The attempt to maintain the homogeneity of the group beyond the stage of elation requires an immense amount of violence that can never abate, for the moment it does the group will fragment. Enemies are needed to project the aggression outside the group. Hannah Arendt describes the endless cycles of terror as new enemies have to be invented to keep the homogeneity of the group by projecting the aggression outside (see Chapter 1).

When sado-masochism fails to preserve the object, domination is replaced by extermination. The last human differentiation between oppressors and oppressed that characterises an authoritarian state is substituted by the homogenised group (the master race) and the Untermensch (the sub-human) that characterises fascism. Extermination replaces domination.

Terror is the underside of the manic group – a necessary part of the aim for homogeneity. Euripides shows this with horrific accuracy. When the stranger is apprehended in paradise elation is substituted by terror.

Notes

* From *Nineteen Eighty Four: A Novel* taken from *The Complete Works of George Orwell* edited by Peter Davison, published by Secker & Warburg © the estate of the late Sonia Brownell Orwell. Reprinted by permission of The Random House Group Limited.
1 I refer here to Mussolini's well-known aphorism: 'Everything within the state, nothing outside the state, nothing against the state.'
2 Sandor Fernczi believed that human beings always craved for the aquatic element from where life originated and that even ordinary intercourse was an attempt, albeit a symbolic one, to return to mother's belly, to the prenatal state of well being and expansion that the aquatic environment of the womb offers (Ferenczi 1924).
3 Klein sees Fabian's colonization of other men as a quest for a good father but unable to find him because of his immense envy and greed. This 'good father', however, is an idealised creation of Fabian's mind who seems to be in flight from his mother as if being imprisoned in another man's body would be preferable than being imprisoned in a woman's body. This perhaps is the fascist dilemma.
4 It remains to be explored whether the mutual projection between the sexes makes sure that woman is not a dangerous maenad that threatens men with dismemberment and that femininity is a weak and non violent state.

Part IV

Masculinity and fascism

Chapter 8

Masculinity and the fascist state of mind

'War is to man what maternity is to woman.'
(Benito Mussolini quoted in Bollas 1993)

In Part I of this book I examined the boy's struggle to establish his masculine identity at a time when his differentiation from mother is difficult due to the excessive use of projective identification. Mourning for the loss of the breast and, of accepting his difference from mother are the twin demands made on him as he grows up and differentiates himself from mother. Having a good relationship to father helps him in this difficult negotiation of separateness, attachment and loss.

However, differentiation brings with it separation, loss, responsibility and guilt. A deep wish for non-differentiation and merging with the object remains in all human beings men or women. This wish is symbolically satisfied in religion, art and in loving and sexual relationships.

However, the wish for non-differentiation in boys can easily become a dangerous feminine wish to be one with mother which spells the death of his masculinity. In the previous chapters I have looked at the deeply repressed wishes for non-differentiation within the male individual and the delusional internal world that can be created (in *Bacchae* and in Schreber for instance) when these wishes become dominant. One way that these wishes can be satisfied without a loss of masculinity is within certain male homogeneous types of groups. The fascist group with its stress on the sameness of its members and its stress on the extermination of the outsider, is an extreme type of a homogeneous group and follows the extreme traumatic circumstances of the First World War and the traumatic effects of the Depression of the 1930s in Germany.

I have argued that traumatic circumstances often undo precarious solutions both within the individual and within society, in this way plunging the individual into feelings of helplessness and fears of annihilation. Feelings of humiliation have the same traumatic effect on the individual leaving him feeling helpless as his ordinary defences collapse and a kind of 'death' is threatening the ego. In this case the individual may become a small helpless child wanting a mother to retreat to as Michael Roper reports examining the stories of many traumatised men in First World War (Roper 2009); or he might turn this trauma into a new retreat that both endorses and denies his wish for an undifferentiated state. This new retreat is fascism.

I shall examine these issues in what follows.

Masculinity, humiliation and violence

As we have seen fascism uses violence not only as a way of defeating its opponents but, more importantly, as a way of creating the new virile man. I have examined this issue in my clinical example in Chapter 1 but I shall look at this once again here.

On the use of violence by men Anthony Clare writes:

> Government think-tanks, international and national commissions, local task forces and clinical workshops sit and solemnly deliberate on the origins of human violence and often the most obvious feature – that it is the activity engaged almost exclusively by men – receives no attention.
>
> (Clare 2000: 38)

He comments that across cultures a man is more than 20 times 'likely to kill a man than a woman is to kill a woman, and a man is even more likely to kill a woman than a woman is to kill a man' (ibid.: 38). Clare also considers rape and sexual abuse as 'the commonest and often the most severe forms of physical abuse by men on women' (ibid.: 43). He goes on to examine organized violence such as wars, genocides and ethnic violence and atrocities. Clare rejects the biological explanations and comes down on the side of socialization and gender stereotypes (Clare 2000: 68).

However, we do not have to go down the route of either the biological or the socialization thesis to explain male violence. Psychoanalysis, although it has retreated from this thorny subject can, nevertheless, give us some explanations. As we have seen in Chapter 4, Klein talks about the boy's 'excessive protestations of masculinity' and the use he makes of his aggression to assert his threatened masculinity and his sense of humiliation as he is faced with his feelings of inferiority towards the mother (Klein 1928).

In this sense, aggression and violence can be seen as masculine defences against feelings of humiliation and dissolution of identity. We would expect therefore to find that males who are insecure in their sense of self and in their masculinity would feel easily humiliated and, under certain circumstances, use violence to bolster their masculinity (the patient in Chapter 2 is an example of this). It is as if violence makes the insecure or humiliated male respectable.

Studies on violent fundamentalist groups cite shame, humiliation and feeling disrespected as the most consistently present feature in the development of terrorism (Alderdice 2002; Varvin 2003; Chodorow 2003). National or group trauma and humiliation is closely related to this loss of identity and narcissistic investment (Volkan 2003, 2003). Another characteristic mentioned in studies on terrorism is that most terrorists are overwhelmingly young dissatisfied men (Varvin 2003; Akhtar 2002, 2003; Alderdice 2002).

Salman Akhtar writes: 'The leader is usually a traumatized and charismatic individual … The followers are usually *single, sexually inhibited young men*, equally

traumatised themselves and struggling to achieve a sense of selfhood and a cohesive identity' (Akhtar 2002: 91; italics mine). Paxton mentions that the leader is
always male and refers to fascism as a 'masculine fraternity' (Paxton 2004).

One author who linked masculinity, humiliation and violence is Nancy
Chodorow. In her paper 'Hate, humiliation and masculinity' she connects masculine vulnerability to terrorism, nationalism and fundamentalism (Chodorow 2003:
102). As I have looked at this paper in Chapter 5 I shall only remind the reader of
Chodorow's description of the 'fault-lines' of masculinity. She defines these as:

1   masculinity defined by a negative statement – as *not-female*, that is the male
     as defensively separating from, and warding off, the female 'other' and defin-
     ing himself as not-female; and
2   maleness as adult man rather than boy-child, not humiliated, shamed or
     defeated by another man (ibid.: 103).

The first component which is part of the defensive separation from mother – male
as not-female – constitutes a main part of most contemporary authors understanding of the vulnerability of masculinity (see Chapter 5). The second component is
the main dynamic of the positive Oedipus complex and constitutes Freud's main
understanding of the 'repudiation of femininity', that is femininity as submission
to another man which equals femininity and castration (Freud 1937).

For Chodorow any threat or humiliation that the individual or the ethnic or
religious community or nation endures, becomes also a threat to masculinity.
Humiliations – which include defeat in war and occupation of a country as well as
the helplessness that accompany them – have the unconscious meaning of feminisation and of loss of selfhood. The humiliation of the group with which one identifies
becomes a personal humiliation. This is true for ordinary warfare and ethnic and
nationalist violence as well as for childhood fist-fights. But she sees the extreme
violence of the holocaust and of other genocides as involving both components of
masculinity – the fear of humiliation by a man *and* the 'regressive pull' and fear of
the fusion with mother. In this sense her analysis helps us to link phenomena at different levels – the level of individual identity, the level of group identity (cultural,
religious) and the level of national identity. We can also differentiate phenomena
at the oedipal level that include a traumatic defeat by a father or brother on the one
hand; and the wish to delete and erase the trauma by a merging experience with
mother on the other. In this sense there are two ways in which a man can become
feminised: (1) by merging with mother – an omnipotent wish and (2) by being belit-
tled by father or other males – which threatens to render him helpless and throw him
back to being mother's baby and expose his wish for a merging experience with her.

In this sense we can follow the chain from humiliation to helplessness to a
merge with mother, feminisation and the reaction through violence. Violence now
defines the male.

The wish to go back to mother following a traumatic event is movingly explored
by Michael Roper in his study of soldiers' response to trauma in the First World

War (Roper 2009). Roper found that very often, under extreme stress or trauma, a return to a state of infantile dependence occurred and often the word 'mother' was the last word the soldiers uttered as they lay dying. It is as if trauma had the power to dissolve the myth of heroic masculinity. What was left was a vulnerable human being feeling like a little child wanting to be taken into mother's arms. Roper quotes Wilfred Bion's description of his own regressed fears and longings at a moment of extreme anxiety:

> The strain had a very curious effect; I felt that all anxiety had become too much; I felt like a small child that has had a tearful day and wants to be put to bed by its mother; I felt curiously eased by lying down on the bank by the side of the road, just as if I was lying peacefully in someone's arms.
>
> (Quoted in Roper 2009: 1)

And a German soldier crashed by a tank and being delirious moaning 'Mutter, Mutter, Mutter' and approached by an English soldier who held his hand and whispered 'All right son, it's all right. Mother's here with you' (ibid.: 2).

The clash here with ideas of heroic masculinity could not be stronger. The little boy wanting to be enveloped in mother's arms is hardly a model of the hero 'standing alone'. For men secure in their sense of self these experiences may strengthen their understanding of themselves and their own vulnerability. However, for others these experiences may be a source of utter humiliation and 'unmanning' at a time when masculinity was seen as a capacity to fight and die 'like a man'.

However, this less than heroic masculinity finds a container within the army and the camaraderie of fellow soldiers. Going back to civilian life many men declared that they missed the intimacy of comradeship and of shared experience. Adjusting to civilian life after a time at the front is notoriously difficult. The army with its shared experience acts as a container not only for extreme anxiety but also for male anxieties.

At the time of writing the shocking statistics about ex US soldiers who fought in Afghanistan taking their own lives dominate the headlines. The fact that more US soldiers died by their own hands after they had been discharged from the army than in battle, speaks volumes about traumatic experiences not contained within a group (or in any other way). The army that had caused their trauma was also the container for their trauma. The loss of this container drives many men to suicide or mental illness.

Men, groups and homogenisation

We can begin to understand why male groups are so important for men, so much so that as we have seen Lionel Tiger attributed a genetic wiring to the male drive towards group formation. Tiger, like Robert Bly (Bly 1990) has been very influential in the USA triggering more male groups to be formed where men searched for their 'lost' masculinity (Parker 1997).

But how can we explain this attraction of males to groups in a psychoanalytic way? I suggest that the answer can be sought in the realm of narcissism. An explanation of group phenomena in terms of narcissism has been offered by many theorists and examined in Chapters 6 and 7 (Freud 1921; Bion 1961; Anzieu 2001; Kernberg 2003a, 2003b; Hinshelwood 2006, 2007). In this sense individual narcissism becomes invested in the group and in the leader with whom they identify. To answer the aforementioned question of how masculinity can be 'lost' we can say that it is male narcissism (phallic narcissism) that has been lost or wounded and seeks its re-instatement within a male group led by a male leader.

We can say that individuals with wounded narcissism seek groups to restore their narcissistic integrity. If we take into account the boy's primary narcissistic wound *vis-à-vis* the mother (Chapters 4 and 5) we can see why insecure men, that is men who have not worked through this early narcissistic trauma, are attracted to groups or ideologies, and why very insecure men are more likely to join groups as a way of bolstering their masculinity as well as their fragmenting personality. Religious and political fundamentalism thrives on group narcissism (Hinshelwood 2006, 2007; Kernberg 2003a) which seems to restore the early narcissistic illusions of wholeness and omnipotence. National and group humiliations re-kindle the narcissistic trauma and drive some men towards extreme military groups where masculinity is underwritten by violence.

The restoration of narcissistic omnipotence is part of the function of religion. The combination of religious elements with the worship of violence is the terrain of fascism.

According to Klaus Theweleit, Hitler basically offered a new religion. He writes:

> It seems to me misleading to see the Fuehrer as a demagogue – or his speeches as theatrical. Both terms deny not only the needs of the participating crowd but above all the undeniable fact that the Fuehrer is bestowing a gift on his people. He offers them a religion – not a substitute, but a real one.
>
> (Theweleit 1989: 413)

In relation to this Theweleit quotes from Albert Speer's diaries:

> But it was when the ritual was finally agreed upon – indeed it was almost canonized – that I first became aware that the whole thing was meant to be taken literally. I had always believed all these parades, processions, and initiation ceremonies to be part of a virtuoso propagandistic review. It was now clear that for Hitler it was a matter of founding a church.
>
> (Speer quoted in Theweleit, footnote 53: 475)

The fascist religion that Hitler offered had to do with the fusion of males together and the fusion of the group with the Fuehrer. In this fusion the worship of purity coupled with the worship of violence and war became the 'making of the man'.

Theweleit examined the drive for fusion as a main characteristic of fascist groups. In his book *Male Fantasies* (1987, 1988) he looks at the novels of some men from the Freikorps[1] and examines the main themes that emerge out of these novels. In relation to the key themes of these texts he writes: '... I described the impulse towards fusion as a key dynamic of fascist organization formation and fascist propaganda ...' (vol. 2: 213). In relation to this Theweleit sees the basic dynamic as a longing for a 'unification with maternal bodies, within which it can become "whole", born to completion' (ibid.: 213). However, he goes on to say that this kind of fusion is 'marked by revenge, which, as we have seen, cannot fail to transform the artificial and violent symbiosis that is to follow into a relationship of domination' (ibid.: 213).

In another passage he writes: 'Almost all authors discussed in this study provide similarly celebratory accounts of the sameness of the soldier males' (ibid.: 350).

This kind of mass identity that is created through the 'sameness of soldier males' uses aggression, violence, militarist language and militarist paraphernalia to make sure that we make no mistake that these are real men – hard, military and ready to die. But even death is not a quiet affair but has to happen in an explosion, with a bang, and with the violent dissolution of body and mind. Theweleit dwells on this characteristic of the fascist mind – the wish for an explosion, which becomes a moment of violent fusion, a moment of an anti-erotic dissolution of the ego. He quotes one of the formulations favoured by the Freikorps: 'To smash the world to pieces, and then perish' (ibid.: 350). In another place he puts it like this:

> The texts of the soldier males perpetually revolve around the same central axes: The communality of the male society, non-female creation, rebirth, the rise upwards to hardness and tension; the phallus rising to a higher level. The man is released from a world that is rotten and sinking (from the morass of femaleness); he finally dissolves in battle.
>
> (Ibid.: 361)

Although Theweleit's study has been criticised on many grounds (for instance that The Freikorps were not fascists and not everybody who belonged to the Freikorps went on to join Hitler's NSDAP and that Hitler himself never joined the Freikorps) I think that his analysis of the fusion sought in the pre-fascist and fascist groups is very insightful and revealing of the underlying forces and contradictions involved in the fascist state of mind.

Masculinity and feminisation

The fear of feminisation and of not being proved to be a man seems to have been a widespread masculine fear in Wilhelmine Germany (Santner 2000), and probably in the whole of nineteenth-century Europe and can be linked to what Alexander Mitscherlich has called the 'fatherless society' (Mitscherlich 1973). Mitscherlich linked this to the fact that fathers in modern society are, on the whole, absent from the household as work has progressively moved from the home to the workplace. In this sense children grow up without a personal engagement with a father who sets boundaries and creates frustration but who is present to work this through with his own children. In the place of the personal father a series of rules and severe discipline stepped in to fill the gap. In this way the obedient individual is created who lacks strong emotional ties and who is ready to substitute the group for the family as a place of emotional fulfilment. This leads inevitably to a mass society yearning for an authority figure.

This seems to support my argument that male group phenomena are used, not only to bond men together as Lionel Tiger has suggested (Tiger 1969), but more importantly to supply a ready made male identity for the fatherless sons. Mitscherlich does not refer to the development of masculinity but his analysis of the mass society and the 'sibling society' or 'fatherless society' touches on the father vacuum in the development of masculinity within modern society and therefore on the development of systems which promote the homogenisation of men as one big organizm larger than life. This bigger-than-life masculinity is always in fear of contamination by women and those representatives of the feminised man – the Jews.

The Jew as the feminised man was a stereotype of nineteenth-century Germany, and more widely, Europe, and was connected with the fact of circumcision which was seen to be feminising the male. This led to the Jew being seen not only as feminised and degenerate but also as diseased, or more than that, as the disease itself (Santner 2000; Gilman 1993; Geller 1992).

Eric Santner talking about Gilman's work writes: 'According to Gilman florid fantasies about the consequences of circumcision abounded in nineteenth century European culture in general and in medical discourse in particular' (Santner 2000: 110).

And:

> In the medical discourse of the nineteenth century ... circumcision was as evil as it was inescapable for the Jew because it led to the specific diseases that corrupted the individual and eventually the body politic ... The linked dangers of sexuality, syphilis, and madness were constantly associated with the figure of the male Jew. [...] Central to the definition of the Jew was the image of the male Jew's circumcised penis as impaired, damaged, or incomplete, and therefore threatening to the wholeness and health of the male Aryan.
>
> (Gilman cited in Santner 2000: 111)

But Gilman's work also talks about the link between 'circumcision, feminisation, and antisemitism' in European culture (Santner 2000: 110).

We can now see the chain of associations Hitler used in *Mein Kampf* between Jews, disease, degeneracy, Germany's defeat in First World War, and the contamination and weakening of German blood. We are now in a position to complete the last link which links the Jew to the feminized male and the feminine part of the self. In this chain of associations the fear of feminisation is projected onto a minority which is then seen not only as abject, but also as contaminating and as threatening the health of the nation. The discourse was now one of disease and contamination versus health and purity of blood.

In an article entitled 'What does man want?, or the political meaning of the phallus' Daniel Boyarin examines the masculinity problems in colonised territories. In this article Boyarin quotes Franz Fanon:

'What does a man want?

What does the black man want?

At the risk of arousing the resentment of my coloured brothers, I will say that the black is not a man.'

(Fanon 1967 quoted in Adams and Savran 2002: 280)

This citation by Franz Fanon exploring the influence of colonialism on the colonised male expresses this influence as unmanning. Boyarin comments: 'The racial other lacks the phallus; "he" is always castrated' (Boyarin quoted in Adams and Savran 2002: 280). He continues by comparing the colonised male with the European Jews and the perception in both cases that they were 'castrated'.

I shall not go into the Fanon thesis of the divided colonised subject and the self-contempt that this engenders as he tries to emulate the master country's culture. What is important for my argument here is how much humiliation in males is linked to being feminised, unmanned or castrated.

However, Boyarin also looks at the original intention behind the custom of circumcision. Commenting on rabbinic literature he comments: 'Circumcision was understood somehow as rendering the male somewhat feminine, thus making it possible for the male Israelite to have communion with a male deity' (Boyarin quoted in Santner 2000: 118).

We now begin to understand that the loathing of the Jew in European culture is not a straight forward affair and that envy has a great part to play. If the Jew by the virtue of being feminised comes closer to God, he is obviously to be envied and all the sacrifices that the European male has had to make – such as being removed from mother prematurely and undergoing a series of harsh training to toughen up – may look rather futile. The envy of the Jew, and of woman, can only be counteracted by hatred and loathing.

A look at the protagonist of National Socialism, Adolf Hitler, may throw some more light on the relationship between insecure masculinity and the fascist state of mind. In his book *The Mind of Adolf Hitler* (1973)[2] the psychoanalyst Walter Langer examines, among other things, Hitler's sexuality and gender identity. Contrary to most people's expectations he sees Hitler as having a 'strong feminine component in his physical makeup' (ibid.: 172).

Langer continues:

There is every reason to suppose that during his early years, instead of identifying himself with his father as most boys do, he identified himself with his mother ... Many writers and informants have commented on his feminine characteristics – his gait, his hands, his mannerisms, and his way of thinking. Hanfstaengl reports that when he showed Dr Jung a specimen of Hitler's handwriting, the latter immediately exclaimed that it was a typically feminine hand.

(Ibid.: 172)

Langer comments on his 'over submissiveness' in the army, his 'extreme senti-mentality, his emotionality, his occasional softness, and his weeping' and suggests that his fear of cancer is also an indication of his identification with his mother as his mother died of cancer.

Ian Kershaw reporting on the impression Hitler made on those who knew him quotes Helene Hanfstaengl's remark to her husband 'believe me he is an absolute neuter, not a man' (Kershaw 1998: 187). Kershaw also adds that her husband Putzi Hanfstaengl who was a close friend and supporter was convinced that Hitler was impotent (ibid.: 187). Hitler's avoidance of intimate relationships and his fear of women are well documented (Kershaw 1999; Hayman 1997; Fromm 1974). His disgust and repugnance of sexual activity but also his fascination with the sub-jects of sex, homosexuality, and prostitution is also well documented (Kershaw 1999: 45–6). But Kershaw insists that the rumours about Hitler's sexual perver-sions and 'sordid sado-masochistic practices' are based on 'dubious evidence' and that there is no solid evidence to corroborate this (p. 46).

After examining the scarce evidence that exists about Hitler's sexual life Erich Fromm concludes: 'Whatever the nature of Hitler's perversion, the details hardly matter, nor does his sexual life explain anything more about him than what we know already. In fact, the credibility of the scarce data we have on his sexual life rests mainly on our knowledge of his character' (Fromm 1974: 548).

'It is remarkable', Erich Fromm writes, 'that quite a few women who had been close to Hitler committed – or tried to commit – suicide: Geli Raubal, Eva Brown (twice), Renee Muller, Unity Mitford, and a few, more doubtful cases quoted by Maser' (Fromm 1974: 548).

His relationship with Geli Raubal his 18-year-old niece, is perhaps the only one that resembled a normal human relationship. (We can deduce the incestuous theme here). People around him reported that he looked like a man in love. The absolute control he attempted to exercise over her reminds one of the young Hitler as described by his friend Kubizek (see Chapter 6). The relationship lasted for 4 years until Geli's controversial death – suicide or murder. After her death Hitler looked like a broken man and as far as we know he never loved another woman again.

On the subject of intimacy Langer writes about Hitler:

> He has cut himself off from the world in which love plays any part for fear of being hurt, and what love he can experience is fixated on the abstract entity – Germany, which, as we have seen, is a symbol of his ideal mother.
>
> (Langer 1973: 167)

Langer's book *The Mind of Adolf Hitler* has been severely criticised by historians when it was finally published in 1973 for its historical shortcomings (Pick 2012). But the book seemed to have survived the criticism and became an unexpected best seller in the 1970s. From the psychoanalytic viewpoint, however, we can only admire the insightfulness with which Langer understood Hitler's internal world in its contradictions and deadly denials.

Conclusion

In this chapter I have brought together several components of both masculinity and fascism. My argument is that insecure masculinity and humiliation and, therefore, violence, are linked, and they are linked via the same route that makes masculinity insecure and vulnerable in the first place. This is the wish for merging and the wish to erase the reality of difference, separateness and loss. These wishes, and the fears attached to them, are evoked especially in times of individual or social and political crisis as the traumatised self seeks refuge in mother's protective body.

As I hope to have shown, the wish for merging activates the death instinct and in the male activates the castration complex as a buffer against the death instinct (Jones 1932). Merging with mother becomes now a matter of castrated masculinity. In the fascist state of mind the state of merging, which is a state of narcissistic elation, takes place within a wholly masculine container – the male violent or militaristic group. This homogenised militarist group is a compromise formation that allows males to have a narcissistic, merging experience without being feminised. This homogenised group is necessarily paranoid and touches on a psychotic state of mind. Plurality itself is experienced as contaminating because it contains femininity not only as the 'other', but as a desirable and therefore threatening state. Fragments of expelled femininity are everywhere and have to be exterminated. Hence, the metaphor for the 'enemy within', the Jew is not one of whole objects but of millions of parasites or viruses as Hitler's *Mein Kampf* exemplifies (I shall examine this in Chapter 9).

My exploration of the fascist state of mind brings together two different modes of functioning in a malignant way, that is in a way that destructiveness becomes dominant and assumes perverse qualities: (1) a sado-masochistic mode and (2) a delusional/homogenised mode. Both are ways the male tries to deal with the femininity inside.

The sado-masochistic mode is a surrender of the ego to a harsh superego Freud named this kind of superego a 'pure culture of the death instinct' (Freud 1923a: 53) and Bion called it an 'ego-destructive superego', or a 'super' ego devoid of any morality (Bion 1962: 97).

We can say that this functioning has been in evidence in the 'normal' cultural personality structure in Germany during the last decades of the nineteenth century and until the end of the First World War and has been described as the 'authoritarian character' or the 'authoritarian personality' (Horkheimer 1936; Fromm 1941; Adorno 1950; Reich 1933; Mitscherlich 1973; Money-Kyrle 1978).

It is necessary to say that the authoritarian state of mind is not, in my opinion, a fascist state of mind. However, I suggest that the totalitarian state of mind presents itself as a seduction to liberate the individual from this slavery of the superego present in the authoritarian state of mind. In this sense, the authoritarian personality predisposes the subject towards a totalitarian, homogenised state of mind where the slavery of the superego is abolished. The fusion with the Fuhrer abolishes, however, if only momentarily, the sado-masochistic mode, together with the object itself, and establishes omnipotence as the predominant personality trait. The Fuehrer himself has undergone the same kind of fusion – first with the omnipotent part of himself – the 'Great Mother', Nature, History – and then with his followers. Any relation to reality can now be relinquished as the ego is merged with the superego and the superego with the ego-ideal and with the id in the delusional mother/baby union. Any ego functioning is hijacked by the totalitarian 'Fuehrer' and can exist only in relation to totalitarian aims. However, since fascism, as we have seen, cannot exist in a pure state an oscillation between a sado-masochistic state and a homogenised state characterises the fascist state of mind. Submission and homogenisation co-exist and give the fascist state a different dynamic from that of an authoritarian dictatorship both within the psyche and in society.

I suggest that the authoritarian personality acted as a kind of 'psychic retreat' (Steiner 1993) for the German people to contain aggression and guilt and the terrors of the core complex from the mid nineteenth century up to the end of First World War. Under conditions of extreme trauma and humiliation psychic retreats can be destroyed and the individual is thrust into a confusing world. Such a national trauma was, for Germany, the defeat in the First World War and the humiliating terms that were imposed on her by the allies. Added to these, the Crash in 1929 and the Depression that followed acted as further traumatic situations.

The dissolution of the ego's defences in traumatic circumstances means that the individual is exposed to primitive anxieties of annihilation and loss of identity including the loss of a secure gender identity. The masochistic surrender of the ego to the superego which had been up to the end of the war the normal 'cultural type' (Dicks 1972) meant that the ego remained weak and unable to face traumatic changes in the environment, especially the loss of a strong, non-humiliated authority. The new retreat was to embrace fascism and a charismatic leader with whom one was invited to merge, and who promised the destruction of the traumatic reality and the rebirth and regeneration of the nation. The surrender to a leader who promised his followers a part of himself and participation to a new rebirth, spelled the creation of a different kind of retreat which had all the hallmarks of a pathological organization with psychotic traits (Segal 1972; Steiner 1993). This surrender is different from the submission to the superego. This kind of surrender does away with the superego and with any differentiation within the self. The omnipotence that it creates claims to be liberation.

What I am describing could be any cult or religion as well as extreme political ideologies. However, what distinguishes fascism, and other extreme fundamentalist/terrorist ideologies, from a peaceful religious cult is the use of organized violence and militarism, not as a means to an end but *as an ideal in itself*. It is simultaneously a religion and a gang.

The fact that my emphasis has been on masculinity and the ego-syntonic use of violence in masculine identity does not preclude women from this state of mind. However, violence in women is not, on the whole, ego-syntonic and does not enhance their feminine identity. Of course, as supporters of violence or of violent parties like the Nazi Party women vicariously experienced their own aggression and their own sense of omnipotence. Claudia Koonz shows how as supporters of the National Socialist Party in Germany women have been ardent campaigners and contributed a great deal to the success of the Party. I shall examine her contribution to the understanding of women's part in National Socialism in Chapter 9.

Here I offer a tentative hypothesis about the relation between the fascist state of mind and masculinity. I suggest that the fascist state of mind is a 'compromise' solution between a wish to merge (which is experienced as a feminine wish) and a wish to bolster masculinity. It is a compromise solution in the sense that a symptom according to Freud is a compromise solution.[3] In this sense the wish is not given up but appears in a disguised form: The child's wish to merge with mother is not given up as impossible. Instead it appears in its disguised form as a delusional 'male merge' within an all male omnipotent group led by an omnipotent Fuehrer. Instead of dealing with reality the group is now taken up by several basic assumptions[4] at the same time – the messianic delusion co-existing with the fighting mode and the dependence mode creates the mixture of ideas that is fascism. The persecution of those seen as weak, soft or feminine is now inevitable.

In the next chapter I shall expand on the fraudulent identity of the fascist based on this hotchpotch of delusional ideas.

Notes

1 The Freikorps were right wing private armies or warlords that roamed Germany after the WWI and attacked socialists, communists and trade unionists. Eventually they were disbanded or absorbed into the Nazi movement. Hitler did not belong to the Freikorps. Klaus Theweleit uses their writings to understand proto-fascist and fascist emotions and ideas.
2 Walter Langer, a psychiatrist and a psychoanalyst, was approached in 1941 by the USA Intelligence Services and was given the task to provide a psychological profile of Adolf Hitler which could predict his likely moves and development. The result was a secret report which later became the book *The Mind of Adolf Hitler* (1973).
3 For Freud a symptom was a compromise between the gratification of a wish and its denunciation.
4 Bion distinguished three basic assumptions as best describing a regressed group: dependence, fight/flight and pairing.

Chapter 9

Pact with the Devil

The fascist state of mind and the manufacturing of masculinity

'Alles was ich bin, bin ich durch euch allein' (All that I am, I am through you alone)

(Adolf Hitler addressing the crowds; quoted in Joachim Fest 1973)

'You are now the master race here. Nothing was yet built up through softness and weakness ... That's why I expect, just as our Fuehrer Adolf Hitler expects from you, that you are disciplined, but stand together hard as Krupp steel ....'

(Rudolf von Alvensleben quoted in Kershaw 2000: 231)

I am approaching the end of this study and I would like to examine in some more detail the dynamics of the internal world which, in my opinion, best describe the fascist state of mind. Following from the previous chapter this is a more detailed exploration of the unconscious dynamics of the fascist solution.

The destruction of the object

As we have seen from Chapter 1 the historian Robert Paxton sees the essence of fascism not in its ideology or policies but as a series of 'mobilising passions'. Among these passions the primacy of the group, the community and the leader are central. In this the special relationship between leader and the group is of paramount importance. I have attempted to describe this relationship in Chapters 6 and 7 but I shall elaborate further here.

Nowhere we can see the essence of this relationship better as in the following words used by Hitler often to address the crowds: 'Alles was ich bin, bin ich nur durch Euch allein' (All that I am, I am only through you alone) (Fest: 922). The wording of this simple sentence is very interesting. It does not say for instance 'all that I am, I owe it to you'. Instead it says 'all that I am, I am *through* you'. We can take this as a rhetorical device designed to evoke strong feelings in the crowds. But I think that these strong feelings reveal a bigger truth than is not obvious in the first instance.

The truth which Hitler reveals in this statement, calculated to evoke deep emotions in the crowd, is the inter-dependence of the leader and the group, or in this case the Fuehrer and his followers. In this particular group, the fascist group, the interdependence is total. The one cannot exist without the other.

The regressive group (Bion called it a 'basic assumption group') takes shape under the leader who gives expression to the longings and the grievances of the group. But, as Hitler well knew, and the above quote expresses, it is not only the group that comes to life through the leader, but also the leader comes to life *through* the group and therefore cannot outlive it.

Interestingly many authors predicted Hitler's suicide long before his downfall. The psychoanalyst Walter Langer, for instance, wrote in 1973 in his study on the mind of Hitler that the most likely outcome for Hitler would be suicide. And Sebastian Haffner writing in 1940 expressed the same view seeing Hitler as the 'suicide par excellence'. Writing on a heated conversation between Hitler and Goebbels, Haffner reports Hitler as saying: 'When the Party falls to pieces I shall end it all in five minutes with a pistol' (Haffner 1940/2009: 13). And he continues: 'Hitler is in the privileged position of one who loves nothing and no one but himself' (ibid.: p. 14).

I think that Haffner well understood that somebody who has no ties and owes nothing to anybody is an empty vessel, a self empty of internal objects. This empty vessel was filled, in Hitler's case, by the group – the German people, the Party, the Army – and could not outlive the group's demise.

The group and the leader share a common illusion, which through the amplification of the group becomes a delusion, based on primitive phantasies and wishes. Bion called this phenomenon valency and saw it as a fundamental part of the basic assumption group (Bion 1961). I have suggested that the illusions – primitive wishes and anxieties – that the fascist group shares with the fascist leader constitute the essence of the fascist state of mind.

Hitler, like any leader of a basic assumption group, knew instinctively that he shared these primitive wishes and anxieties with the group and set out to mobilise them. The historian Neil Gregor comments on the common misunderstanding of the word propaganda as a kind of brainwashing. He writes: 'For Hitler, propaganda was clearly intended not to dupe people into believing something they did not already believe …. The function of propaganda was thus not to dupe but to mobilise what was already latent' (Gregor 2005: 107).

Carrying this further, we can say, as I have tried to show in the earlier chapters, that the primitive longings of a total immersion into a bigger entity, a group or an ideology, in phantasy the body of early mother, are part of the primitive longings of human beings, and that such a group, by satisfying these primitive longings, releases a sense of elation and expansion in the members of the group. This part of fascism based on human (primitive) sociality is part of all of us. The manipulation and perversion of this very human trait is part of the success, and finally the demise, of fascism. In this state of elation violence, and its idealization, becomes part of the elation of belonging to the group and becomes normalised. Other violent fundamentalist groups share this characteristic.

Consider, for instance, the words thought by an aspiring terrorist in Sebastian Faulks' novel *A Week in December*. The aspiring terrorist is the young Hassan, a middle class intelligent graduate, as he walks towards his intended target: the intended target being a mental hospital where he was going to plant a bomb knowing that innocent people would die:

> He'd read accounts of Islamist groups in the *Kafir* press and he'd read fine writing about what went on in the heads of 'terrorists'; he'd seen a 'drama-documentary' in the cinema about the planes that crashed into the towers. What no one talked about, no one seemed to understand, was the joy – the pure exhilaration of belief.
>
> (Faulks 2010: 289)

And consider this passage from *Mein Kampf* where Hitler describes an ordinary man entering a mass meeting of believers in National Socialism:

> When from his little workshop or big factory, in which he feels very small, he steps for the first time into a mass meeting and has thousands and thousands of people of the same opinions around him, when, as a seeker, he is swept away by three or four thousand others into the mighty effect of suggestive intoxication and enthusiasm, when the visible success and agreement of thousands confirm to him the rightness of the new doctrine and for the first time arouse doubt about the truth of his previous conviction – then he himself has succumbed to the magic influence of what we designate as 'mass suggestion'.
>
> (MK: 435)

Now this exhilaration and joy is only possible because the murderousness of the group is directed outside the group. The manufacturing of enemies is therefore a fundamental trait of fascism. These two things, the elation and the paranoia go hand in hand as Melanie Klein showed in describing the paranoid-schizoid position.

Such an aforementioned group is not based on feelings of dependence on the leader as a father or mother. Bion challenged Freud's model of the group as a family and contested that only groups that approximate normality, that is 'work groups' can be thought of along the lines of a family model. Basic assumption groups are led, not by the leader, but by the psychotic mechanisms described by Melanie Klein as part of the paranoid/schizoid position (Bion 1961). Fears of fragmentation and paranoid fears are therefore rampant. Any stability in such groups would come, not from their paranoid/elated core which is psychotic and unstable, but from the pathological organization which is built to create some stability out of the volatile situation of a basic assumption group. I suggest that for fascism it is the sado-masochistic organization, otherwise called the 'authoritarian character'. As I have already discussed, sado-masochistic organizations are more stable structures as their purpose is the preservation of the object, albeit in a rigidly controlled way. The elated/paranoid state of mind on the other hand has as its purpose not the preservation of the object but the destruction of the object – or to put it more clearly *the destruction of the differentiation between subject and object in the elated state, and the extermination of the object in the paranoid state.*

The sado-masochistic type of relationship described in the authoritarian character model is no doubt a part of the fascist group. However, as I have suggested in the previous chapter this is not an adequate explanation of the fascist group. I shall not repeat here the authoritarian personality thesis but briefly remind the reader that Fromm who coined the term the 'authoritarian character' saw it as the subjection of the ego to a powerful and cruel superego, or 'the simultaneous presence of sadistic and masochistic trends' (Fromm 1941: 220) so that a person would submit to those above him and oppress to those below him.

Talking of the qualities necessary in a Nazi leader Ley, the leader of the German labour front says: 'We want to rule and enjoy it .... We shall teach these men to ride horseback ... in order to give them the feeling of absolute domination over a living being' (quoted in Fromm 1941: 222–3).

Speaking of the masses Hitler compares them to a woman wanting eagerly to submit to the stronger man: 'Like a woman ... who will submit to the strong man rather than dominate the weakling' (quoted in Fromm: 220).

But while the leaders enjoy the power over the masses, the masses themselves rest content in their conviction that they are the 'master race' and have the divine right to dominate the world. The hatred and contempt of weakness and the wish to dominate is ubiquitous in everything the Nazis said or did.

It is hardly necessary to illustrate further Hitler's and the Nazis' belief in sadistic domination. What is less obvious, however, is Hitler's and the Nazi's masochism. One could say 'that they protest too much' as if what they wish to hide is the masochism in themselves.

However, the masochistic trends were no less present and ubiquitous. Although they are projected onto 'the masses' or (the 'feminine' masses as Hitler calls the masses) the masochism of Hitler himself reveals itself, as Fromm argues, in the way he submits to the superior power of Fate, Necessity, History, Nature.

Fromm writes about the authoritarian character of the Nazi regime:

> A hierarchy was created in which everyone has somebody above him to submit to and somebody beneath him to feel power over; the man at the top, the leader, has Fate, History, Nature above him as the power to which to submerge himself.
>
> (Fromm 1941: 225–6)

Evidence of Hitler's sexual masochistic trends is scant as the women he was involved with were either gagged, or committed suicide. Ian Kershaw comments that such evidence as it exists is unreliable. However, Fromm refers to his deferential attitude towards women of the upper class. He refers to Hanfstaengl's account of the way Hitler fell on his knees before his wife and 'called himself her slave and deplored the fate that had given him, too late, the bittersweet experience of meeting her' (Fromm 1974: 548).

There is also some evidence by the actress Renee Muller who gives an account of a sexual encounter with Hitler in which he fell on his knees and begged her to kick him. 'She demurred, but he pleaded with her and condemned himself as unworthy, heaped all kinds of accusations on his own head, and just groveled in an agonizing manner. The scene became intolerable to her, and she finally acceded to his wishes and kicked him. This excited him greatly and he begged for more and more...' (Zeissler quoted in Fromm 1941: 548).[1]

In relation to sado-masochism Fromm writes:

> It may sound like a contradiction but the sadist is a submissive person, and yet not only is it not a contradiction – it is, dynamically speaking, a neces-sity. He is sadistic because he is impotent, unalive, and powerless. He tries to compensate for his lack by having power over others by transforming the worm he feels himself to be into a god.
>
> (Fromm 1974: 389)

However, the authoritarian personality thesis does not go far enough in explaining the total homogenisation and destruction of the individual implied in the fascist state of mind. What I want to stress in this chapter is the unconscious dynamics of the state of mind described by both the young terrorist in Sebastian Faulks' book and the state of mind described in the passage from *Mein Kampf* mentioned above – the merging of the individual with the omnipotence of the ideology or the leader, the merging of the individual with the group – because, I argue, it constitutes the central seduction of fascism. It is, I believe, the state of mind that Melanie Klein describes in her paper 'On identification' (see Chapter 7) which involves a 'pact with the Devil'. It is a total manic state in which the central phantasy is one of totally appropriating the object and becoming it. *The self is now in the place of the object.* As the object disappears the self feels omnipotent. As Fabian takes over the different characters in Green's novel, they become him, that is they disappear as separate objects. But he also disappears as himself – a person with particular characteristics. The pact with the Devil achieves the erasure of both the subject and the object. A new creature comes into being which is neither a subject nor an object, but neither is a result of their union.

Out of this unholy marriage between the subject and the Devil, or the group and the leader, a kind of Frankenstein's monster is born – a creature that looks human and has all the characteristics of being human but has no parents, no internal objects, no attachments – a lone and destructive android. It can reproduce only by cloning and duplication.

Hitler's lack of an internal world, the emptiness inside the Fuehrer, the fact the 'he *is* Germany' (see Hess' appeal to the crowds in the 1934 Nuremberg rally) makes him a 'non person' and a 'neuter' – as one of his friends referred to him (Kershaw 1998: 187). Sexual reproduction – the creation of a new being out of two creatures whose difference is essential for this creation – the model for all cross-fertilization of ideas and emotions – is exterminated through the pact with the Devil. The endless duplication that is a characteristic of totalitarian thinking is at the heart of fascism. In this way difference is erased, first in the mind and then endless attempts are made to achieve a homogenisation in society. Mary Shelley in her creation of a monster was thus describing not only a danger of science 'going mad' but also the paradox of Modernity – the advance of science and rationality on the one hand, and the establishment of the myth of the male hero, the man 'who stands alone', the man without parents or internal objects – the monster of a man created by another omnipotent man – on the other.

This attempt to erase internal objects and achieve de-differentiation amounts to a monstrous creation which is an idealization of death. Sebastian Faulks' hero brings together these two longings in the foregoing passage. So does Euripides in *Bacchae*.

As Freud observed when such longings take over, violence is not far off. He called this longing for death the 'death instinct' and saw it operating silently within the organism, normally counter-balanced by the life instinct – the two instincts co-existing in a state of fusion. If, for whatever reason (often a personal or national trauma), a de-fusion occurs the death instinct will be directed outside as aggression and destructiveness (Freud 1920, 1930).

The word 'instinct' implies a biological entity and that was Freud's original formulation. Melanie Klein accepted the biological basis of the death instinct but other Kleinian psychoanalysts used it mainly to describe destructive phenomena played out in the consulting room without any implication that they had their origin in biological forces. They did, however, connect it with the destruction of the object and of parts of the self. Psychoanalysts like Herbert Rosenfeld, Donald Meltzer and Wilfred Bion explored this deadly trend of human beings in purely psychological terms based on Melanie Klein's concept of projective identification.

In chapters I explored Klein's concept of projective identification mainly through her paper 'On identification' published in 1955. However, Klein introduced her concept of projective identification first in 1946 and described it as splitting off unwanted parts of the baby's ego and projecting them into the object/ mother who then became the bad object, thus triggering a paranoid reaction in the baby. Klein saw projective identification as the main defence of the paranoid-schizoid position.

> Much of the hatred against parts of the self is now directed towards the mother. This leads to a particular form of identification which establishes *the prototype of an aggressive object relation*. I suggest for these processes the term 'projective identification'.
>
> (Klein 1946: 8; italics mine)

'In psychotic disorders' Klein continues, 'this identification of the object with the hated parts of the self contributes to the intensity of the hatred directed against other people' (ibid.: 8).

However, Klein also described the projection of good parts of the self into the object. This leads to the idealization of the object which is part of early object relations and helps the child to develop good relations to his objects and integrate his ego. If this tendency to idealise is excessive it leads to impoverishment of the ego and to excessive dependence.

> As a result the ego may be felt to be entirely subservient to and dependent on the internal object – only a shell of it. With an unassimilated idealized object there goes a feeling that the ego has no life and no value of its own.
>
> (Ibid.: 9)

The impoverishment of the ego through excessive projective identification leads to its inability to assimilate objects. These unassimilated objects are now experienced as alien objects within the self and the ego feels as if it is ruled by them. In this sense Klein describes both idealization and paranoia through her new concept. 'The phantasy of forcefully entering the object gives rise to anxieties relating to the dangers threatening the subject from within the object' (ibid.: 11).

Klein's new concept had its origins in her earlier work (1928, 1932) where she described the baby's phantasised attacks on mother and the child's attempts to take over her riches and appropriate them for himself (see Chapter 5). Claustrophobic and paranoid fears of being imprisoned within mother's body and being attacked from within have their origin in these phantasised attacks with a special consequence for the boy: '… the fear of being imprisoned (and especially of the penis being attacked) inside mother is an important factor in later disturbances of male potency (impotence) and also underlines claustrophobia' (1946: 12).

We may be able to make some sense of Fabian's need to colonise other men (see Chapter 7) and get inside their body as a counter-balance of being inside mother's body. The male need to identify with a man – especially if the early processes described here are excessive – would be overwhelming. Fabian's pact with the Devil appears like a life-saving solution. Leaving his own body and his mother behind Fabian creates more and more distance between his real self/body/mother and his new manufactured self. This ghost of a self may seem powerful to start with until the omnipotence slowly wanes and the reality of a fragmented impoverished and imprisoned self slowly shows through the gaps.

The fascist group's identification with the fascist leader seems equally life saving. The group and the leader projecting into each other the perfect masculine self and evacuating any weakness into outside groups evade for a while anxieties about annihilation, fragmentation and feminisation. It is as if the fault lines of masculinity had come apart and deadly anxieties have required deadly solutions.

I shall not go into the historical and social conditions under which the 'fault lines of masculinity' can come apart, but these conditions have generally been described by historians and social scientists as 'national humiliation', 'national trauma', 'cultural crisis', 'humiliated authority', 'authority vacuum', 'fatherless society' and so on.

The total projective identification between the leader and his followers mimics the way the small child attempts to take over mother's riches and identify with her, or rather *be* her (Klein 1928). In this the child denies his own smallness, his need for mother and dependence on her and ultimately his envy of her. If one *is* the object one has neither need nor envy. One has and is everything.

This is a description of total mania, megalomania and omnipotence. At the same time, however, it is a 'wish for death', for it implies the eclipse of the subject who is now lost inside the object he has taken over. In Klein's paper (and in Green's novel) this is portrayed vividly as Fabian gets more and more distant from his own self/body which is more and more weakened and moribund and finally results in Fabian's death (see Chapter 7).

The attempt to take over the object's assets and claim them as one's own is an ordinary infantile process to deal with dependence and helplessness. In ordinary terms it is usually seen in the cute grandiosity of the toddler and has been described in a very different way by Margaret Mahler and Heinz Kohut (Mahler *et al.* 1975; Kohut 1971). This omnipotence (interspersed with impotence) is normally worked through within a bigger context that includes the father, the siblings, and the parents as a couple. In other words it is worked through in what psychoanalysis calls the 'Oedipus complex'. In this sense the Oedipus complex is the locus where, not only love and hate, but equally importantly omnipotence is worked through and relationships with objects are established within the psyche. On the other hand the destruction of the object in total projective identification spells the destruction of all relationships.

I suggest that the destruction of the object – or to be more accurate the destruction of the subject – object relationship and the destruction of a relationship to an 'other' who has a relationship with somebody else, an other who is free from our omnipotence – is a description of the death instinct expressed in an object-related language. The one-ness that is created through total projective identification is the essence of totalitarianism.

In this sense the 'longing for death' is always one aspect of the human project and the 'totalitarian temptation' is always there as an option.

I suggest that until the First World War this 'longing for death', or the wish for de-differentiation, had been contained within the personality by the sado-masochistic structure of the authoritarian character. This type of internal structure has been masterfully portrayed by Franz Kafka in his novels and short stories. The destruction of the ego under the weight of a superego that had developed into a 'pure culture of the death instinct' has been chillingly portrayed in his novel *The Trial*. The internal process described in *The Trial* is a process whereby aggression remains within the self and the deadly superego in its omnipotent aspect finally destroys the ego. It is a description of deadly melancholia (Freud 1917) and moral masochism (Freud 1924b). It is a description of the authoritarian character carried to its logical conclusion. The omnipotence of the superego finally crashes and destroys a weak and masochistic ego.

I suggest that the fascist solution reverses the aforementioned process whereby the object devours and ego and creates a different kind of chilling reality. The fascist solution consists of the ego devouring the object and taking possession of its assets. In this destruction of the object, which I believe Rosenfeld described under 'destructive narcissism', the self becomes omnipotent. The subject is now not just in possession of the object but ultimately devours it. In this substitution of the object by the self there is a mad promise: to destroy the world and build it anew in the image of the self. It is megalomaniac and destructive on a big scale. The self, in devouring the object (or the internal objects), is elevated to the master of the world. Such a self is not only a murderous self but it is also an empty self in a world devoid of objects.

Emptiness, omnipotence and paranoia

The emptiness of a leader like Hitler has been commented upon by many percep-tive observers. Ian Kershaw reflecting on 'the emptiness of the private person' Hitler, quotes Joachim Fest who referred to Hitler as an 'unperson' (Kershaw 1999: XXV). Albert Speer who was for years in Hitler's inner circle, comments on Hitler's inability to make any personal relationships and on his inability to let anybody come close to him (Speer 1970: 133, 156). Alan Bullock remarks: 'It may well be doubted whether Hitler, absorbed in the dream of his own greatness, ever had the capacity to love anyone deeply' (1962: 396). On the subject of con-cern for other human beings Bullock observes:

> Indifferent towards the sufferings of others, he lacked any feelings of sym-pathy, was intolerant and callous, and filled with contempt for the common run of humankind. Pity and mercy he regarded as humanitarian clap-trap and sign of weakness. The only virtue was to be hard, and ruthlessness was the distinctive mark of superiority.
>
> (Ibid.: 397)

This absence of any concern about human beings follows from the emptiness of his internal world. The objects that ordinarily form the internal world of indi-viduals are absent in Hitler's internal life. What is put in the place of the object is a bigger than life self, unreal in its expansiveness and hubris. The deadness of the internal world makes death the real quality underneath the pompousness and the masquerade.

'We have seen the only stable idea behind Hitler's policy'. Sebastian Haffner writes, 'It is, in a word, Hitler'. And in another place '... the only stable element in Hitler's politics, is their devotion to his own person. Resentment, career, and satisfaction of a theatrical urge to see his own ego in many banal radiant roles of doubtful taste' (ibid.: 12). Haffner quotes from Hitler's conversation with Papen in 1932 (Germany's Kanzler at the time): 'I am now over forty, I must rule', and to the British Ambassador in 1939: 'I am now fifty. I would rather have the war now, than when I am fifty five or sixty' (ibid.: 11).

This emptiness at the centre of the fascist leader is sought to be filled by the group, the Party, the nation. He is to be one with them and they are to be one with him. He stands and falls with the group. Standing alone and apart of the group the leader is nothing – an 'unperson'.

We can only assume that the men of his inner circle were, if not exactly, 'empty vessels', at least had an ideal of the omnipotent self as an 'empty vessel' – a man, a hero who stands alone. (The hero who stands alone was an ideal of masculinity in the late nineteenth and early twentieth centuries.)

This internal emptiness as an ideal (an internal world without objects), creates a masquerade of projected objects that may be taken as real but which are nevertheless a mirage. The only 'real' object is the will to power. This may explain the 'shifting' ideology of Hitler's Party, the constant change of policies and the belief in omnipotence. Speer comments that if there was any insanity in Hitler it was his unshakable belief in his 'lucky star' (ibid.: 483) – that come what it may he is bound to win. His disregard for the facts is graphically portrayed in the film *Downfall* (based on eye witnesses' accounts of Hitler's last days in the bunker) where a trembling and doddering Hitler moves imaginary armies on the map in front of his generals who nod and exchange uneasy glances while the soviet army is outside Berlin and the allies within a few days away.

Whether Hitler was insane or not is a question that preoccupied many diplomats, politicians and writers after his ascent to power (Pick 2012). However, contemporary psychoanalysis is influenced by Bion's way of seeing a psychotic and a non-psychotic part of the personality co-existing in all of us, and that it is the predominance of the one over the other that determines whether a person is psychotic or neurotic (Bion 1957). Bion also saw basic assumption groups acting on psychotic mechanisms so that the psychotic bits of the leader would join the psychotic bits of the group (1961). If we allow ourselves to think in terms of group processes we might be able to avoid the question whether Hitler was insane or not. Hitler was certainly not insane in terms of psychiatric criteria, but the psychotic part of his personality was certainly amplified by group processes and the trauma of a whole country. There is some doubt whether he maintained the sense of reality the last few months of his life but he was certainly sane enough to know what awaited him if he lived to see the German capitulation.

Freud saw psychosis not just as a denial of reality – this occurs also in neurosis he tells us. After a long discussion in his paper 'The loss of reality in neurosis and psychosis' (1924a), he summarises the difference between neurosis and psychosis thus: 'neurosis does not disavow the reality, it only ignores it; psychosis disavows it and *tries to replace it*' (Freud 1924a: 185; italics mine).

This 'destruction the world' phantasy and the re-creation of it from scratch is also discussed by Freud towards the end of the Schreber case. Freud discusses here Schreber's delusion at the peak of his illness that the world was coming to an end and he comments:

> The patient has withdrawn from the people in his environment and from the external world generally the libidinal cathexis which he has hitherto directed on to them. Thus everything has become indifferent and irrelevant to him, and

has to be explained by means of secondary rationalization as being "miracled up, cursorily improvised". The end of the world is the projection of this mental catastrophe; his subjective world has come to an end since *his withdrawal of his love* from it.

(Freud 1911: 70; italics mine)

And he continues with a quote from Goethe's *Faust* where the spirits address Faust after he has clinched his pact with Mephistopheles:

Weh! Weh!
Du hast sie zerstoert
die schoene Welt,
mit maechtiger Faust!
sie stuerzt, sie zerfaellt!
Ein Halbgott hat sie zerschlagen!
. . .
Maechtiger
der Erdensoehne,
Praechtiger,
haue sie wieder,
in deinem Busen baue sie auf!

Woe! Woe!
Thou hast it destroyed
The beautiful world
With powerful fist!
In ruins 'tis hurled,
By the blow of a demigod shattered!
. . .
Mightier
For the children of men,
More splendid
Build it again,
In thine own bosom build it anew!
    (Goethe, *Faust*, Part I, Scene 4)

'And the paranoiac', Freud comments, 'builds it again, not more splendid, it is true, but at least so that he can once more live in it. He builds it by the work of his delusions' (Freud 1911: 70–1).

Freud, of course, speaks of psychosis here, not of political extremism or fascism (which was yet to come). That fascism in its extreme totalitarian ambitions had something in common with psychosis is maybe a controversial point but one that has been considered in this study, in terms of the type of relationship between the leader and the group described above, which puts psychotic mechanisms at the centre of the picture.

The wish to destroy the world and re-build it from scratch is certainly part of the fascist ambition. This grandiose plan to rebuild the world (or Germany) from scratch was nowhere better portrayed than in Hitler's megalomaniac plans to re-build Berlin as a 'model city'. The monumental scale of the planned buildings surpassed anything that European architecture ever designed. In the middle of the destruction of the old world (during World War Two) Hitler began the 're-building' of Berlin.

The exhibits of this 'model city' were set up in the Academy of Arts in Berlin. Most of these were huge models on a scale of 1:50 or 1:100 repro-duced by cabinetmakers in every small detail. The model of the 'big boulevard' for instance went on for about 100 feet through the exhibition rooms of the Academy of Arts.

Albert Speer, Hitler's architect who designed the buildings according to Hitler's plans, quotes him as saying: 'The Champs Elysees is three hundred and thirty feet wide. In any case we'll make our avenue seventy odd feet wider' (Speer 1970: 123).

The 'grand boulevard', as it was known, led to a group of grandiose buildings that were central to the power holding of the Third Reich. These were the Chancellery, the High Command of the Armed Forced and the Secretariat of the Party.

At one side of the boulevard was the 'Arch of Triumph' – a structure of immense proportions: 'five hundred and fifty feet wide, three-hundred and ninety-two feet deep, three hundred eighty-six feet high and towering over all the other buildings. In comparison the Arc de Triumph is only one hundred and sixty foot high' (ibid.: 199).

But to crown all these grandiose buildings the big Dome was planned at the other end of the boulevard dominating the whole townscape. The great Dome was a building the like of which the world had never seen. It was to be 'the biggest building in the world' which 'would have loomed against the sky like some green mountain' (ibid.: 222). The dimensions of the Dome are truly unimaginable.

> This structure, the greatest assembly hall in the world ever conceived up to that time, consisted of one vast hall that could hold one hundred fifty to one hundred eighty thousand persons standing.... The idea was that over the course of centuries, by tradition and venerability, it would acquire an impor-tance similar to that St. Peter's in Rome has for the Catholic Church.
>
> (Ibid.: 222)

Speer continues: 'The volume of this structure amounted to almost 27.5 million cubic yards; the Capitol in Washington would have been contained many times in such mass. These were dimensions of an inflationary sort' (ibid.: 224).

There were also the new railway stations planned to the north and the south of the city. 'Emerging from it the visitor would face a basin of water thirty-three hundred feet long and eleven-hundred and fifty feet wide, across which the great dome was to be seen a mile away' (ibid.: 203).

There would also be three enormous buildings to stand at the western side of the lake: the new Berlin Town Hall (15,000 feet long) flanked by the new High Command for the Navy and the new Berlin Police Headquarters. A new German War Academy was to be built on the eastern side of the lake.

Speer describes Hitler's childlike delight in viewing the models and making plans for the future. He had a connecting corridor built between the Chancellery and the Academy so that late at night he and Speer, sometimes accompanied by other guests, would visit the Academy and view the models.

> 'We would set out armed with flashlights and keys', Speer writes. 'In the empty halls spotlights illuminated the models. There was no need for me to do the talking, for Hitler, with flashing eyes, explained every single detail to his companions .... He loved to "enter his avenue" at various points and take measure of the future effect .... These were rare times when he relinquished his usual stiffness. In no other situation did I see him so spontaneous, so relaxed ...'
>
> (Speer: 196)

The dimensions of the boulevard, the Arc of Triumph, the surrounding buildings and finally the great Dome were, like everything else in Hitler's life, dreamlike. Not that the buildings were not achievable. But the 'dream' was bound to the other 'dream' of conquering the world, raising it to the ground and rebuilding it. That the 'dream' continued to be active not just before the war but also during the most violent war humanity ever saw was truly extraordinary.

It is as if Hitler and his entourage were living in a parallel universe. Speer reports how when he went to visit Hitler during the Stalingrad campaign in 1941 Hitler wanted to discuss the buildings with him. Speer reports that 'he (Hitler) would not hear of any restrictions and refused to divert the material and labor for his private buildings to war industries anymore that he would consider calling a halt to his favourite projects, the autobahns, the party buildings and the Berlin project'. Speer continues: 'Hitler told me bluntly: "The building must begin even while this war is still going on. I am not going to let the war keep me from accomplishing my plans"'(ibid.: 259).

What is striking about these buildings, however, is their non phallic character. The dome, if anything, could be seen as a huge breast or a huge womb. The design of a whole city, roads, buildings etc., are a whole environment, a new mother created at will – perfect and grandiose under the son's control. Creator and creation are united in a grandiose total environment.

As I have argued this delusional grandiosity is part of the unconscious phantasy of having taken over the omnipotent object and having become it. This process, however, has an underside: a delusional paranoia. It can hardly be otherwise because the destruction of the object in total projective identification involves the subject *becoming* the object and, in this way, never being able to get rid of it. The phantasy that the object enraged with its demise will come back as a parasite within the subject is a consequence of this whole process. The re-projection of a hostile and intrusive object creates paranoia. The subject is now endlessly invaded by the object which demands the subject's destruction. The unimaginable violence that certain groups and individuals perpetrate may be an attempt to get rid of the intrusive object which, when re-projected, becomes the centre of paranoia. The difficulty is that, if the subject's power and omnipotence relies on having devoured the object, he can never get rid of it. The object, hostile and alien, threatens the subject with contamination and demolition. In this sense mania can very quickly and unpredictably turn into paranoia.

As the boy takes over the object/mother he cannot differentiate himself from her. Her femininity pollutes him and contaminates his masculinity. If the Devil has breasts as Haizman describes him/her (see Chapter 4) the male subject can only find salvation in the community of men. For Haizman it was the community of brothers. For Hitler and the fascists it was the fascist group – the Party, the Army – the 'masculine fraternity' (Paxton).

Hitler's paranoia is nowhere better revealed as in those passages in *Mein Kamp* and in the *Second Book* where he speaks of the Jews. The Jews as the intrusive object that invades the pure self/body/community of the German people is the pinnacle of Hitler's paranoia as well as of his castration and annihilation anxieties.

The Jews

It is important to state that Hitler's type of anti-Semitism differed from the traditional type common in the nineteenth-century Europe. Neil Gregor explains this difference in the following way. In the traditional anti-Semitism, as existed in the whole of Europe for many centuries, the Jews were seen as a religious community, not a separate race, and were portrayed as capitalists or financiers who controlled the economy and manipulated everything. This image was also used by Hitler in his accusation of the Jews as profiteering from the war. There was also the image of the Jews as decadent, libertines, licentious and pornographic responsible for the erosion of traditional values. This is also present in nineteenth-century pamphlets, jokes and stories involving Jews. This image of the Jew was also used by Hitler (Gregor 2005: 57–8).

But there is a new image which permeates Hitler's writings. This is the image of the Jew as a parasite that attaches itself to the German body and sucks its blood. Parallel to this basic image, a variety of other images of non-human organisms, or micro-organisms, are used to describe the Jews, such as vipers, spiders, bacillus, virus, foreign bodies, serpents. What they all have in common is that they attack and poison or contaminate the German blood.

This new kind of anti-Semitism did not accept that the Jews were a religious community. If being Jewish amounted to having a certain religion or culture, then the Jews could be assimilated into German society once they changed their religion or culture. This had been the position of many nineteenth-century liberals. But this position was absurd for Hitler who saw in the Jew an irreducible entity, a biologically determined evil. In fact, for Hitler a converted or assimilated Jew was more dangerous, since he could camouflage his real self and lulled society into security while he attached himself to the pure German body and sucked and contaminated its blood (Gregor: 64–5).

Neil Gregor, in his book *How to Read Hitler* attempts to answer the question whether the genocidal message is already obvious in *Mein Kampf*, which was published in 1925, long before Hitler came to power, and whether the holocaust was a logical consequence of Hitler's ideology as expressed in it. He answers the question in the affirmative, that is as the Jews are seen as vermin and virus the logical conclusion is that they need to be exterminated.

The following passage from *Mein Kampf* demonstrates this new type of anti-Semitism and the explanation that Hitler provided:

> Since the Jew never possessed a state with definite territorial limits and therefore never called a culture his own, the conception arose that this was a people which should be reckoned among the ranks of the nomads. This is a fallacy as it is dangerous ... No, the Jew is no nomad; for the nomad had also a definite attitude towards the concept of work which could serve as a basis for his later development in so far as the necessary intellectual premises were present. In him the basic idealistic view is present, even if in infinite dilution, hence in his whole being he may seem strange to the Aryan peoples, but not unattractive. In the Jew, however, this attitude is not at all present; for that reason he was never a nomad, but only *always a parasite in the body of other peoples*. That he sometimes left his previous living space has nothing to do with his own purpose, but results from the fact that from time to time he was thrown out by the host nations he has misused. His spreading is a typical phenomenon of parasites; he always seeks a new feeding ground for his race.
>
> This, however, has nothing to do with nomadism for the reason that a Jew never thinks of leaving a territory that he has occupied, but remains where he is, and he sits so fast that even by force it is very hard to drive him out. His extension to ever-new countries occurs only in the moment in which certain conditions for his existence are present, without which – unlike the nomad – he would not change his residence. He is and remains the typical parasite, a sponger who like a noxious bacillus keeps spreading as soon as a favourable medium invites him. And the effect of his existence is also like the spongers: whenever he appears, the host people dies out after a shorter or longer period.
>
> Thus the Jew of all times has lived in the states of other peoples, and there formed his own state, which, to be sure, habitually sailed under the disguise of 'religious community' as long as outward circumstances made a complete revelation of his nature seem inadvisable. But as soon as he felt strong enough to do without the protective cloak, he always dropped the veil and suddenly became what so many of the others previously did not want to believe and see: a Jew.
>
> (Ibid.: 275–7; italics mine)

Like any paranoiac Hitler speaks here, as in most of *Mein Kampf*, with an authoritative voice as if he is pronouncing 'the truth' or as if he is laying down the 'laws of nature' and of society and no doubt can be allowed to enter his mind. The images are paranoid and concern the attacks on the pure German body by millions of micro-organisms leading to its weakening and its depletion of energy. So the enemy here is not a whole object but rather the object is splintered into thousands of fragments that threaten to enter the pure German blood. I argue here that the process is not just one of splitting and projection, but one of ego and object *fragmentation* and the projection of the fragments outwards to create 'bizarre objects'.[2]

Let us look at this extract in more detail.

The main images here are the nomad and the parasite. The nomad seems to be a whole object – 'other' to the Aryan people 'but not unattractive'. Like the American Indian Winnetou in Karl May novels[3] that Hitler admired and read avidly, the nomad seems to be like the noble savage. The Jew, however, is another matter. He cannot be honoured with the same traits of idealism as the nomad. He is not an 'other'. He is a *parasite*. The difference is important in distinguishing Hitler's brand of racism which is not just fuelled by hatred of the other. A parasite exists only by attaching itself to other organisms. It needs a host. This foreign body is attached to the wholesome German body sucking all its strength away – and there is an implication that there are millions of them – like the 'noxious bacillus' or in other passages the virus, the vermin, the maggots. I argue that the images of thousands or even millions of minute organizms attacking the German body can only be projections of a fragmented self and object united, that is a 'bizarre object'.

In my reading this is a fragmented image of a mother/son union that is most desired and most feared because it feminises the subject and pollutes and weakens the German blood. This contradiction at the heart of the fascist – the wish and its fear – remains unresolved. Its seeming solution is minute splitting and projection of the fragments that return and persecute the object.

I have already discussed in Chapter 8 the work of Gillman, Boyarin and Santner who examined the image of the Jew as a feminised male in nineteenth-century Europe. I have also discussed in Chapter 4 the dread of feminisation in the boy and the adult man, especially the man of Modernity.

So when Hitler speaks about parasites entering the German body, whose body is he talking about? The mother Germany's (female) body he talks about at the opening paragraphs of *Mein Kampf*, or the German men's bodies which have been feminised, 'softened'? Is the virus attacking the mother-(land) or her sons? And, if there is a merged state, can we make such a distinction? Are parasites the contents of the mother's belly? Or the mother herself? Or the self as the parasitic baby entering the mother and sucking her blood? Or the fragments of the ego that is destroyed in the service of the delusion of a union with mother – the fragments that return as bizarre objects to persecute the subject? In my reading all these are part of the symbolic equation of the parasite entering the body – an overdetermined concrete symbol, or symbolic equation, of persecutory bits of self and bits of object glued together.[4]

The vicious circle that this creates in the mind is obvious as the attacked, damaged or exterminated fragments persecute the owner of these fragments and more expulsion and extermination is seen as necessary to eradicate the split off fragments of the self as they attempt to return to their owner. I also suggest that this is an unsolvable dilemma for Hitler and the totalitarian Nazi psyche, and one that inescapably leads to paranoia and the sanctioning of mass murder. For, what is wished for, a union with mother, is also that which threatens with feminisation and annihilation.

Hannah Arendt (1951: 46) saw totalitarianism as in constant need of new enemies (see citation in Chapter 3). Nick Temple (2006) also wonders whether totalitarianism, and the totalitarian state of mind, is in need of constant enemies (see Chapter 3). As both Klein (1946) and Bion (1957) showed the need for enemies is inbuilt in these processes of splitting, fragmentation, expulsion and persecution. I further suggest that this weakened and fragmented self can only survive within the homogeneous group and borrow, so to speak, the bigger group identity. And, of course, a homogeneous group is by definition a paranoid group as any differences, real or perceived, threaten the homogeneity of the group. The vicious circle is now complete.

As we have seen Hitler was not a masculine, tough guy kind of man, pursuing the theme of feminine identification Langer refers to Hitler's excessive submissiveness to his superiors in the army, to his persistent fear of cancer (from which his mother had died), his obsession with cleanliness which was a characteristic of his mother and closes this section by asking whether this phenomenon might not have been a frequent one in Germany:

> If further research on the subject should corroborate this evidence, it might prove of extreme value to our psychological warfare program insofar as it would give us a key to the understanding of the basic nature of the German male character and the role that the Nazi organization plays in their life.
>
> (Langer 1973: 173)

In other words, if there were general fears about masculinity among the German males of the time it would explain why there would be such a need to differentiate themselves from the 'effeminate' Jews especially at a time of national identity crisis. For the moment my focus is on Hitler himself and what we can deduce from his writings. However, my main point in looking at the above passage from *Mein Kampf* is to point out the fragmentation of both ego and object, so that what is expelled is not a whole object but a fragment of the self/object which after it has been expelled becomes a bizarre object that persecutes the owner of this object.

Neil Gregor examines Hitler's false analogy between the mating of Germans and Jews and the mating of different species in nature. By making this analogy Hitler claims a scientific law that forbids the intermarrying between Germans and Jews which he called 'blood mixing'. For Hitler the mating of German and Jew is as unnatural as the mating between a cat and a dog. But also what is unthinkable in this kind of new anti-Semitism is that a Jew could ever be assimilated into the culture and become German. In Hitler's thinking 'a Jew could no more become German', Gregor tells us 'than a dog could become a cat' (Gregor 2005: 62). Part of this was the idea that an assimilated Jew was a dangerous delusion. 'It was a sham anti-Semitism which was almost worse than none at all; for it lulled people into security', Hitler writes. 'They thought they had the foe by the ears, while in reality they themselves were being led by the nose' (MK: 110).

Also the mating of different races polluted the race and led to 'blood poisoning': '... all great cultures of the past perished only because the originally creative race died out from blood poisoning' (MK: 262).

I suggest that in describing the unbridgeable gap between Jew and German as one between dog and cat Hitler is describing another unbridgeable gap – the one between male and female. This unbridgeable gap makes his own wishes to be one with his mother both an absurdity and an abominable cause of pollution: Were it to become true it would pollute his own masculinity. We can speculate that Hitler's well-known fear of normal sexuality (Kershaw 1999, 2000; Fromm 1974; Langer 1973) has its roots in this concrete fear that to 'mate' with a woman is to become polluted – in my argument to become feminine.

As I have already mentioned Hitler's metaphors are not mere metaphors but rather 'symbolic equations'. At this concrete state, different levels of functioning get compressed into one and no differentiation between them is possible. I suggest that the metaphors of a union between mother and son and the metaphors of a union between Germans and Jews get confused in Hitler's concrete mind and have to be violently separated because they give rise to fears of de-differentiation, confusion, and contamination.

I also suggest that incest, mating, a return to the womb and a taking over the object in a total projective identification also get confused with each other. His own wishes to have his mother to himself (incest wishes), his wish to return to the womb (narcissistic parasitical phantasy), his wish to merge with her (homogenisation/annihilation phantasy) and his wish to take over her riches and her power (colonising phantasy) can neither be differentiated nor transformed. They just collapse into each other and are projected out, and those who carry this mish-mash of bits of self and object should be exterminated.

The term Hitler used for different races coming together was 'mixing of blood'. We can understand in psychoanalytic language as blood mixing the union of man and woman, not related by blood, to create a child (in contrast to incest or a merge with mother where mother and son share the same blood). I suggest that the mixing of blood is abhorred by Hitler as it evokes the hated father and the hated parental procreative couple which prevents his union with mother. This hatred of the parental procreative couple is an ordinary feature of normal development which is usually to some extent overcome through the working through of the Oedipus complex and the internalization of the parental couple, so that in normal development what comes to be abhorred is incest not the 'alien' blood. I suggest that for Hitler this hatred of the parental couple and of the father remained unaltered and entered his ideology as a paranoid fear of the alien blood. It has also become one of the cornerstones of his ideology as he advocated the control of sexuality and of the couple by the state in his particular version of eugenics.

The emptiness of Hitler's internal world is strewn with the dead objects that form the furniture of his world. The reproduction of this dead internal world is ultimately what fascism is about.

Notes

1 As we know Renee Muller committed suicide shortly after this meeting with Hitler.
2 Bion described an active psychosis as a fragmentation of the ego and a projection of the fragments into objects so that they are engulfed by them or are engulfing them. These objects that now seem to be alive are seen to be spying and undermining the individual. Bion named these objects 'bizarre objects' (Bion 1957).

    In arguing this, I argue that a psychotic process is in operation whereby the differentiation between mother and son is eclipsed by an attack on the perceiving ego the way Bion conceptualized it in his classic paper 'The differentiating of the psychotic from the non-psychotic personalities' (1957). In this sense a wish is fulfilled (the merge with mother) at the expense of reality (separation from mother, sex differentiation) – as Freud maintained in his paper 'Loss of reality in neurosis and psychosis' (1924). However, this merged state threatens to annihilate the individual and to feminise the male. Under the unbearable burden of contradictory demands (i.e. the wish to merge with mother on the one hand; and fears of annihilation and feminisation/castration on the other) the ego fragments, and the fragments enter those who are seen as suitable to carry these projections – in the first instance the Jews.
3 Karl May was a nineteenth century German writer who, like Hitler, wrote his works in prison. He wrote adventure novels, read mainly by children, about places he had never been, like America and Iraq. His hero Winnetou is a 'good American Indian' who sides with the 'good' white men against the exploitative and evil white men. He represents something like the noble savage.
4 Hanna Segal coined the term symbolic equation for this fusion of symbol and object.

Chapter 10

Epilogue – hollow men

> We are the hollow men
> We are the stuffed men
> Leaning together
> Headpiece filled with straw. Alas!
> (T.S. Eliot, Reproduced by kind
> permission of Faber & Faber)

I have looked at the heart of the fascist state of mind and described the devastation left behind by the destruction of the object as emptiness. But hollowness is probably a better description. Hollowness is the quality created by the destruction of the object.

T.S. Eliot writing in 1925, the year of the publication of *Mein Kampf*, very accurately portrays the hollowness of a generation of men who survived the First World War – the hollow men, 'leaning together', with an empty mind, puffed up like stuffed animals.

For Eliot it was not inner violence which characterised these men but hollowness. Fascism had just been born in Italy 6 years before and Hitler's assumption of the leadership of NSDAP took place in July 1921. In 1925 *Mein Kampf* had just appeared in print. The celebration of violence as life enhancing had already begun. The lost men of this generation were attempting to 'come alive' through violence and militarism. In Germany the hollow stuffed men were transformed by 1934 into the armoured regimented young men forming a mechanical sea of moving and saluting steel in Nuremberg. The fascist group, and later the army, was the place where real men were made, where trauma was transformed into deadly aggression. Why such a change did not take place in Britain or France is a question I do not attempt to tackle here, as this study is not a sociological or historical study. Suffice it to say that the humiliation of Germany in the war played a big role in the formation of fascism and the military style of the regime. The humiliation of Italy after the war, has also been important in the formation of Italian Fascism, as Italy failed to secure the border territories which were promised to her in the Treaty of London in 1915.[1]

Eliot portrays the traumatic consequences of a catastrophic war as lifelessness, emptiness and 'sightlessness'. From internal deadness to a deadly ideology is perhaps less of a leap than is apparent in the first instance. The false, enforced liveliness of fascism, its hysterical vitalism, coupled with its ultimate genocidal reality, reveal the grim dead internal landscape. The murder of anything soft, loving and feminine in men was a big part of the training of men during fascism:

> Confronted with the Jewish-democratic idea of a blind worship of numbers' Hitler writes in *Mein Kampf*, 'the army sustained belief in personality. And thus it trained what the new epoch most urgently needed: men. In the morass of a universally spreading *softening* and *feminisation*, each year three hundred and fifty thousand vigorous young men sprang from the ranks of the army, men who in their two years' training lost the softness of youth and achieved *bodies hard as steel*.
>
> (MK: 255; italics mine)

We can see here the association of the Jews with democracy, softness, and feminisation as opposed to the army who makes real men out of the soft, feminised democratic ones. But to simplify and distort reality to such a degree one has to be blind. Eliot continues:

> The eyes are not here
> There are no eyes here
> In this valley of dying stars
> In this hollow valley
> This broken jaw of our lost kingdom.
>
> (Ibid.: 79)

Eliot describes here a blindness that is a kind of depression, a kind of withdrawal from life, a kind of deadness. The blindness of the fascist is, however, of a different kind. It is a blindness that is a deliberate distortion of reality.

One way this kind of blindness can be achieved is by the destruction of the ego as the part of the personality that perceives reality (as Bion showed). The fragmentation of the ego and the projection of the fragments onto the 'other' create a distortion of reality that is the most deadly part of the fascist state of mind. For this distortion of reality creates the most destructive aggression known to humanity – the reduction of the human other to a 'part-object', or a 'bizarre object' – a disposable sub-human entity which needs to be exterminated.

Standing together, armoured and hollow, the fragmented, hollow men melt into one big homogenised whole. Bion called this phenomenon *agglomeration*.

Beta elements and bizarre objects, he said, cannot combine to create bigger, articulated units that we can call thinking. But this does not mean that they cannot combine at all. They can combine through agglomeration – sticking together rigidly, creating a shield, the beta screen (Bion 1962a: 21–2).

This rigid system, very similar to a pathological organization, prevents disintegration and establishes some kind of relationship to an object, however, primitive and rigid. 'Thanks to the BETA-SCREEN the psychotic patient has a capacity for evoking emotions in the analyst' Bion writes.

I suggest that fascism in the mind and in society, with its totalitarian tenets of a homogenised society, has the quality of a beta-screen able to glue the fragments of a disintegrating personality/community/nation together and evoke strong emotions to the participants. The mad quality of the beta screen is betrayed by its being impermeable to reality. The rigidity with which the beliefs are held, points to them being the glue of the personality.

Of course a fascist regime, as opposed to a fascist state of mind, has to face some kind of reality in order to survive. If a fascist regime is to be realised, the use of compromises, lies, intrigues, false alliances is part of a *realpolitik* that both Hitler and Mussolini were able to pursue. However, the beta-screen of the basic tenets persists. For Hitler the beta-screen was the purity of blood; the fears of contamination and the weakening of the pure German blood by the Jews; the policy to exterminate the Jews; the pursuit of a pure race/community/nation; a policy of expansion to the East and the creation of 'living space'; life seen as a Darwinian struggle for survival where only the strongest survive. The glue to all these tenets is violence and a masculinity that is hard, unyielding, un-democratic, and uncompromising. Take away this belief in violence and militarism, in creating real men, and the whole edifice of fascism collapses.

This pure masculinity is cleansed of all foreign bodies that might weaken it and feminise it. The separation of sexes that the Nazis sought to achieve, and the confinement of women to the home point to this fear of the contamination by the feminine. The gender apartheid they created betrays their fear of women and the feminine.

Although women supported the Nazi cause as much as men, they did this from a position of a disenfranchised, soft and non-threatening femininity. Within these invisible walls they embraced a feminine domain which they called theirs – making a home, raising children, participating in local women's pursuits. Most women adapted to this separation of functions and were content to acquire more influence within their own domain. But when a woman made the mistake of attempting to participate with men in decision making 'the alarms went off' Koonz writes, 'and she faced a storm of ridicule. Autonomy existed only in relation to the women within their sphere and did not translate into bargaining power in male administration' (Koonz 1987: 13).

I do not intend to look into the ways men and women participated, adapted to or cooperated with the Nazi regime. My point here is that the separation of sexes was one of the cornerstones of internal Nazi policy in this way betraying the fear and hatred of woman's power and the fear of contamination by the feminine that I have seen as a fundamental fascist trait. Softness, as the above quote from *Mein Kampf* shows, was linked with women and with feminised men and the purpose of a hard military training was to create real men hard as steel.

That this false virility through militarism is one of the fundamental traits of fascism is part of the main argument of this book. Yet the contradiction remains: the fact that I have looked at the fascist state of mind as if it were a 'masculine' phenomenon while at the same time I have asserted that this is a state of mind common to all of us men or women. I would like to clarify further these seemingly contradictory assertions.

I have already discussed this issue but let me recap here.

It is true that the emptiness, and the *wish* for emptiness and homogenisation, that forms part of deep early longings to which both the traumatised individual and the fascist returns, is common to both men and women. This substratum of the fascist state of mind – what Bollas and Chasseguet-Smirgel are describing, that is the wish to simplify the mind, to wipe out the contents of the mind, the wish to return to a place of no conflict and no frustration, the wish to demolish the ego and be part of a bigger entity – all this is part of a universal wish and a universal danger. In its extreme it is part of the death instinct as understood by Freud. This universal death wish can be activated in times of trauma and national humiliation.

That national trauma and humiliation can be experienced as castration and feminisation is a particularly male problem which acts as a secondary trauma. This secondary trauma of a humiliated and castrated masculinity activates the fascist machinery to create 'real men' through military discipline, homogenised in their hyper-masculinity and partaking to the glory of the one leader.

I have argued that this state of mind is one of being within a masculine womb, a place where one exists only as part of a bigger whole – the army, the Party, or the para-military group. I have also argued that this masculine womb both satisfies and denies the original wish to be within a bigger whole, ultimately the mother's body.

It might be objected that I have based my book too much on Nazi Germany and particularly on what we can deduce from Hitler's personality. For instance can we deduce from Hitler's personality that he is the prototype of the 'fascist state of mind'? Or are we entering a circular argument here whereby I define a fascist state of mind by looking at Hitler's personality, and at the same time, I explain Hitler's personality by assuming the predominance of the fascist state of mind in him?

I have no comprehensive answer to this danger except to say that I hope I am not guilty of this particular sin, and that I used Hitler and certain striking features of his personality, only as *illustrations* of a certain state of mind. This state of mind that I called 'fascist' was not deduced from Hitler's personality but from the whole 'rhetoric' of fascism, from its aims and 'mobilising passions', as well as from psychoanalytic theories of the 'fascist' or 'totalitarian' state of mind.

That each real fascist regime will inevitably stress different characteristics of these 'mobilising passions' is obvious. The ferocity and violence with which the passions will be pursued is also bound to vary. The balance within the personality and within a country will determine the final form that a regime, internal or external, will take. In Italy for instance the existence of the Catholic church, and of the monarchy, created a balance of powers that prevented a wholesale fascism from being established despite Mussolini's rhetoric. In one sense Hitler carried out Mussolini's rhetoric, as well as his own, to its logical conclusion in an attempt to create a totalitarian regime.

I have looked at the different components of fascism mainly following Robert Paxton's 'mobilising passions' – the primacy of the group and the community, the primacy of the leader (always male), a sense of overwhelming crisis, a sense of grievance and an adherence to some kind of Darwinian struggle. I have added to these the sense of a masculinity in danger which needed to be salvaged from the morass of femininity, a femininity desired and wished for by the little boy and the traumatised man alike. It is in this sense that I have connected the fascist state of mind with the manufacturing of a new, hyper-masculinity while *at the same time* it satisfied the longed for femininity not only with the submission to the Fuehrer, but more importantly, with the merge, in phantasy, with the Great mother/Germany as the opening lines of *Mein Kampf* testify to (see Chapter 2).

This primitive phantasy of a merge with mother (intensified and made more concrete in times of crisis and massive trauma), created two things: (1) a new moral panic about the intactness of masculinity and the danger of its being contaminated by feminine longings; and (2) a new military and para-military mass movement to create 'real men', a movement that was more charismatic and more malignant than anything the world had hitherto known. As I have suggested, this military movement differed from other authoritarian military regimes in its quasi-religious quality in this way betraying its roots in infantile longings and infantile phantasies of a merge with mother. This quasi-religious quality that both satisfied these longings and protected against them at the same time was, I believe, the big seduction of fascism.

We can examine Neo-fascist groups today, certain violent fundamentalist groups and regimes and certain terrorist groups which preach the extermination of the 'other' in terms of some universal tendencies in human beings that I have described in this book. Moreover the wish to simplify the world is in every one of us. In this sense there is no last chapter of fascism. We all live under its shadow and with the possibility of its re-inventing itself under a new cloak and a new rhetoric, both in our internal world and in society.

Note

1 Although Italy was with the winning side in the Second World War, she nevertheless did badly in the final negotiations for territory. The Italian delegation returned from the Peace Conference in Paris in 1919 humiliated as Italy was not granted the land that was promised to her when she entered the war in 1915. The Americans had not signed the Treaty of London in 1915 and Woodrow Wilson now argued that the frontiers of Italy should be decided on ethnic grounds.

References

Abelin, E.L. (1975) 'Some further observations and comments on the earliest role of the father', *International Journal of Psychoanalysis*, 56: 293–302.

Adams, R. and Savran, D. (eds) (2002) *The Masculinity Studies Reader*, Malden, MA: Blackwell.

Adorno, T.W., Frenkel-Brunswik, E., Levinson, D. J. and Nevitt Sanford, R. (1950) *The Authoritarian Personality*, New York: The Norton Library.

Akhtar, S. (2002) 'The psychodynamic dimension of terrorism', in Covington, C., Williams, P., Arundale, J. and Knox, J. (eds), *Terrorism and War: Unconscious Dynamics of Political Violence*, London: Karnac.

——(2003) 'Dehumanization: origins, manifestation, and remedies', in *Violence or Dialogue: Psychoanalytic Insights on Terror and Terrorism*, London: International Psychoanalytical Association.

Alderdice, Lord (2002) 'Introduction', in Covington, C., Williams, P., Arundale, J. and Knox, J. (eds), *Terrorism and War: Unconscious Dynamics of Political Violence*, London: Karnac.

Alizade, A.M. (ed.) (2003) *Masculine Scenarios*, London: Karnac.

Anzieu, D. (2001) 'Freud's Group Psychology: background, significance, and influence', in *On Freud's 'Group Psychology and the Analysis of the Ego'*, London: The Analytic Press.

Arendt, H. (1951) *The Burden of our Time*, London: Secker & Warburg.

——(1977) *Eichmann in Jerusalem*, New York: Penguin Books.

Benjamin, J. (1990) *The Bonds of Love*, London: Virago.

Bion, W.R. (1956) 'Development of schizophrenic thought', *International Journal of Psychoanalysis*, 37: Part 4.

——(1957) 'The differentiation of the psychotic from the non-psychotic personalities', *International Journal of Psychoanalysis*, 38: Parts 3 and 4.

——(1958) 'On hallucination', *International Journal of Psychoanalysis*, 39: Part 5.

——(1959) 'Attacks on linking', in *Second Thoughts*, London: Karnac.

——(1961) *Experiences in Groups*, London: Karnac.

——(1962) *Learning from Experience*, London: Karnac.

——(1963) *Elements of Psychoanalysis*, London: Karnac.

——(1977) *Two Papers: The Grid and Ceasura*, London: Karnac.

Bly, R. (1990) *Iron John: A Book About Men*, Shaftesbury, Dorset: Element Books.

Boehm, F. (1930) 'The femininity complex in men', *International Journal of Psychoanalysis*, 11: 444–70.

Bohleber, W. (2003) 'Collective phantasms, destructiveness, and terrorism', in Varvin, S. and Volkan, V. (eds), *Violence or Dialogue?*, London: International Psychoanalytical Association.

Bollas, C. (1993) 'The fascist state of mind', in *Being a Character*, London: Routledge.

Bracher, K.D. (1969/1973) *The German Dictatorship*, London: Penguin Books.

Breen, D. (1993) *The Gender Conundrum*, London: Routledge.

Britton, R. (1989) 'The missing link: parental sexuality in the Oedipus complex', in Steiner, J. (ed.), *The Oedipus Complex Today*, London: Karnac.

Bullock, A. (Revised edition 1962) *Hitler: A Study in Tyranny*, London: Penguin Books.

Butler, J. (1999) *Gender Trouble*, London: Routledge.

Campbell, D. (1999) 'The role of the father in the pre-suicidal state', *International Journal of Psychoanalysis*, 76: 315–23.

Canovan, M. (2000) 'Arendt's theory of totalitarianism: a reassessment', in Villa, D. (ed.), *The Cambridge Companion to Hannah Arendt*, Cambridge: Cambridge University Press.

Cardoza, A. (2005) *Benito Mussolini: The First Fascist*, New York: Pearson/Longman.

Chasseguet-Smirgel, J. (1985) *Creativity and Perversion*, London: Free Association Books.

——(1986) *Sexuality and Mind*, London: Karnac.

Chodorow, N. (2003) 'Hate, humiliation and masculinity', in Varvin, S. and Volkan V. (eds), *Violence or Dialogue*, London: International Psychoanalytical Association.

Clare, A. (2000) *On Men: Masculinity in Crisis*, London: Chatto & Windus.

Connell, R.W. (1995) *Masculinities*, Cambridge: Polity Press.

——(2000) *The Men and the Boys*, Cambridge: Polity Press.

Davids, F. (2002) 'Fathers in the internal world: form boy to man to father', in Torwell, J. and Etchegoyen, A. (eds), *The Importance of Fathers*, Hove: Brunner-Routledge.

De Grand, A.J. (1995) *Fascist Italy and Nazi Germany: The 'Fascist' Style of Rule*, London: Routledge.

De Felice (1977) *Interpretations of Fascism*, Cambridge, MA: Harvard University Press.

Diamond, M. J. (1998) 'Fathers with sons: psychoanalytic perspectives on "good enough" fathering throughout the life cycle', *Gender and Psychoanalysis*, 85: 45–64.

——(2004a) 'Accessing the multitude within: a psychoanalytic perspective on the transformation of masculinity in mid-life', *International Journal of Psychoanalysis*, 85: 45–64.

——(2004b) 'The shaping of masculinity', *International Journal of Psychoanalysis*, 85: 359–80.

Dicks, H. (1972) *Licensed Mass Murder: A Socio-psychological Study of some SS-Killers*, London: Sussex University Press in association with Heineman.

Euripides (1998) *Bacchai*, Translated by Frederic Raphael and Kenneth McLeish, London: Nick Hern Books.

Faulks, S. (2010) *A Week in December*, London: Vintage.

Ferenczi, S. (1924) *Thalassa: A Theory of Genitality*, London: Karnac, 1989.

Fest, J. (1973) *Hitler*, Berlin: Propyläen.

Figlio, K. (2000) *Psychoanalysis, Science and Masculinity*, London: Whurr.

——(2010) 'Phallic and seminal masculinity: a theoretical and clinical confusion', *International Journal of Psychoanalysis*, 91: 119–39.

Fogel, G.I. (2006) 'Riddles of masculinity: gender, bisexuality and thirdness', *Journal of American Psychoanalytic Association*, 54: 1139–65.

Freud, S. (1905) 'Three essays on the theory of sexuality', S.E. VII.

——(1909) 'Analysis of a phobia in a five-year-old boy', S.E. X.

——(1911) 'Psychoanalytic notes on an autobiographical account of a case of paranoia (dementia paranoides)', S.E. XII.
——(1913) 'Totem and taboo', S.E. XIII.
——(1917) 'Introductory lectures on psychoanalysis', S.E. XV.
——(1918) 'From the history of an infantile neurosis', S.E. XVII.
——(1920) 'Beyond the pleasure principle', S.E. XX.
——(1921) Group psychology and the analysis of the ego', S.E. XVIII.
——(1923a) 'The ego and the id', S.E. XIX.
——(1923b) 'A seventeenth-century demonological neurosis', S.E. XIX.
——(1924a) 'Neurosis and psychosis', S.E. XIX.
——(1924b) 'The economic problem of masochism', S.E. XIX.
——(1924c) 'The dissolution of the Oedipus complex', S.E. XIX.
——(1924d) 'The loss of reality in neurosis and psychosis', S.E. XIX.
——(1925) 'Some psychical consequences of the anatomical difference between the sexes', S.E. XIX.
——(1926) 'Inhibitions, symptoms and anxiety', S.E. XX.
——(1927) 'Fetishism', S.E. XXI.
——(1930) 'Civilzation and its discontents', S.E. XXI.
——(1931) Female sexuality', S.E. XXI.
——(1933) 'Femininity', S.E. XXII.
——(1937) 'Analysis terminable and interminable', S.E. XXIII.
Fromm, E. (1941) *Escape from Freedom*, New York: Holt, Rinehart and Winston.
——(1974) *The Anatomy of Human Destructiveness*, Harmondsworth: Penguin Books.
Frosh, S. (1994) *Sexual Difference: Masculinity and Psychoanalysis*, London: Routledge.
——(1997) 'Screaming under the bridge: masculinity, rationality and psychotherapy', in Ussher, J. (ed.), *Body Talk*, London: Routledge.
Gaddini, E. (1976) 'On father formation in child development', *International Journal of Psychoanalysis*, 57: 397–401.
Geller, J. (1992) 'The unmanning of the wandering Jew', *American Imago*, 49: 227–62.
Gentile, G. (1934) 'From the origins and doctrine of fascism', in Adrian Lyttelton *Italian Fascisms*, London: Harper & Row.
Gilman, S. (1993) *Freud, Race and Gender*, Princeton, NJ: Princeton University Press.
Glasser, M. (1985) 'The weak spot: some observations on male sexuality', *International Journal of Psychoanalysis*, 66: 405–14.
Goethe, J.W. (1808) *Faust: Part I*, translated by Philip Wayne, Harmondsworth: Penguin Books, 1963.
Green, J. (1950) *If I Were You*, translated by J.H.F. McEwen, London.
Greenson, R. (1968) 'Dis-identifying from mother: its special importance for the boy', *Internaltional Journal of Psychoanalysis*, 49: 370–4.
Greenspan (1992) 'The second other', in Cath, S., Gurritt, A. and Ross, J. (eds), *Father and Child: Development and Clinical Perspectives*, Boston: Little Brown.
Gregor, N. (2005) *How to Read Hitler*, London: Granta Books.
Grosz, E. (1990) *Jacques Lacan: A Feminist Introduction*, London: Routledge.
Grunberger, B. (1971) *Narcissism*, translated by Joyce Diamanti, Madison, CT: International Universities Press.
——(1989) *New Essays on Narcissism*, translated by David Macey, London: Free Association Book.

Haffner, S. (1940/2009) *Germany Jekyl and Hyde*, translated by Wilfrid David, London: Abacus.

Hayman, R. (1997) *Hitler and Geli*, London: Bloomsbury.

Hinshelwood, R.D. (2006) 'Racism: being ideal', *Psychoanalytic Psychotherapy*, 20: 84–96.

——(2007) 'Intolerance and intolerable: the case of racism', unpublished manuscript.

Hitler, A. (1925) *Mein Kampf*, translated by D.C. Watt, London: Pimlico, 1993.

——(1928) *The Second Book*, translated by Krista Smith, New York: Enigma Books.

Horkheimer, M. (ed) (1936) *Autorität und Familie*, Paris: Librarie Felix Alcan.

——(1932) 'The dread of woman', in *Feminine Psychology*, New York: W.W. Norton.

Horney, K. (1971) 'The flight from womanhood', in *Feminine Psychology*, New York: W.W. Norton.

Irigaray, L. (1974) *Speculum of the Other Woman*, translated by G.C. Gill, Ithaca, NY: Cornell University Press, 1985.

——(1977) *This Sex Which is Not One*, translated by G.C. Gill, Ithaca, NY: Cornell University Press, 1985.

Jacques, E. (1955) 'Social systems as defence against persecutory and depressive anxiety', in Klein *et al.* (eds), *New Directions in Psychoanalysis*, London: Tavistock Publications.

Jones, E. (1932) 'The phallic phase', in Ernest Jones, *Papers on Psychoanalysis*, London: Maresfield Reprints, 1948.

Kernberg, O. (2003a) 'Sanctioned social violence: a psychoanalytic view', Part I, *International Journal of Psychoanalysis*, 84: 683–98.

——(2003b) 'Sanctioned social violence: a psychoanalytic view', Part II, *International Journal of Psychoanalysis*, 84: 953–68.

Kershaw, I (1993) *The Nazi Dictatorship: Problems and Perspectives of Interpretation*, London: Arnold.

——(1998) *Hitler:1989–1936 Hubris*, London: Penguin Books, 2001.

——(2000) *Hitler: 1936–1945 Nemesis*, London: Allen Lane, The Penguin Press.

Klein, M. (1928) 'The early stages of the Oedipus complex', in *Love, Guilt and Reparation and Other Works*, London: Hogarth Press.

——(1930) 'The importance of symbol formation in the development of the ego', in Klein, M., *Love, Guilt and Reparation and Other Works*, London: The Hogarth Press.

——(1932) *The Psychoanalysis of Children*, London: Hogarth Press.

——(1946) 'On some schizoid mechanisms', in *Envy and Gratitude and Other Works*, London: Hogarth Press.

——(1955) 'On identification', in *Envy and Gratitude and Other Works*, London: Hogarth Press.

Kohut, H. (1971/1987) *The Analysis of the Self*, Madison, CT: International Universities Press.

Koonz, C. (1987) *Mothers in the Motherland*, London: Methuen, 1988.

Kristeva, J. (1986) 'Women's time', in Toril Moi (ed.), *The Kristeva Reader*, Oxford: Blackwell.

——(1989) *Black Sun*, New York: Columbia University Press.

Langer, W. (1973) *The Mind of Adolf Hitler*, London: Secker & Warburg.

Lax, R.F. (2003) 'Boy's envy of mother and the consequences of this narcissistic identification', in Alizade, A.M. (ed.) *Masculine Scenarios.*

Le Bon, G. (1895) *La psychologie des Foules*. Paris: Felix Alcan.

Leowald, H.W. (1962) 'Internalization, separation, mourning and the superego', *Psychoanalytic Quarterly*. 31: 483–504.

Lifton, R. (1999) The *Protean Self: Human Resilience in an Age* of *Fragmentation*, Chicago: University of Chicago.

Lousada, J. (2006) 'Glancing over the shoulder: racism, fear of the stranger and the fascist state of mind', *Psychoanalytic Psychotherapy*, 20: 97–104.

Lyttelton, A. (1973) *Italian Fascisms: From Pareto to Gentile*, London: Harper & Row, 1975.

McDougall, W. (1920) *Group Mind*, Cambridge: Cambridge University Press.

Mahler, M., Pine, F. and Bergman A. (1975) *The Psychological Birth of the Human Infant*, London: Maresfield Library, 1985.

Meltzer, D. (1968) 'Terror, persecution and dread', *International Journal of Psychoanalysis*, 49.

——(1992) *The Claustrum*, Perthshire: Clunie Press.

Menzies-Lyth, I. (1992) *Containing Anxiety in Institutions*, London: Free Associations.

Mitchell, J. and Rose, J. (1982) *Feminine Sexuality*, London: Macmillan. p. 58

Mitscherlich, A. (1973) *Society without the Father*, translated by Eric Mosbacher, New York: Jason Aronson.

Mommsen, H. (ed.) (2001) *The Third Reich: Between Vision and Reality*, Oxford: Berg.

Money-Kyrle, R. (1978) *The Collected Papers of R.E. Money-Kyrle*, edited by Donald Meltzer and Edna O'Shaugnessy, Strath Tay, Petrth: Clunie Press.

Morgan, D. and Ruszczynski, S. (2007) *Lectures on Violence, Perversion and Delinquency*, London: Karnac.

Niederland, W. (1984) *The Schreber Case: Psychoanalytic Profile of a Paranoid Personality*, Hillsdale, NJ: The Analytic Press.

Ogden, T. (1992) *The Primitive Edge of Experience*, London: Karnac Books.

Orwell, G. (1949) *Nineteen Eighty Four*, Harmondsworth: Penguin Books, 1954.

O'Shaughnessy, E. (1988) 'A clinical study of a defensive organisation', in *Melanie Klein Today*, Vol. I, London: Tavistock and Routledge.

O'Sullivan, N. (1983) *Fascism*, London: J.M. Dent & Sons Ltd.

Parker, I. (1997) *Psychoanalytic Culture*, London: Sage.

Paxton, R. (2004) *The Anatomy of Fascism*, London: Penguin Books.

Perelberg, R. (2009) 'Murdered father; dead father: Revisiting the Oedipus complex', *International Journal of Psychoanalysis*, 90: 713–32.

Person, E. (2006) 'Masculinities, plural', *Journal of American Psychoanalytic Association*, 54: 1165–86.

Pick, D. (2012) *The Pursuit of the Nazi Mind*, Oxford: Oxford University Press.

Reich, W. (1933) *The Mass Psychology of Fascism*, Harmondsworth: Penguin Books, 1975.

Rice, A.K. (1969) *Learning for Leadership*, London: Tavistock.

Rice, K. (1965) *Learning for Leadership: Interpersonal and Intergroup Relations*, London: Karnac.

Riviere, J. (1929) 'Womanliness as a masquerade', *International Journal of Psychoanalysis* 9: 303–13.

Roiphe, H. and Galenson, E. (1981) *Infantile Origins of Sexual Identity*, New York: International Universities Press.

Roper, M. (2009) *The Secret Battle: Emotional Survival in the Great War*, Manchester: Manchester University Press.

Rosenfeld, H. (1965) *Psychotic States*, London: Karnac.

——(1971) 'A clinical approach to the psychoanalytic theory of the life and death instincts: an investigation into the aggressive aspects of narcissism', *International Journal of Psychoanalysis*, 52: 169–78.

———(1987) 'Destructive narcissism and the death instinct', in *Impasse and Interpretation*, London: Routledge.

Santner, E. (2000) *My Own private Germany: Daniel Paul Schreber's Secret History of Modernity*, Princeton, NJ: Princeton University Press.

Sayers, J. (1997) 'Adolescent bodies – boy crazy memories and dreams', in Ussher, J.M. (ed.), *Body Talk*, London: Routledge.

Schatzman, M. (1973) *Soul Murder: Presecution in the Family*, Milan: Feltrinelli.

Schreber, D.P. (1903/2000) *Memoirs of my Nervous Illness*, translated by I. Macalpine and R. Hunter, New York: New York Review Books.

Segal, H. (1955) 'Notes on symbol formation', *International Journal of Psychoanalysis*, 38: 391–7.

———(1972) 'A delusional system as a defence against the re-emergence of a catastrophic situation', *International Journal of Psychoanalysis*, 53: 393–401.

Segal, L. (1990) *Slow Motion: Changing Masculinities. Changing Men*, New Brunswick, NJ: Turgers University Press.

Seidler, V. J. (1989) *Rediscovering Masculinity*, London: Routledge.

———(1993) *Unreasonable Men: Masculinity and Social Theory*, London: Routledge.

Silverman, K. (1992) *Male Subjectivity at the Margins*, London: Routledge.

———(2002) 'Masochism and male subjectivity', in Adams, R. and Savran, D. (eds), *The Masculinity Studies Reader*, Malden, MA: Blackwell.

Speer, A. (1970/1995) *Inside the Third Reich*, London: Phoenix.

Spillius, E. (1988a) *Melanie Klein Today, Volume 1: Mainly Theory*, London: Tavistock/ Routledge.

———(1988b) *Melanie Klein Today, Volume 2: Mainly Practice*, London: Tavistock/ Routledge.

Steiner, J. (1987) 'The interplay between pathological organizations and the paranoid-schizoid and depressive positions', *International Journal of Psychoanalysis*, 68: 69–80.

———(1993) *Psychic Retreats*, London: Routledge.

Stoller, R. (1968) *Sex and Gender*, London: Maresfield Reprints.

———(1975a) 'Symbiosis anxiety and the development of masculinity', in Stoller, R. (ed), *Perversion*, London: Karnac.

———(1975b) *Perversion: The Erotic Form of Hatred*, London: Karnac, 1986.

Stoltenberg, J. (1999) *Refusing to be a Man: Essays on Sex and Justice*, London: Routledge.

Target, M and Fonagy, P. (2002) 'Fathers in modern psychoanalysis and in society: the role of he father in child development', in Trowell, J. and Etchegoyen, A. (eds), *The Importance of Fathers*, Hove: Breunner-Routledge.

Temple, N. (2006) 'Totalitarianism – the internal world and the political mind', *Psychoanalytic Psychotherapy*, 20: 105–14.

Theweleit, K. (1987) *Male Fantasies*, Vol. 1, translated by Stephen Conway in collaboration with Erica Carter and Chris Turner, Oxford: Polity Press.

———(1989) *Male Fantasies*, Vol. 2, translated by Chris Turner, Erica Carter in collaboration with Stephen Conway, Oxford: Polity Press.

Tiger, L. (1969) *Men in Groups*, Melbourne: Nelson.

Todd, A. (2002) *The European Dictatoships: Hitler, Stalin, Mussolini*, Cambridge: Cambrdge University Press.

Trowell, J. and Etchegoyen, A. (eds) (2002) *The Importance of Fathers*, Hove, East Essex: Brunner-Routledge.

Turquet, P. (1967) *The Use of Groups in Training*, London: Karnac.

——(1975) 'Threats to identity in the large group', in Kroeger, W. C. (ed.), *The Large Group*, London: Constable.

Ussher, J. M. (ed.) (1997) *Body Talk*, London: Routledge.

Varvin, S. (2003) 'Trauma and its after effects', in Varvin, S. and Volkan, V. (eds), *Violence or Dialogue*, London: International Psychoanalytical Association.

Villa, D. (ed.) (2000) *The Cambridge Companion to Hannah Arendt*, Cambridge: Cambridge University Press.

Volkan, V.D. (2003) 'Traumatized societies', in Varvin, S. and Volkan V.D., *Violence or Dialogue*, London: International Psychoanalytical Association.

Weiniger, O. (1906) *Sex and Character*, London: Heinemann.

Wieland, C. (1996) 'Matricide and destructiveness: infantile anxieties and technological culture', *British Journal of Psychotherapy*, 12: 300–13.

——(2000) *The Undead Mother: Psychoanalytic Explorations of Masculinity, Femininity and Matricide*, London: Karnac, 2002.

——(2005) 'Human longings and masculine terrors: masculinity and separation from mother', *British Journal of Psychotherapy*, 22: 71–86.

Winnicott, D.W. (1945) 'Primitive emotional development', in *Through Paediatrics to Psychoanalysis*, London: The Hogarth Press.

——(1954) 'The depressive position in normal development', in Winnicott, D.W. (ed.) *Through Paediatrics and Psychoanalysis*, London: The Hogarth press.

——(1956) 'Primary maternal preoccupation', in *Through Paediatrics to Psychoanalysis*, London: The Hogarth Press.

——(1960) 'Ego distortion in terms of true and false self', in *Maturational Processes and the Facilitating Environment*, London: The Hogarth Press.

——(1962) 'Ego integration in child development', in *Maturational Processes and the Facilitating Environment*, London: The Hogarth Press.

——(1963) 'From dependence towards independence in the development of the individual', in *Maturational Processes and the Facilitating Environment*, London: The Hogarth Press.

——(1971/1974) *Playing and Reality*, Harmondsworth: Penguin Books.

Index

Made in the USA
Monee, IL
04 January 2021

56365025R10109